P9-EMB-832

Democratic Teacher Education

SUNY Series,
Democracy and Education

George H. Wood, Editor

Democratic Teacher Education

Programs, Processes, Problems, and Prospects

**Edited by
John M. Novak**

STATE UNIVERSITY OF NEW YORK PRESS

Production by Ruth Fisher
Marketing by Theresa A. Swierzowski

Published by
State University of New York Press, Albany

© 1994   State University of New York

For information, address the State University of New York Press,
State University Plaza, Albany, NY 12246

Library of Congress Cataloging-in-Publication Data

Democratic teacher education : programs, processes, problems, and
    prospects / edited by John M. Novak.
        p.   cm. — (SUNY series democracy and education)
    Includes bibliographical references and index.
    ISBN 0-7914-1927-4. — ISBN 0-7914-1928-2 (pbk.)
    1. Teachers—Training of—United States. 2. Democracy—Study and
teaching—United States. 3. Teaching—Philosophy. I. Novak, John
M. II. Series.
LB1715.D45 1994
370.71′0973—dc20   93-26763
                                                                            CIP

10 9 8 7 6 5 4 3 2 1

CONTENTS

PREFACE

At a recent conference on teacher education an invited presenter, a noted sociologist of education, claimed there are two basic perspectives, the macro and the micro, for making sense of teacher education. From the macroperspective, teacher education will provide, in appropriate numbers at the least expense, candidates with the lowest qualifications allowable by society. The idea here is that teacher education is a factory-like enterprise responsible for filling out the societal work-order for bodies in the classroom by churning out, in some standardized form, agents of the state who could get the job done. From the microperspective, teacher education is seen as the way for individuals to attain or maintain middle-class status. The point here is that teacher education is an avenue for many to a quasi-professional occupation which allows the rights and privileges thereof.

When I asked the speaker if teacher education could also be viewed as a way to help create a more democratic way of life, he said he knew of no such places where this was really taking place and he would be very suspicious of claims that this was actually being done. For, as he said, rhetoric is easy in such matters; social and individual realities are much more recalcitrant. Rhetoric, reality, and recalcitrance being what they may, there are individuals, networks, institutions, and institutes attempting to develop democratic practices in teacher education. Many teacher educators are trying to practice what they preach, reflect on what they do, and develop insights and strategies that will help transform schools, institutions, and society in democratic ways, toward democratic ends. Their work is not easy and their results are not guaranteed. However, without some recognition and articulation of their work, their democratic projects run the risk of being swept away by factory-like institutions training merely status-seeking individuals.

This book is a deliberate attempt to focus attention on the creative work and struggles of democratic teacher educators. Through a description of the programs in which they are involved, the processes they develop, the problems they encounter, and the prospects opened up to them, it is hoped that the democratic possibilities for education can be examined, kept alive, and expanded.

Democratic possibilities are also kept alive because of a series of edifying conversations and an enlivening spirit. Our Democratic Education Discussion Group at Brock University has been a conversant source of stimulation and inquiry. Thank you to the many faculty and students who have participated. Thank you also to Dean Terry Boak for providing the structure, possibilities, and interest needed for the writing of this volume. Democratic educational leadership in difficult financial times is a sign of personal and institutional hope. Also a special thanks to Priscilla Ross and Ruth Fisher of SUNY Press. They have brought a caring touch, rather than a heavy hand, to the democratic delivery of this book. And finally, a loving thank you to Josephine, Linda, and Natalie Novak. The three generations of nurturing you represent have shown me that the spirit of democracy is much more than words.

INTRODUCTION

The Talk and the Walk of Democratic Teacher Education

John M. Novak

Where should we begin in our pursuit of democratic ideals? If democracy is to become a way of life in contemporary North American society, we certainly need to have schools with strong democratic commitments. This is no easy task. However, if we are going to have democratic schools, we certainly need teachers with the knowledge, skills, and attitudes necessary for developing sustained democratic ways of educating. This too is no easy accomplishment. Following this line of logic still further, if we are going to seek and sustain democratic teachers, we will also need to have democratic teacher educators: committed and down-to-earth teachers of teachers who can call forth democratic possibilities in a wide variety of situations. This book focuses on the delicate and precarious work of democratic teacher educators, but also by necessity connects with democratic projects in schools and society.

In this book we will look at the unique and complex work of a varied collection of democratic teacher educators from throughout North America as they describe their attempts to transform public schools, higher education, and societal practices. Using a diverse group of democratic educational projects, we will tap into the ways democratic teacher educators from large state institutions, small rural colleges, urban private universities, new academic programs, and special teacher development centers are working to create the resources and opportunities for teachers to develop the perspective, skills, support, and confidence necessary to promote sustained democratic practices. The diverse work of these teacher educators has important implications for down-to-earth democratic theory and practice.

Democratic teacher educators have to be down-to-earth as they develop theories, principles, and strategies for making democratic practices take hold. Their focus is on the deliberate process of preparing, sustaining, and transforming those involved in classrooms and other learning settings with the attitudes, knowledge, and skills necessary for them and their students to meaningfully participate in the self-rule of all in their society. This too is certainly no easy task. It is even more difficult because teacher educators involved in such participative democratic projects not only have to "know their stuff," they also have to model and make available for inspection their approaches to democratic teaching. These teachers of teachers feel the pressure and obligation not only to "talk the democratic talk" but also to "walk the democratic walk." This doubly difficult task requires sound thinking, solid interpersonal skills, and thoughtful articulation. However, they do not have to start from scratch because a democratic tradition is available to them. Their work can be seen as continuing and extending the democratic project of John Dewey.

Democratic Talk

Certainly, any talk of democratic teacher education has to involve John Dewey and his evolving conceptualization of democracy. Dewey, the author of the seminal text, *Democracy and Education*,[1] saw the vital links among democracy, philosophy, and education and focused a great deal of his professional work on the articulation of this seamless web. For Dewey, a social philosopher through and through, democracy is a type of associative living which enables us to hold things in common by way of communication and thus live in community; "philosophy is the theory of education as a deliberately conducted practice";[2] and education is the laboratory in which we can see what difference philosophical insight can make in the practice of living a meaningful life. Thus, Dewey's democratic educational philosophy emphasizes the importance of maintaining, protecting, and enhancing deliberative and self-correcting communicative practices in and out of schools for the sake of sharing, savoring, critiquing, and extending the goods found in experience.

No ivory tower speculator, from 1896 to 1904 Dewey tested and refined his philosophical, democratic, and educational ideas in his work with the Laboratory School at the University of Chicago. Putting ideas into practice and testing and refining both ideas and practices as a result of reflective inquiry were integral to the Deweyan method. So strong was Dewey's interest in this self-correcting educational method and its connection to philosophy that he once wrote to his wife, "I sometimes think I will drop teaching philosophy directly, and teach it via pedagogy."[3] Although he did not drop teaching philosophy directly, his talk and thoughts were constantly in democratic and educational places.

But why is this Deweyan concept of democracy important? What light does it shine on the work of the democratic teacher educators highlighted in this volume? Quite simply, Dewey developed a cogent and comprehensive notion of participative democracy that is essentially linked with a pragmatic approach to experience, inquiry, and education. Each of the chapters in this text comes in contact, often implicitly, with Deweyan notions of participative democracy, pragmatism, experience, inquiry, and education. Let's turn first to Dewey's notion of participative democracy.

In a recent and extensive biography of John Dewey, Robert Westbrook[4] uses the concept of democracy as the integrating idea in Dewey's lifework. According to Westbrook, Dewey's philosophical work began in, and returned to, an attempt to more clearly articulate the implications of a democratic way of life. Westbrook thinks Dewey was quite successful and states emphatically in the introduction of his book:

> Among liberal intellectuals of the 20th century, Dewey was the most important advocate of participatory democracy, that is, of the belief that democracy as an ethical ideal calls upon men and women to build communities in which the necessary opportunities and resources are available for every individual to realize fully his or her particular capacities and powers through participation in political, social and cultural life.[5]

It should be noted that Dewey's participatory democracy, with its vital link to the quality of everyday social life and the character development of all people, is very different from the notion of democracy proffered by the late Allan Bloom in *The Closing of the American Mind: How Higher Education Has Failed Democracy and Impoverished the Soul of Today's Students*.[6] For Bloom, a strong critic of Dewey's approach to education and democracy, democracy is important because it is the best way for the best to get to the top. Higher education has failed because it has lost sight of the truths which enable the best to succeed. From a Deweyan perspective, this is a very limited and questionable notion of democracy. For Dewey, "democracy is the name of a way of life of free and enriching communion in which free social inquiry is indissolubly wedded to the art of full and moving communication".[7] Thus, for Dewey, democracy serves as an ethical ideal worth seeking because of its communicative and educative effects. Seeking this ethical ideal was deeply grounded in Dewey's pragmatism.

Dewey's pragmatism is a down-to-earth philosophy that focuses on the integration of theory and practice, and provides alternatives to time-worn pursuits. In doing so, it goes against the grain. For example, rather than pursuing THE GOOD, THE TRUE, and THE BEAUTIFUL, it could be said that Dewey's pragmatism is more interested in seeking the better, the warranted, and the enlivening. This difference is not mere semantics but instead has serious implications for our orientation to everyday endeavors. For example, by seeking the "better" in concrete situations Dewey felt we could appreciate what is good in situations and build on the tensions, realities, and ideals also present in these same situations. By seeking the warranted, we could think in terms of communicating that which we can make intersubjectively available and give evidence for, but, in the process, always remain open to the possibilities of correcting or refining our perspectives (or even of perceiving the importance of viewing things from very different vantage points). By seeking the enlivening, we could become aware of aesthetic possibilities in our everyday situations and try to creatively experiment so as to make these possibilities actualities. Thus, Dewey's pragmatism is grounded in everyday life practices and the desire to use experience and creative inquiry to construct a life worth living, a life with many and varied connections to others that seeks deeper and more meaningful experiences.

Experience and inquiry are the essence of Dewey's pragmatic democratic education. For Dewey, experience represents the totality of our transactions with our environment and the felt quality of our existence. It is the noncognitive live connection from which thinking begins and returns as we deal with life situations. Quite simply, what Dewey seeks is "education of, by, and for experience."[8] Inquiry is the deliberate process of examining felt difficulties in experience. To inquire in order to bring the better, the warranted, and the enlivening into our experiences involves the self-correcting use of reflection, imagination, experimentation, observation, and judgment. It should be noted that these same qualities of inquiry are demonstrated in the best of scientific and aesthetic thinking and, from a Deweyan perspective, should serve as basics for a down-to-earth focus for democratic education.

Returning full circle, participative democracy to Dewey is an important ethical ideal because it is the best means for getting educated, that is for getting smarter about things that matter and processes that enhance life experiences. This goes well beyond the view of education offered by Mortimer Adler, an early critic and late admirer of Dewey. Adler dedicates his *Paideia Proposal*[9] to Dewey for holding steady on the vital connection between democracy and education. However, although Adler offers practical suggestions and strong policy proposals for the realization of more equality in public education, he is only touching the surface of the ubiquity of Dewey's notion of democratic education, change, and values.

Dewey's pragmatic democratic educational philosophy is no value-free philosophy of mere change. It is vitally concerned with the responsibility of "conserving, transmitting, rectifying, and expanding the heritage of values we have received";[10] it is grounded in values people bring to situations, but it does not stop there. The values people bring to situations are the down-to-earth starting places for much of our inquiry. The practice of participating in, questioning, and bettering these values is much of what education is all about. Certainly this involves what we do in classrooms and how we structure our schools, but it also goes well beyond this to all aspects of our cultural life. That is, we get smarter about life and develop our individuality and connectedness when we engage in cultural practices as thoughtful and creative participants capable of sustained inquiry and conversation. This is the shared value of democracy and education; this is what connects the talk about pragmatism, experience, and inquiry. Putting this talk to work is the goal of the democratic teacher educators in this volume.

Democratic Walks

Although Dewey spent most of his professional life deepening his conceptualization of democracy, and a significant part of it encouraging democratic work in schools and in the larger society, he was well aware of the practical complexities involved in democratic teacher education. His Lab School, a bastion of democratic experiences and experimentation, was not open to or for the production of new teachers. Dewey felt that the work in the Lab School required competence well beyond what new candidates could be expected to display. Also, Dewey's personal teaching style, which was memorable to only a few, could, at best, be called traditional. Although his lectures were certainly rich in democratic content, he was not a classroom embodiment of democratic pedagogy.

To further complicate matters, Dewey's essential democratic educational ideas are much more easily professed than practiced. There is a seductive consummatory quality in being able to sound Deweyan. Perhaps because it takes some intellectual effort to understand and articulate Deweyan thoughts, teacher educators who are so inclined may sometimes feel they need not, or can not, go any further. They may feel that just articulating the words has the power to bring about democratic change. Dewey was aware of this. As Alan Ryan points out, "Dewey himself thought that teacher training institutions often paid lip service to his ideas, but that he had made very little difference to the practice of elementary schools."[11] This certainly must have been discouraging to a philosopher of democratic change. However, Dewey, true to form, tried to find ways to learn from this experience. This led him in his later years to more deeply articulate the concept of democracy and the necessity for, and difficulties with, working in schools and society in democratic ways. Difficulties and all, Dewey stayed committed to the concept that the cure for the problems of democracy is not less democracy but more democracy.

The teacher educators in this book have taken up and extended Dewey's call for more democracy. They too have gone against the grain in developing down-to-earth ways to extend experience and inquiry through democratic participation. In addition, they have focused a significant part of their work on the daily activities of teachers and have attempted to create, display, and defend democratic ways of becoming and continuing to be a democratic teacher. The programs and processes they are working with are not without their problems, as they so honestly point out, but examining their work certainly adds to the prospect of developing wider-eyed democratic talk and more substantive and imaginative democratic walks.

The following 13 chapters are divided into programs and processes. Although this clear-cut division does not exist in the chapters themselves or in the actual work of these democratic teacher educators, this differentiation enables us to see the importance of organizing and networking for democratic ends in addition to the quality of interpersonal relationships and deliberative skills that are necessary to function democratically in the classroom.

NOTES

1. Found in *John Dewey: The Middle Works, 1899-1924*, Vol. 9, 1916, edited by Jo Ann Boydston (Carbondale and Edwardville: Southern Illinois Press, 1980). Dewey said this was the best statement of his social philosophy up to that time. In the 20s and 30s he deepened his notion of democracy by showing its connections to aesthetic, social, psychological, epistemological, "metaphysical," and religious issues.

2. Ibid., p. 342.

3. Quoted in Robert Westbrook, *John Dewey and American Democracy* (Ithaca: Cornell University Press, 1991), p. 95.

4. Ibid. On the jacket for this book, Richard Bernstein says "This is without doubt the finest, most comprehensive, and informative book on Dewey that has ever been written." No small praise from a noted pragmatist who also has written a book on Dewey.

5. Ibid., pp. xiv-xv.

6. Allan Bloom, *The Closing of the American Mind: How Higher Education Has Failed Democracy and Impoverished the Soul of Today's Students* (New York: Simon and Schuster, 1987).

7. Westbrook, p. xviii.

8. John Dewey, *Experience and Education* (New York: Collier, 1963), p. 29.

9. Mortimer Adler, *The Paideia Proposal* (New York: Macmillan, 1982). Dewey is one of the three in the dedication. The other two are Horace Mann and Robert Hutchins. Adler writes they "would have been our leaders were they alive today" (p. v). Perhaps they might have been our leaders, but I do not think they would have been leading toward the same end.

10. John Dewey, *A Common Faith* (New Haven: Yale University Press, 1934), p. 87.

11. Allan Ryan, "Twenty-First Century Limited," *New York Review* (November 19, 1992), p. 23.

SECTION I

Programs

INTRODUCTION

Democracy does not just happen. It takes commitment, coordination, down-to-earth efforts, learning from experience, and support. The seven chapters in this section show a variety of imaginative organizational approaches for developing democratic perspectives. The unity in their variety comes from the commitment to democratic ideals, attempts to give all involved a voice in the effort, learning from mistakes, and the supportive arrangements that have been created.

A democratic supportive arrangement is embodied in George Wood's chapter about the history, principles, and structure of the Institute for Democratic Education (IDE). This innovative and burgeoning network of democratic teacher educators, classroom teachers, administrators, and community organizers works by first focusing on the practical concerns of teachers and only moving to larger democratic rationales when teachers see the need. The working principles of IDE emphasize building on teacher needs and understanding that people with problems can often provide the best solutions. A long-range perspective is stressed for maintaining democratic connections.

Foxfire Teacher Outreach is another program that builds on teachers' needs and problem-solving ability. Using Maxine Greene's *Dialectic of Freedom*[1] as a philosophical base, Hilton Smith and ten others dialogically describe the genesis and daily work of this non-traditional approach to democratic teacher development. As these participants show, teaching democratically involves a commitment to be open to and creatively live with the professional and personal changes that occur.

Along the lines of change, Cecilia Reynolds, director of Women's Studies at Brock University, argues that many of the basic operations of the university itself work against developing democratic practices and hence make it difficult for people to become democratic educators. In particular, restricted access, discipline boundaries, and hierarchical structures negate many democratic intentions. Women's Studies, she feels, is particularly important for democratic teacher educators because it challenges all of these taken-for-granted practices and offers alternatives. Some of the basic rules of the university regimen may need to be changed if democratic teacher education is going to be able to offer substantive alternatives.

Moving to alternatives within the university, Thomas Kelly describes the rationale and workings of the Secondary Teacher Education Program (STEP) at John Carroll University. After elucidating some key unifying concepts in this pre-service program, Kelly shows how these concepts are connected to some selected roles of democratically minded secondary teachers.

9

Some of the special features of this program involve practical ways to negotiate authority and conflict, develop multicultural experiences, and become involved in public service and advocacy. These down-to-earth practices do not just happen, they need to be planned, implemented, and evaluated.

In a similar vein, Keith Hillkirk describes the inception and the design of the Teacher Education for Civic Responsibility (TERC) experimental program at Ohio University. Going through the TERC curriculum year by year, he shows the integration and faculty collaboration needed to make this voluntary experiment work. Democratic teacher education, he points out, needs experimentation and evaluation. His work also shows the importance of having faculty, students, and school personnel who are committed to democratic experiments.

Experiments come in many forms, some of them mandated. Barbara McEwan of Oregon State University, in an ironically titled chapter, "Deliberately Developing Democratic Teachers in a Year," shows what might be done to develop democratic teachers even in the midst of top-down mandates in less than desirable situations. Her work details the daily commitment to democracy as seen in the procedures for selecting students and schools, the process of matching students, teachers, and schools, and the innovative aspects of the college classes in this newly organized program.

Finally, in the last chapter in this section, Cynthia McDermott describes the democratic projects of the Action Responsibility Institute (ARI) at California State University, Dominguez Hills. Working with mostly emergency-credentialed elementary teachers, ARI promotes empowerment strategies for teachers and students that focus on the need for community and noncompetitive production. Strongly emphasized in this program is the need to articulate, put into practice, and mutually examine the democratic commitments necessary to work in commutarian ways. The notion that "we are all in this together" is not just talked about but lived through sustained teacher practices.

But enough of this talk about the walk of these programs. Let's look at the programs themselves.

NOTE

1. Maxine Greene, *The Dialectic of Freedom* (New York: Teachers College Press, 1988).

One

The Institute for Democracy in Education
Supporting Democratic Teachers

George Wood

In the ongoing debates over the future of schools and school reform, little is said about the role of alternative education sites for practicing teachers. The assumption often seems to be that we can just mandate school change and teachers will follow along, alternatively, that state departments of education, colleges, universities, and in-service development shops will help teachers adjust to their new places in reformed and/or restructured schools.

In my way of thinking, such approaches are wrongheaded for several reasons. First, the really lasting reforms or changes in the daily lives of kids in school will only occur when teachers themselves want change. No matter whether the pressure for change is state mandate or parental demands, if the classroom teacher does not want to change, it will not happen. She or he may acquiesce to a few more forms to fill out, or to a different time schedule or a new evaluation package, but the basic structure of classroom life will only change when a teacher either allows or makes it happen.

The second problem is that reform programs that ignore classroom teachers ignore one of the best resources for change. Myles Horton, founder of the Highlander Center, put it best when he said that it is the people with the problems who can best solve them.[1] Put in the context of public education today, nobody understands the systemic problems of public education better than classroom teachers. By hearing what teachers say and helping them find their own solutions, we can begin to solve them.

This means we need new sites for teacher development. More specifically, we need to find multiple ways to help practicing teachers name their own problems and solve them. These can and often will be places where the democratic promise of public education is reclaimed. What follows is a brief history of such an alternative site, The Institute for Democracy in Education (IDE), and the lessons we have learned through its development.

11

A Short History

"The Institute is teacher lounge talk the way it ought to be." That is how Barb Hayes, an elementary special educator in rural Amesville, Ohio, describes the work of IDE. Because we began as a conversation among educators and continue, at our best, to carry on that discussion, it is probably the best place to start when thinking about what IDE is and why it has been successful as an alternative education site for teachers.

IDE began when a group of teachers in rural southeastern Ohio decided to fight back. It was 1984, one year after the release of "A Nation At Risk" and teacher-bashing was rapidly becoming a national sport. The recommendations for school reform were as harsh as the criticism being heaped on teachers. Proposals were being launched (many of which have since been enacted) calling for more external control of the school day by administering more standardized tests, mandating new curricula, and regulating even more tightly the daily schedule. Ohio was no exception to the national mood as the state assembly passed multiple bills to further regulate teachers', and students', lives.

Realizing that their only hope was to organize their own alternatives to this onslaught, a group of teachers within an elementary school started a small study group. Their goal was simple and direct: to find a way to reclaim what it was about teaching that brought them into the field in the first place. Their concern was that reforms of the day were working in ways that directly circumvented both their abilities to meet the needs of their students and the fundamental purposes of public education.

On the first count, one of the teachers summed it up best: "It's my job to set up my classroom in ways that meet the needs of each child. I am the one closest to their educational development and needs. But I'm having a hard time doing that when someone in Columbus (the Ohio state capital) tries to tell me what to teach, when to teach it, and how to measure what a kid learns." This teacher, who worked with second graders, was pointing out something profoundly anti-democratic about much of the school reform movement. The agenda seemed to be moving decision making to a more centralized, and hence more removed from public control, bureaucratic structure. Teachers were left to be mere functionaries, carrying out directives over which they had no control and into which they had little, if any, input.

The second concern that pulled these teachers together was with what the reform movement was saying about the purpose of public education. Virtually every reform proposal was laced with language that made it clear that the main reason to be concerned about public education was economic. But nothing was said about the democratic or public mission of schools. Closely related to the first concern, the issue here was that if the main reason for school reform is just to prepare better workers, then the civic, democratic mission would be overlooked.

Both of these sentiments were summed up by a kindergarten teacher
who was instrumental in the early meetings of the group:

> My goal is to help my kids become active, involved members of their
> community. I try to reach this by having them be active, involved mem-
> bers of our classroom and school and neighborhood. But what I'm being
> told now is that what we are really to do is just get kids ready to take tests
> so we can make better cars than the Japanese. So I'm told to drill, and
> sort, and measure; and whether or not my kids can think, cooperate, be
> creative, or work for a common goal is irrelevant.

To combat this trend, this group of elementary school teachers began to
study reform reports that were at odds with the official school reform agenda.
Among these were the works of John Goodlad, Ernest Boyer, and Ted Sizer.
Their study led them to the works of John Dewey[2] where they found an organizing principle that became the foundation of all their work.

It was through Dewey that they came upon the ways in which democracy
and the preparation of democratic citizens can tie together the life of the school.
Using his idea that we learn from our experiences much more than what we
learn from texts, these teachers began to see the links between their disenfranchisement and the narrowing of the school curriculum all more clearly. Their
goal became to work for ways in which the experience of all members of the
school community—teachers, students, administrators, parents, and community
members—was as democratic (thus democratically empowering) as possible.

At this point it became apparent to this small group (numbers fluctuated
between six and 15) that the types of changes they envisioned would have to be
fairly broad based. Further, other teachers in the Athens County, Ohio area
were also expressing a desire to get involved in progressive, democratic school
reform. In order to build a network county-wide, an invitation was sent out to
area teachers. Simply put, they asked their colleagues if they would be interested in giving up two weeks of summer evenings, without university credit or
pay, to discuss how to put theories of public education for democracy into
practice. Imagine their surprise when more than 40 area teachers, administrators, and parents showed up the first night.

For two weeks the group read Dewey, talked of their struggles in their
schools and, most importantly, planned for action to take when they returned in
the fall. These action plans included moving to school-wide Whole Language
literacy programs, involving faculty more in the hiring of new faculty, com-
munity-action projects involving students, project-based approaches to teaching, and formalizing the group into some sort of an ongoing organization. This
last agenda item was added by a secondary school teacher who, halfway
through the week, announced: "I have to tell you, this is what I've been waiting
for. A chance to work with colleagues in a way that does more than just change

schools—it will change lives. And I can't leave this group and go back out on my own—we have to stick together for the long haul."

From that sentiment the Institute for Democracy in Education was born. The mandate from these teachers was simple and direct: Get the group together informally, put out a newsletter, bring in a speaker or two, support teachers working to make democratic change. Above all our mission was to *respond* to teacher requests, *not* to be about building a large institution that generated its own program.

With that mandate, we began by holding a series of meetings during the 1986-1987 school year on democratic approaches to teaching reading and writing. This made sense as a starting point because so many of the teachers involved in IDE were experimenting with their language arts curriculum. However, rather than inviting so-called experts to talk *to* teachers, we invited teachers who were having success with Whole Language and similar approaches to talk *with* their colleagues. This effort was so successful that from these sessions emerged a program called our "Teacher Roundtables." Held monthly on a Friday evening (yes, Friday) they are a time for teachers just to share ideas, problems, frustrations, and triumphs in their classrooms. The Roundtables, seldom with an agenda and open to all comers, are a cornerstone of what we do.[3]

We also began a small newsletter—two pages, mimeoed front and back, stapled and addressed on someone's dining room table. Our agenda was to give teachers a place to write for other teachers. Thus, virtually everything in the newsletter was written by and for classroom teachers.

Finally, we also agreed to continue to meet in the summer. In a seminar setting we would gather to reinvestigate the theories and principles behind what we do and how these ideas work out in practice. All this was taken on by our small, but enthusiastic, band of three dozen classroom teachers. We knew we wouldn't change the world tomorrow, but we did know we were in this together for "the long-haul."

At this writing, nearly six years later, IDE is alive and well. It has become a membership organization of over 700 members in nearly every U.S. state and Canadian province and in Europe and Africa. In addition to a national office in Athens, Ohio (located at Ohio University), there are fourteen (and growing) regional offices in the United States and Canada. The newsletter has grown into a quarterly journal *(Democracy and Education)* which we supplement with a members' newsletter *(IDE Reports)*, curriculum packets, booklets, and occasional papers. The summer workshop has grown into a national conference attracting educators and parents to Athens from all around North America and Europe. Finally, we are now entering a new phase of our work, direct service to students through developing a student-teacher environmental network (called Project Common Ground) and a summer camp offered free to low-income kids where teachers can try out new teaching projects.

Through all this we have tried to maintain our core identity. All of our workshops are offered in response to teacher requests and presented by teachers. The journal is written primarily by teachers, and conference presenters are virtually all school people. And our offices and student projects are started only at the request of educators in the area. In what follows, I want to try and set out why this orientation to working from the ground up is so important and how it has sustained us.

Small Steps on the Path to Change

There is no doubt that IDE has been able to play a major part in the continuing education of democratic teachers. Further, we have been successful in helping democratically restructure numerous classrooms and schools. As both an advocacy and support organization, we have been able to make a difference in the lives of teachers and their students.

This is not to say that we have not experienced failures. In fact, one of the lessons we have learned is how difficult progressive school change is in the current political climate. While numerous calls are made for school reform, what many of these erstwhile reformers seem to be after is just doing more of the same. The press is on for higher standardized test scores above all else, with the assumption that everything will work out if we just work harder at what we are currently doing. Thus, taking our lead primarily from the Japanese, the call goes out for more days in school, more school hours in the day, more homework after school, and more testing during school. In this environment a progressive, democratic educator often finds that even the smallest change must face mountains of bureaucratic over-regulation.

Given this orientation, it is not surprising to find that the reforms most often touted are of the type that leave the overall structure of teaching and learning untouched. Even outstanding programs such as Whole Language approaches to literacy, cooperative learning, or the Foxfire approach are often sold to teachers as a quick fix to low test scores. Unfortunately, it is only when such approaches yield these results that they are deemed legitimate for classroom use.

Given this climate of test and measure, quick-fix approaches to school change (and, by necessity, teacher development), it is difficult for progressive educators to find a place for their agenda. When we take seriously the democratic mission of schooling it means rethinking the very day-to-day experience of children and their teachers. It means ensuring that they all engage in developing a genuine sense of school community and that what is learned is used to make a difference in the world outside the school. All of this necessitates going beyond tinkering with the school as it stands.

But such restructuring is much more difficult work than many school reformers seem to understand. The institutional inertia alone prevents an easy transition to a progressive solution to our current educational challenges. This may be why quick-fix solutions are so readily embraced. But none of those by themselves, will make a lasting difference in the type of citizens we produce unless they are part of an overall strategy to reclaim the democratic purpose of schooling.

How then, in the face of these pressures, is IDE able to help educators develop progressive practices? Perhaps most fundamentally it is because we do recognize how difficult our task is. As an organization made up primarily of teachers, our visions of a democratic future are tempered by the reality of daily work in schools. Because of that our orientation is toward small steps on the road to change. Our programming, literature, conference, etcetera do not promise six easy steps to a restructured school or ten rules for every teacher. Rather, we offer real teachers who often find themselves taking one step backward for every two forward. In so doing we actually make it easier for educators to take hold of a vision of a democratic future for schools. It is not a fully elaborated plan for every teacher to follow lockstep to some nirvana. No, we've all been down those roads of false promises before. Rather, our project is to make a road together by working for a vision and hope we all share.

As a follow-up to this general orientation, we also make it a point to begin with a focus on the practical. Our workshops and publications are not primarily theoretical, focusing on abstract discussions of empowerment or critical theory. Rather, we start with what people are doing to help empower children. How does a project-centered approach to teaching engage students in taking control of their learning? How can community service projects actively engage students in making a difference in their neighborhoods? In what ways does cooperative learning facilitate breaking down barriers between students of different academic abilities? What children's literature can be used to help children cross ethnic, racial, socioeconomic, or gender lines?

Through beginning with the do-able, we help all teachers enter into the conversation about what our schools and classrooms could be. No one is excluded because we begin with the language and experiences that virtually every teacher shares. It is a way of giving all participants equal footing by starting from a terrain they know best—the classroom. From there we can go on to imagine and work for more democratic schools through talking about *why* we do what we do.

It is that transition in our discussions, from technique to rationale, that moves our work beyond the quick-fix approaches mentioned above. When we turn to the purpose of change, of going beyond just trying to raise test scores, then we move toward how these practical, short-term solutions take us another step closer to the type of school or classroom we desire. What we have learned in our work is to keep the end in sight but to begin with what we can do tomorrow.

Beyond the pragmatic concern of wanting to engage as many educators as possible in our efforts, our orientation toward celebrating the work of classroom teachers has a philosophic underpinning as well. Early in this essay I recounted the argument of Myles Horton that problems are usually solved most effectively from the ground up. Certainly this is the promise of democracy. But it is not just a blind hope or fantasy. Tempered by experience, we have come to see that when people are well informed and free from manipulation, the paths of action they choose are often the most effective.

This is certainly the case when it comes to schooling. Consider the wide range of attempts to dictate school structure from the "outside." Such efforts have, for example, given us the multiperiod school day with little time to really work with students, textbooks which are an insult to most teachers' and students' intelligence, and standardized tests which miss so much of the educational experience yet claim to be a measure of all we do. Virtually every school structure we have today that has not succeeded has been imposed on classrooms by either educational "experts," state or federal policymakers, or bureaucratic functionaries.

On the other hand, consider just a few of the recent teacher-initiated or teacher-led campaigns for school renewal. These include the Whole Language movement (which has reinvigorated reading and writing instruction), project-based instruction, holistic assessment, portfolio assessment, process writing, hands-on mathematics instruction, the essential schools programs, peer mediation, community service programs, and the list goes on and on. Every one of these efforts have made a genuine, positive difference in the lives of children. And each of these, if not directly developed by teachers, has only been possible because teachers saw them as solutions or alternatives to the situations they faced.

Furthermore, in the cases mentioned above, these grassroots movements have worked on the side of democratic education. Each one provides students with experiences that enable them to take control of their own learning, to get involved and make a difference in the world around them, and to see themselves as part of a community. Contrast these to the bureaucratically imposed or mandated reforms that reward conformity and individualism and teach skills in isolation from the world. There is little doubt which set of initiatives provide the experiences that future citizens need.

To summarize, our work over the past seven years has taught us three things about the democratic education of teachers. First, progressive democratic educational change is difficult and hard work, a task only for those with a view toward the long run. Second, the best start on the road to change is with small steps, focusing on the practical work of classroom teachers as our model. Third, we more often respond to the needs of teachers rather than initiate programming on our own because we know the best answers come from the people with the problems.

Next Steps

Perhaps the most important work to be carried out today in terms of democratic education is with teachers currently in the field. Given their experience and authority, they will be central to any changes that occur within our schools. Additionally, if our means are to be consistent with our ends, reforms for democratic education must come about democratically. The emphasis should be on the bottom up, as slow as that process can often be.

My own sense now is that many educators are ready to begin down the road toward progressive, democratic schooling. Frustrated with the way things are, their hands tied by the increasing bureaucratization of schooling, many teachers see that their own liberation is tightly linked to that of their students. What they lack, what teachers involved in IDE lacked, is the vision that something different is possible.

In a very real sense the work of the Institute for Democracy in Education is about creating that vision. By providing educators with examples drawn from the practices of other teachers, we help demonstrate that change is possible. And once a teacher of school begins down that road, we work to support those efforts no matter how limited they are. As Bill Ayers (a long-time member of IDE) put it, "We're here to support any move, no matter how small, toward democracy."

What's next? For IDE that is always a difficult question. Looming on the horizon appear to be more attempts to limit the work of progressive teachers through national standardized testing and a national curriculum. Additionally, as the ranks of the poor continue to grow and school funding continues to shrink, the job of any teacher, progressive or not, becomes more difficult. Our task will be to help educators fight against these roadblocks while continuing to develop democratic practices.

Beyond IDE, it's imperative that progressive educators find more and more ways to work together. Such efforts can be readily supported by universities through small steps such as access to copying equipment, rooms, and resources. But more importantly it takes a commitment by teacher educators to become learners. We must seek out and spend time in the classrooms of progressive, democratic teachers and learn from them. And then we need to focus not on one more theoretical article or research piece produced only in the search for tenure, but to get involved up to our elbows in the messy and often unsettled world of the public schools. Because it is to other teachers that teachers will turn for models of democratic change, not to theoreticians. And recounting such efforts and successes is what is vitally important to democratic education today.

NOTES

1. See Myles Horton, *The Long Haul* (New York: Doubleday, 1990).

2. Particularly useful were Dewey's *Experience and Education* (New York: Collier, 1963), *The Child and the Curriculum,* and *The School and Society* (Chicago: University of Chicago Press, 1990).

3. For information about IDE (including our meetings and membership) write or call: IDE, 119 McCracken Hall, Ohio University, Athens, OH 45701; Telephone: 614-593-4531.

Two

Foxfire Teachers' Networks
(Viewed Through Maxine Greene's
The Dialectic of Freedom)[1]

Hilton Smith

In *Dialectic of Freedom*, as in all her work, Maxine Greene addresses issues—difficult, evasive issues like freedom. Some educators try to escape the implications of her treatment of those issues by characterizing them as "philosophy," and choose to burrow instead into "practical" matters. The route of education reform is littered with the wasted hulks of reforms guided by such rudderless thinking. Greene's perspective combines the tough-minded epistemology of American pragmatism with a rich appreciation of the beauty people are capable of in all endeavors, from all cultures. Foxfire practitioners share the same perspective, so it is not surprising that there is such a resonance between the insights in *Dialectic of Freedom* and the discoveries by those of us involved in Foxfire's Teacher Outreach program. More importantly, that shared perspective has the potential for a revealing examination of this program.

Many readers know, at least vaguely, that "Foxfire" refers to a high school cultural journalism program started by Eliot Wigginton in Appalachian Georgia more than 25 years ago. In recent years, stimulated by the experiences of adapting Wigginton's program to a variety of student constituencies, classroom practitioners developed a more complete *approach* to instruction, applicable to all grade levels, all content areas, and, as far as we can tell, all student constituencies.[2] In 1986, the Foxfire Fund, Inc. accepted a grant with the challenge to disseminate that approach through a "teacher outreach" program. Rather than providing an extensive explication of the nuts and bolts of the program, provided elsewhere,[3] we scattered them throughout this essay to illustrate key points. Readers thus participate in something like a constructionist approach to an understanding of the program. As a safety net, we provide several appendices at the end to tidy up the picture.

21

We constructed this essay through a participatory process which illustrates how we do most of our work. The coordinators of the Foxfire-affiliated teachers' networks read an initial draft. Several of them and some networks' members then provided responses which appear as Commentaries within the text. That allows us to honor the variety of perceptions which energizes the dialectics described in the essay, without trying to meld them into a hybrid analysis that would homogenize our unique personal perspectives. All the contributors are identified following the text, pages 40-41.

> The rebellious teacher, the "reflective practitioner" is asked to tramp down dissonant conceptions of what education might be and perhaps ought to be in a chaotic, uncertain time. We do not know how many educators see present demands and prescriptions as obstacles to their own development, or how many find it difficult to breathe. There may be thousands who, in the absence of support systems, have elected to be silent.[4]

In her introduction to *The Dialectic of Freedom*, Greene says that the book is "an effort to tap the multiple realities of human experience," to "remind people of what it means to be alive among others," and "to reawaken concern for and belief in a humane framework for the kinds of education required in a technology society."[5] Those phrases so aptly describe the intent of Foxfire and the overarching aims of the teacher networks affiliated with Foxfire that, from that point on, each page of *The Dialectic of Freedom* contains phrases, lines, and paragraphs that leap out as if in bold print to describe our Teacher Outreach venture. Greene's analysis of the dialectic of freedom—tensions between world views, dilemmas encountered while trying to decide between moral "oughts" and "practical" courses of action—seem to resonate with the collective experiences of all of us involved with Foxfire's Outreach program.

Her analysis seems particularly relevant to the aims, struggles, and continuing dialectics within the networks which form as support systems for teachers who participate in Foxfire courses for teachers and implement the approach in their own classrooms. In the networks, members are "enabled to test their own capacities, to use their minds," while "refusing to remain immersed in the taken-for-granted and the every-day." At the same time they refuse to approve freedom "as an indulgence of the instinctual and the irrational," becoming caught up, instead, "in the striving toward their own 'completion'—a striving that can never end."[6]

"Dialectic" in this context captures the tensions, dilemmas, and opportunities inherent in building teachers' organizations in which the voluntary participants are guided by their own interpretations of both the guiding pedagogy and the "difficult and resistant world" in which they seek to practice that pedagogy. The dialectic potential is squared by the reality that the guiding pedagogy runs against the grain of the education establishment's operative (if largely unarticulated) presumptions about schooling.[7] Greene's graceful, probing analysis is made more elegant and accessible by her references to literature which illustrate the facets and tensions of humans engaged in the dialectics of freedom. (An example: In Kundera's *The Unbearable Lightness of Being*, Greene finds a vivid illustration of the existential paradox of seeking freedom by deserting the "situated freedom" of familiar surroundings.)

Since Maxine Greene is a philosopher of education, it is not surprising that her book deals straight-on with the roles of schooling in the creation and preservation of freedom. In her introduction, she describes the book (and herself) as "struggling to connect the understanding of education . . . to the making and remaking of a public space, a space of dialogue and possibility."[8] Members of Foxfire networks share her view that "it is through education that preferences may be released, languages learned, intelligences developed, perspectives opened, possibilities disclosed."[9] More salient, even, is Greene's argument that "a teacher in search of his/her own freedom may be the only kind of teacher who can arouse young people to go in search of their own."[10]

Greene's canvas for *The Dialectic of Freedom* is broad: "There is, after all, a dialectical relation marking every human situation: the relation between subject and object, individual and environment, self and society, outsider and community, living consciousness and phenomenal world."[11] Given that broad scope, it occurred to us that it might appear presumptuous to borrow Greene's elegant discourse for a public analysis of a relatively small, classroom-focused education program. A look at the purposes of the networks and the impact on their members tests that presumption.

In the early stages of the Outreach program, from 1986 to, say, 1989, our intentions for the teacher networks (and our attendant perceptions) were simple: After participating in one of our graduate-level courses for teachers, each cohort would form a collegial support group to encourage each other to "Foxfire" their classes and to help them past the doubts, glitches, and obstacles they faced. That certainly happens, but so does much more, as the commentaries by Allen, Varner, and Wilder show.

> I want others to know I've been making real world connections. Sometimes it is simple. After all, a noun is a noun, regardless if you identify it in Gwinnett County or in a housing project nicknamed Little Viet Nam. However, the real world tragedy is that the real world connection must also inform these children that regardless of how well you master all the givens set forth by the powers that be, your life might or might not change for the better. I have the job of selling the educational package without a real guarantee. Please feel free to inform Jimmy [Nations] that being authentic can be very painful. Nevertheless, I have a sense of real growth. I know I

will be a better teacher because of Foxfire. I mean, after all, I know I'm able to formulate the basis of my philosophy firmly within the confounds [sic] of Dewey and I've received a road map for giving my students the gift of storytelling. I *reflect* back over the last two weeks and exclaim "Holy §*@%! I'm prepared. I'm really prepared."

From a journal by Angela Allen, Crossties Network

I think the only way I can do this is to make my class an experimental one—a laboratory to the greatest degree possible. The only things that did drive me last year were the creations of the kids: their poetry, stories, projects. I genuinely get "fired up" by having a part in those sorts of things. I think I should also work on my network of teaching friends. Teachers who are genuinely interested in innovative teaching approaches are hard to come by, but they keep each other going, I am convinced. I need so much to be able to share what the kids in my classroom are doing with someone (or ones) who will appreciate it.

From a journal kept by Laurie Varner, Crossties Network

In the past, the reality has been that most teachers performed their jobs in isolation from fellow teachers, followed the same traditional patterns of instruction taught in their education classes, experienced little or no recognition for their classroom successes, and have very little opportunity to believe their knowledge and expertise is worthy of sharing with others. Trained in the Foxfire teaching approach, members of the Eastern Kentucky Teachers Network have been quietly transforming their classrooms into settings of democratic interaction and their students into learners actively involved in designing their own work.

Challenged by the freedom and participation they observed in their students, teachers began to examine their own professional structures in light of these new discoveries. Just as their students had been given "top down" directives, assignments, and policies in which they had little input, teachers realized that they, too, had been somewhat powerless in the administrative decisions which affected their classrooms. They began to find their "voice" and began contributing ideas to their administrations and faculties based on their experiences.

Jenny Wilder, Eastern Kentucky Teachers Network

By the third year of the Outreach program, the importance of the networks was clear, as the founder of Foxfire, Eliot Wigginton, states in an article on the Outreach program:

> This nurturing function is critical, for with distressing frequency teachers find that a course like ours creates the desire to interact in a different way with students, and gives some of the skills they need, but for the most of them, as with their own students, the actual process of experimentation, implementation, and the building of self-confidence takes time that is often characterized by pain and panic and more than a few false starts.[12]

Typically, as network members implement Foxfire's Core Practices in their classrooms, with attendent reflections on some of their basic notions about schooling, they reach for instructional strategies, classroom management techniques, and more authentic assessment techniques. That begins to affect actual teaching practices in a variety of ways, perhaps nothing more dramatic than changes in how a teacher starts responding to students' questions. On the other hand, it might take the form of a complete rethinking of the possibilities inherent in, say, U.S History, or mounting a challenge of her/his school district's student evaluation policies.

Networks respond by developing what amounts to staff development programs that supplement those provided by the members' schools and school districts. (In some cases they constitute the *only* staff development *program*.) The networks thus evolve into what might be referred to as "quasi-professional" organizations. The commentaries by Wentworth and Jones provide a whiff of the vitality within the networks.

> The structure of schools tends to strew clutter in our paths, so this new way of working together seems freeing and expansive. Everyone uses their talents. Sandra put together a newsletter; Ned and Linda take their students to a presentation; David takes a course on leadership; Andrea checks in on Steve to see how he's doing; ten of us sit down together to write about our work; Alex pressures us to think harder about why we do what we do in our classrooms; an ad hoc committee forms to put together an issue of *Hands On*. When it's time to choose someone to go to a conference, a few people who don't want to go read over the applications and make a decision.
>
> We visit each others' classrooms, talk on the phone, get our students together so they can be resources for one another. The ways we work are fluid and develop out of need. Out of our collective intelligence comes a peculiar kind of democracy made of

trust, passion, attentiveness, justice, and caring support. This kind of democracy works for us because the elements of community are what drive us, not laws, or power, or convention. We are creating a democratic network as we go, with all the flaws and all the exhilaration that comes with risk-taking.

Marylyn Wentworth, Partnership Network

Stimulated by the revelation that two of our network members meet once a week to walk around Green Lake to share their "puzzling stories" about being a Foxfire teacher in an alternative school, someone observed, "And wouldn't that dialogue between two critical friends hold an interesting piece for Hands On?!" Well, you could just see the wheels turning and Ahha's popping throughout the room. The rich dialogue that followed transcended any round-robin sharing by leaps and bounds. We found what each of us was really doing—and that allowed each of us to thoughtfully look at our own classroom practice. Here's an excerpt from that dialogue:

Blanche: Don't we need to talk about more than the good times? What about the dilemma of wasting time?
Michael: We need to share the critical positives *and* negatives.
Sue: I'm struggling with how to get students to see the possibilities of their own work and I catch myself going back to old roles.
Julie: I was evaluated by my administrator who saw what I thought was productive interaction among students, as chaos.
Gayle: Sometimes I know it is chaos in my classroom and not productive work. How do we deal with the chaos and the guilt?
Blanche: I feel guilt when kids are not using time well and yet the presentation is coming up. How do we bring it all together? What are the strategies of getting out of the chaos early on?

Bob Jones, Soundfire Network to Marylyn Wentworth

There's more. Foxfire is an "approach" to instruction, not a method or a curricular variant or a style. Because that approach draws on clearly articulated views about young people, learning, content, and teachers' roles—and because we insist that every participant engage the philosophical underpinnings of those views, most participants come to realize that the reach of those underpinnings applies to much more than her/his classroom. Though the program consciously focuses organizational energies on classroom instruction, the networks' members also start questioning paradigms with which they have viewed most social phenomena, including schooling, politics, and even marital relationships. (Barbara Combs, active member of Network of Empire State Teachers, says she sometimes feels as though she's at a meeting of "teachers anonymous": "My name is Barbara and I . . .")

Within the networks, democratic processes—discussion (deliberation, consensus), projection of consequences, attentiveness to those whose views might not prevail—serve as an *organizational means of mediation*, thereby setting the direction for actions. If we assert that democracy is the appropriate process for society, and if we are sure that democratic skills and attitudes are best learned by using them, then we should use democracy in our classrooms. Similarly, teacher networks provide an organizational context for teachers to practice democracy—"the provision of opportunities for the articulation of multiple perspectives in multiple idioms, out of which something common can be brought into being."[13] If democracy is right for kids and right for society, it is right for us, because in our capacity as teachers, we also mediate. To be effective mediators in our classrooms, we must understand, through experience, democratic processes, not merely talk about them.

Greene reflects on the absence of "serious talk of reconstituting a civic order, a community," about "a widespread speechlessness, a silence where there might be—where there ought to be—an impassioned and significant dialogue."[14] All of us who serve as teachers in public schools understand that we almost never constructively and thoughtfully meet as a faculty to have "significant dialogue" on what we are doing, how we are doing it, and what we *should* be doing. Foxfire networks provide *an ongoing, action-oriented forum* for exactly that kind of dialogue.

In her analysis of the impediments to social change, Greene provides language that describes some of our teacher colleagues "down the hall," complacent in the "regularities" of schooling: "When people cannot name alternatives, imagine a better state of things, share with others a project of change, they are likely to remain anchored or submerged, even as they proudly assert their autonomy."[15] Many of the tensions Foxfire practitioners face originate with those teachers. In a recent assessment of the Outreach program, network members responded on a survey as to whether the effects of "school climate" factors were Supportive, Neutral, or Inhibiting. As you might suspect, they assessed "non-human, intangible" elements like curriculum and teaching load as mostly Neutral and Inhibiting. Their response to the human elements (principals, parents, students, other teachers) contained what was at that time a surprise:

> It appears that virtually all of the "key individuals," or *human resources* are regarded very highly as "Supportive." Some of these folks also appear in the Neutral category, to be sure, but with somewhat lesser numbers behind them. The intriguing exception is *other teachers*—where the combination of Neutral and Inhibiting accounts for half of the responses.[16]

In the networks, in contrast, we free ourselves for "impassioned and significant dialogue" about teaching—an essential activity that schools and school districts never seem to provide, allow, or encourage. It is our way of seeking, as Greene says, "a special sort of understanding" so as to "not be overwhelmed by the necessities and determinants that work on every life."[17] We wrestle with our classroom dilemmas and contextual demons. We seek strategies and tactics to get us past the barriers to a more complete fulfillment of our respective potentials. We argue issues and policies in order to try to make sense of the systemic hazards we face—both real and (sometimes) imagined. We plan courses of action, ways to support each other, and, of course, the next meeting. Thus, we move toward freedom: "A distinctive way of orienting the self to the possible, of overcoming the determinate, of transcending or moving beyond in the full awareness that such overcoming can never be complete."[18]

Greene's broad canvas therefore seems appropriate, especially considering the role she ascribes for "mediation, something that occurs between nature and culture, work and action, technologies and human minds."[19] Teacher networks serve as a collective mediation for professional and some personal concerns for those who share this vision of how schooling could be better for them and their students. (Note, please, "this vision," not The Vision.)

* * *

The problems for education, therefore, are manifold. Certain ones cluster around the presumed connection between freedom and autonomy; certain ones have to do with the relation between freedom and community, most significantly moral community.[20]

Very often, the rhetoric of politicians and many of the rest of us casts freedom as an absence of restraints or prohibitions. Greene calls that "negative freedom," noting that it is often seen as an end unto itself, rather than a condition which enables people to consider purposes, means, and actions. She notes, for example, that some of the early progressive schools were characterized by freedom as unrestrained student behaviors and a lack of social control and academic focus. That situation, as we know, provided part of the motivation for Dewey to write *Experience and Education*.[21] In it, he argues that social control which works *with* students' capacities to cooperatively fashion and enforce classroom order is essential for students to acquire an appreciation of "effective freedom."

That elusive condition Greene describes as "freedom of mind and freedom of action [as] functions of membership and participation in some valued community."[22] That is what we seek in our classrooms and through the networks.

Foxfire networks cannot provide "negative freedom," because the restraints and prohibitions the members face are those of their schools and school districts. The networks *do* provide the inspiration for members to convert those restraints and prohibitions into opportunities for learning, something closer to Greene's description of effective freedom. One example: One member of the Eastern Kentucky Teachers Network and her first-graders developed their own reading program, which moves them faster and more effectively through (and beyond) the district's reading program objectives than the basal. Even so, she is required by her school administration to put her class through a basal reader program on a prescribed weekly schedule. The solution, quickly evolved by the class: They do each week's work in the basal on Monday, with little effort, then work on the meaningful curriculum—theirs—Tuesday through Friday.

Participating in a network is an affirmation of taking responsibility for one's own actions—including the realization that responsibility necessarily entails more than next week's lesson plans. Indeed, the actual fulfillment of an individual teacher's vision of what her/his students can achieve really requires a supportive context in which his/her colleagues at least understand and appreciate the effort, and vice versa. That context is difficult to create in most schools, given the energy-draining and time-consuming programs teachers are expected to deliver.

Creating that context in networks is not necessarily easy or painless, however. For professionals accustomed to the American "silver bullet" paradigm for solving problems, not to mention the intractable realities of our classrooms, network development entails all the discomforts of uncertainty and doubt. Engaging in the seemingly endless discussions about network business—criteria for small grants to members, forming a mission statement, defining membership, deciding whether to offer courses through the local college—manifests grudging acceptance of the impossibility of ever grasping certain truth about any of those issues, and even the difficulty of attaining what Dewey called "warranted assertions" in the absence of certain truth.

> As important, each time he/she is with others—in dialogue, in teaching-learning situations, in mutual pursuit of a project—additional new perspectives open; language opens possibilities of seeing, hearing, understanding. Multiple interpretations constitute multiple realities; the "common" itself becomes multiplex and endlessly challenging, as each person reaches out from his/her own ground toward what might be, should be, is not yet.[23]

The revealing commentaries by Turnbull and Wentworth bring the issues of organizational democracy into a human-level focus. Their networks pursue the elusive benefits of democracy while beset with the exigencies of efficiency and survival, which, in turn, threaten the tenuous bonds between members.

It is a Saturday morning. I join members of our network as
we roll up our sleeves to tackle issues that face us. All our work of
our network is done in this fashion—by the teachers for whom the
outcomes have consequences. We set priorities, make plans of
action and work collaboratively to reach our goals. The foundation
of our organization is consensual decision-making. Our commitment to the democratic process is, however, the very element that
threatens to divide us. The democratic process is effective but it is
hardly efficient. Fewer and fewer teachers are able to dedicate time
and energy to the increasing demands of network business. Now,
less than 20 percent of the membership is actively involved in the
ongoing administrative business of the network. Because all business is handled by those in attendance, less active members are
left out of the loop.

The dilemma, then, is to utilize the skills and dedication of
the administrative core while preventing feelings of overwork and
resentment. We must respect the level of involvement chosen by
others without leaving them out or feeling guilty.

This is the best we've been able to do, but is it democracy?

Dotty Turnbull, Louisville Area Foxfire Network (KY)

If democracy means that individuals can be trusted to work
in the best interest of all; if it means that power is infinite and
grows with the willingness of individuals to offer their personal
power to the collective whole rather than the finite version of
power that accrues to the aggressive few; if it means that all the
business of an organization is conducted in the open, then our network in Maine is a democracy.

The structure of our network would not necessarily be familiar to observers of the democratic process. We don't vote, we use
consensus. We don't have representatives or designated positions
(except for a coordinator); we trust whomever is at our meetings to
do the right thing. We have few rules, no constitution or bylaws.
Rather we have a continuous dialogue. Anyone can be a leader,
anyone can form an ad hoc committee with consensual agreement
from the larger group. We have work to do and we do it with
thoughtfulness, compassion, reflection, and a growing understanding of teaching and learning. We make mistakes, but there is
no censure for error, only another chance to learn.

Perhaps this almost utopian success is because there are only
fifty of us in this network at present. Will the flexibility and trust
continue if we double in size? Will we need the written agree-

ments that become rules and bylaws if we grow larger? Will the feel of a bonded community dissipate? If we find a way to preserve the best of what we presently have, we will have learned a lot more than how to apply the Foxfire approach; we will learn how groups can govern themselves democratically, with a fresh view of what democracy can be.

Marylyn Wentworth, Partnership Network (Maine)

Participating in these networks involves us in a dialectic of those who seek, who define by their actions, freedom. We push against "limits, injustices, exclusion, neglect"; against those who expect and those who prefer compliance; against teachers who prefer job security and closed-door authoritarian classroom control; and against the trophy-like displays of uniform, aggregate achievements of minimum curricular expectations.

Tensions arise from dealing with "outside forces" like school boards, accrediting bodies, and state departments of education. Tensions arise between individual applications of the Foxfire approach and the necessity of maintaining the integrity of the approach so that it doesn't dissolve into an anarchy of individual practices, thus losing all pedagogical resilience and identity.

Anyone who has participated in an endeavor where the participants articulate heretofore suppressed views knows that the result often is the appearance of consensus. When that consensus is acted on, the results reveal the consensus to have hidden the reefs of even deeper-held perceptions and values, potentially divisive. Sorting those out, while maintaining momentum and good will, can be very trying. Many a network meeting has included a wry observation about the tediousness and seeming inefficiency of collective decision-making—followed inevitably with nodded consensus that this must be how our students feel when they try to make classroom decisions about their work or projects.

Tensions develop sometimes between those whose vision of Foxfire is still circumscribed by their own classroom and school, and those who extend the principles underlying the approach to schooling in general, even to an analysis of the educational system in general. The latter are considerably freer and, consequently, more imaginative in their applications of the approach. They take more risks and eschew pat formulas for their classrooms.

We discovered that members of networks who are coaxed into professional activities beyond their normal range experience Gestalt-like extensions of their heretofore limited visions. Now we actively encourage networks' members to make presentations with their students to professional groups, attend the coordinators' trimester meetings with the Outreach staff, and help conduct the Foxfire course for other teachers. Another opening for professional development is our journal for teachers, *Hands On*. Most of the pieces consist of teachers' own case studies of their efforts to implement student-centered instruction in their classrooms. Thus we capture, store, and disseminate a body of classroom experiences—from shining moments to sinking moments to screaming moments—which tend otherwise to simply drift off into the ether of forgotten events.

The effects of those involvements are empowering. They account, in part, for the heightened sense of participating in something much larger than their own school and region. And that often can keep classroom teachers' resolve up when everything around us seems contrary and overwhelming, pulling us back toward default-mode classroom practices. (A regional colloquial expression says it well: "When you're up to your ass in alligators, it's hard to remember that the objective is to drain the swamp.")

Tensions occur within networks when some members want their network to provide organizational support for them to do battle with local boards or state policies or other agencies. That dialectic is classic: between responding to the will of individual members because it is "their organization" and keeping the network focused on the purposes for which it was formed and for which it has resources. Sometimes the result is clarification of purpose, governance, and membership. A few members may quit, angry and disillusioned, so the event is painful and aggravating—but vital.

Those tensions illustrate Greene's distinction between the "individualistic" freedom of laissez faire-type schooling and the Jeffersonian view of freedom through "social intercourse." The latter can "only be maintained out in the open among self-directing (and self-supporting) persons."[24] (Or, in a close paraphrase of the words of one network coordinator, "It ain't for the weak at heart.")

Schooling in the United States manifests tensions arising from the dualistic presence of both views. One quick example: States mandate compulsory attendance for every child, justified on the basis that the society needs "educated citizens" (meaning, often, "workers"). At the same time, in those same schools, school districts mandate reductionist evaluation practices which discourage many students right out of school and away from a real appreciation of learning. Coping with the resulting pedagogical schizophrenia affects decisions we make in our classrooms every day and accounts for many tension headaches—a sure manifestation that a Catch-22 dialectic inhabits the system.

As Greene points out in her analysis of the early abolitionist/civil rights movement, many policies and practices of schooling (including, for example, the reductionist evaluation schemes mentioned above) are based on social Darwinism—the sociological appropriation of Darwinism for the justification of "natural forces" as the primary agent of human conditions. Social Darwinism is like honeysuckle: pretty and persistent, fragrant and deadly to its hosts. In its broad applications, the "survival of the fittest" means that schooling is supposed to prepare individuals to make the best of whatever places the natural forces provided to them: "At best, its function was to transmit from one generation to another a proper understanding of the order of things."[25]

If that sounds familiar, it is because that view, usually unarticulated and covert, pervades American schooling through policies and practices rooted in its self-fulfilling "natural order." Often that has meant for teachers, "[f]or the ordinary person, for the poor and submerged, any dream of freedom had to give way to adjustment to the necessary."[26] In schooling, that usually means teacher-centered, text-focused, test-driven classroom instruction of discrete, unconnected content areas, complete with elitist systems of tracking, grouping, scheduling, and evaluation of student achievement—and administered by a hierarchical management system.

Foxfire teachers, like others who resist that view of schooling, have different hopes for their students—not a misty-eyed fantasy, but a warranted realization that all students are capable of much more than what conventional schooling elicits.

* * *

Greene makes the point that women, whose views of themselves tend to be contained within the confines of socially conventional relationships—daughter, wife, mother, domestic partner—have to "unconceal . . . to create clearings, spaces in the midst of things where decisions can be made."[27] That is powerfully relevant to this discussion since, as of January 1992, 87 percent of the members of Foxfire networks were women. The democratic processes of the networks enable them to express and act on their professional insights, to release energies in ways denied them by male-dominated administrative hierarchies, and to aim the networks in directions most likely to contribute to schools the effectiveness and caring they presently lack.

Attaining that kind of freedom is not as simple as it sounds, however. The very framing of the issues to be discussed, voted on, and implemented by a network can be subtly governed by the educational establishment, mostly men.

What males have thought to be formal truths are grounded, in their cases as well as females, in the concreteness of experience and of encounters in the temporal world. In a *laissez faire* society, however, where those in power relate to one another in contractual and conventional terms, where the private and the affective are excluded, the abstractions take on a pseudo-reality and an apparent objectivity. Women's concrete historical realities, on the other hand, are such that the particularities of everyday life are inescapable. They cannot simply claim their freedom and their rights (at least not ordinarily) and escape the sphere of obligation and concern. When they do so, they very often alienate themselves from what might be called the ground of their being.[28]

Wilder and Priddy speak powerfully and directly about the unshackling effects on women as they allow those kinds of insights into their world views. Wilder's commentary reflects insights from her research about women's issues within the network. Priddy's commentary comes straight from her personal experiences. Could there be more compelling illustrations of the presence of dialectics in individual lives?

The Foxfire approach to teaching is not easy to implement. Needing support, encouragement and resources, these teachers united to form the network, almost entirely women. Now, I hear comments like this, unsolicited: "The network has given me a voice, opportunities to be a part of an organization of teachers operated by teachers."

Personally, the teachers began to examine the structure of their home and family in the light of their new experiences with Foxfire. Their relationships with their children and their husbands developed in new and unexpected ways. Their new sense of self-esteem led to a certain kind of independence in thought and action. They insisted on more participation in the family decisions, expressed more dissatisfaction with the status quo. They began transitions from passive to assertive women; from quiet, reserved followers to confident leaders. Some, determined to remedy unpleasant marital difficulties, made decisions to seek separation and divorce.

Jenny Wilder, Eastern Kentucky Teachers Network

We, as a network, want to do what we, as women, have been taught to do, when tensions and conflicts arise—avoid the issue, hope it will go away—before finally discovering that *we* are responsible here for ourselves. We *are* the network; we are the main authority, after all. And so, "How do we confront this?"

That reminds me of how angry I was the first time I read *The Dialectic of Freedom*, last fall. There were issues going on with my husband, with my father, etc. But most of all it boiled down, simply, to the whole notion of freedom. My father, I need to say, invented women's lib because he had four daughters instead of four sons. He wanted us to be able to do, to work, said he wanted us to think for ourselves. But here was that old notion that "thinking" meant, ultimately, thinking what Daddy wanted you to think. The anger followed by the responsibility: that's the real tension for me. If I say I want this freedom, then I have to acknowledge and accept that I have to be responsible for myself, no longer blame others, *risk* making my own mistakes—in short, make decisions. That is scary as hell for someone who has thought she was free and making her own decisions most of her life, only to realize she has hidden very basic facts from herself.

Melva Sue Priddy, Eastern Kentucky Teachers Network

So the networks honor "women's concrete historical realities."[29] (One example: providing child-care services so women with children may attend two-week long Foxfire training sessions.) They do that, usually with comfort and grace, and they do that without offending male members. Readers may provide their own inferences from that. . . .

* * *

The commentaries by Payne and Starling suggest some of the complexities and cross-currents of the institutional and personal contexts in which network leaders operate. Because Payne's network is relatively new and Starling's network is working toward full affiliation with Foxfire, their narratives also provide some feeling for the difficulties of network start-up.

Of course, the big tension for us is the one between the hierarchical (the university) and the flat (the loose band of dedicated but scattered teachers who are used to working in a system that doesn't mete out rewards of elevated status for their efforts). Orchestrating that dialogue has been like trying to get a Newport matron and a skinhead to like each other—and as dangerous. The University agenda, geared to rewards for public research and posturing, clashes uncomfortably with the teachers' agenda, geared to withstanding anonymity in spite of effort.

What exactly happens when they meet? The University interpretation of the network is to see, at first, a resource guide with a multitude of opportunities for self-promotion and resulting professional security. The teachers, at first, see another marginally interesting here-today-gone-tomorrow ideal they'll have to work like hell for, with no external rewards at all. Maybe a room of happy faces or a few positive calls from parents. Upon revisiting the areas where the clash evidences itself, like a meeting to determine a budget for the network, however, the University (maybe) comes to see a new way to operate collaboratively ("Gee. Wow. Many heads ARE better than one. You mean we can ALL benefit. Well, I never . . ."). And, more quickly, the teachers see those long dead dreams of teaching really meaning something, of making a difference, rising before them, alive and well, because they ARE making a difference—for each other. (A teacher in my current Foxfire class just told me this.) So both sides go back with this new shift in their mental landscapes, and find everything else is moved around now, too. But how much? For the brave, the dialectic multiplies. One thing about growing is, it hurts.

Ann Payne, MountainFire: West Virginia
Foxfire Teacher Outreach Network

We come from three school districts and a university, each with its own agenda for supporting our efforts. In our struggle to infiltrate/collaborate/work with these systems, we've had to be savvy, keeping in mind matters of protocol when approaching the powers in these institutions, and we've had to come to terms with our own power. I think this has been the hardest for us to deal with—recognizing that we do have authority by virtue of our lived experiences and through the validation/endorsement we have received from Foxfire Teacher Outreach.

As a ring leader in this endeavor, I have found myself struggling between deferring to others at the university or the district level and asserting myself too strongly. We actually started working on becoming a network in 1990, after eight Central Florida educators took the Foxfire course in Rabun Gap [Foxfire's home]. At that time, I hoped the university would host the network and I worked with a university professor, trying to collaborate on the process. The relationship wasn't balanced, and the collaboration was clumsy. We kept stepping on each other's toes. Here I was, just a teacher, and there he was, the authority and expert. We pulled and tugged, moving in conflicting directions. We both believed in Foxfire and wanted to share this with teachers, but our missions were different. He wanted to share Foxfire by teaching the course. I wanted to share Foxfire through a support network, making sure that teachers had the support and protection they needed to take the risks necessary to implement Foxfire.

When we taught the course here last summer and the cadre of teachers heartily endorsed the concept of a network, the rules changed and the power shifted. It is no longer my singular voice but our collective voice that asserts what we need from the school districts and the university. Backed by Foxfire Teacher Outreach, our voice has authority. We are beginning to feel that we can impact not only our classrooms, but the system as well.

We've rocked the boat along the way, created disequilibrium. Imagine district-level people having to go through teachers to get to Teacher Outreach! True collaboration requires a leveling of status. We're not level yet, but we don't need to holler quite as loudly for the people up there to hear us. We want to be more than an outside irritation to the system. We want to be more than a little subversive group within the system. If we are successful, our values will permeate the teachers' lounges and our schools will become a safe place for teachers to learn and grow.

Melody Starling, Sunfire Network (Central Florida)

In case it is not already evident, these networks are not franchises, nor is there a pattern for formation, leadership, governance, decision-making, funding, or programs. Each has formed idiosyncratically, reflecting region, state, the happenstance of membership, and the vision of sponsoring, supporting institutions. Networks form through a combination of spontaneous interest by teachers, nurture by Foxfire, and support by host institutions (usually colleges and universities). For the first year or two, most network members manifest concerns about specific issues regarding their classroom practices while implementing Foxfire-style instruction. Those concerns gradually spiral into a growing interest in complementary practices, like whole language, cooperative learning, authentic assessment and reforms of schooling. At some point, described by coordinators as "turning the corner," "attaining momentum," and "taking ownership," members of the network begin to assume interest in and control over the "business" of their network—budgets, fund-raising, planning meetings, getting out the newsletter.

Leadership appears to be the single most influential factor in the pace, direction, and success of a network's spiral. The crucial element of leadership generates a dialectic of its own. In most cases, one of the participants in the course for teachers volunteers to serve as a contact for the group. Often that individual's commitment grows incrementally into a full-time, paid coordinator for the network. In cases where the Foxfire initiative is fully sponsored by a college or university, the leader-coordinator role becomes a job description item for a willing member of the faculty, approved by Foxfire's Outreach staff. In a few cases, the Teacher Outreach staff identifies an individual for the members of the network to consider for the coordinator's position.

Regardless of the selection process, most of the individuals assuming the coordinator's role have evolved into strong, resourceful leaders—effective in ways they never imagined for themselves. That does not always happen, and dissatisfaction with leadership can infect a network, always manifested in quick attrition in membership. (Teacher Outreach engineered one leadership change since the program began in 1986.) Since a prospective network participant has the very attractive option of simply "doing Foxfire" in her/his classroom without the added hassle of taking on an additional responsibility and tedious issues like "Whose network is this, anyway?", it is easy to understand why that happens as often as it does.

As several of the commentaries imply, most teachers have had to accept an authoritarian hierarchy as a condition of their career. While chafing and restricting, that condition becomes such a constant of professional lives that many network participants bring that expectation into the network's operations. They tend to accept whatever leadership is in place, or to reject network participation if the leadership comes across as uninspiring or inept. It seems to take two to three years and some subtle provocations by Teacher Outreach for networks' members to own the matter of leadership in their network.

As the number of networks increases, we may have to attend to the question of leadership to a degree not envisioned in our earlier "benign neglect" phase of organizational development. Clearly aggrieved by the initial leadership situation in his network, Sapp takes Teacher Outreach to task in his commentary.

> Foxfire National [sic] should take a closer look at what Sarason calls the "before-the-beginning" context. "Before-the-beginning" refers to a historical perspective which precedes the physical creation of a new setting. It is true that being inclusive is a key characteristic of new community-building settings. Still, Foxfire National needs to take a closer look at the leadership they allow.
>
> Most of us tend to copy the attitudes, actions, and beliefs of people who are in leadership. My principal during my first year of teaching always stated that "Everything rises and falls on leadership." My experience tells me he was correct.
>
> Foxfire is primarily concerned with the teaching of the Foxfire approach. They don't want the approach bastardized in any way. Foxfire is well aware of how Dewey's philosophy of education was bastardized by early pedagogical reforms who flew the progressive banner. Typically, these groups shared "Dewey's antipathy to the rigidity and extreme didacticism of traditional schooling. Contrary to Dewey's philosophy, however, they have also manifested a tendency to overemphasize the affective side of the child's education, leaving intellectual development largely to chance."[30] Some educators have done this exact thing with the Foxfire approach.
>
> Foxfire National's care about this area has caused some neglect in other important areas. One such vital element they neglect is consideration of community-building skills of their [network] leaders. Do these leaders perpetuate the status quo of top-down leadership that is the antithesis of the democratic spirit of Foxfire? Or are they able to purposely create an environment that nurtures the members of the networks?

> Jeff Sapp, MountainFire

* * *

This quick probe into our program can only begin to engage the perspectives provided in *The Dialectic of Freedom*. However, even that cursory look reveals larger issues and future agendas.

As the program attracts more teachers and new networks, we will have to address in more imaginative ways the tensions that result from accepting (by teaching) mandated curricula which are loaded with values and views contrary to those which connect us in common purposes and a different set of values and expectations for our students and ourselves. Greene describes those common purposes as "stories that open perspectives on communities grounded in trust, flowering by means of dialogue, kept alive in open spaces where freedom can find a place."[31] By the second or third session of our initial course for teachers, the participants begin to envision what they *could* do with this approach. That vision makes even more poignant their frustrations with what they rightly perceive as built-in limits to what they can, in reality, *do*. With experience, they are able to convert the problems into opportunities, though there is always a palpable sense of "Horace's Compromise," of never delivering what we know *ought* to be delivered. Perhaps initiatives like plans to engage Foxfire networks as resources to help deliver various state-initiated education reforms provide some hope of addressing that issue.[32]

A complementary, complicating issue comes from the intersection of the program's goal and the realities of school districts. The goal: For schools and school districts to acknowledge and support the Foxfire approach as *one* of the valid approaches to instruction. The reality is that the cooperation and collaboration necessary to achieve that goal can easily result in the approach being diluted, then absorbed into the formless regularities of conventional schooling. Another scenario: the current superintendent, supportive and sympathetic, is caught in the pattern of biennial turnovers so characteristic of that position; the new superintendent is neither sympathetic nor supportive; the Foxfire element gradually disappears, to join the other rusting hulks of moribund reforms.

Both of those concerns suggest that we are still uncertain about the issue of autonomy vs. freedom, about whether our fragile strength can prevail against the momentum of prevailing practices.

Our part of the dialogue about schools, though much larger than we envisioned in 1986, seems timid when weighed against Greene's view of dialogues which engage the public in explorations of what education could be. (But then, does *anyone* do that?) We seem awkward at times in our relationships with the broader communities within and around our schools. We have not yet found the language or the modes to convey the potential of the Foxfire approach to parents, leaders of communities, or educators accustomed to positivist-inspired constructions of schooling. We are certain that nearly everyone resonates with "learning by doing" and that such resonance can evoke recessive values and visions in support of schooling unshackled from our present factory-inspired modes. Until we, or someone, develops the means for large, informed public dialogue about schooling, we do what we can where we can. Perhaps the barrier lies in residual dualisms that haunt our world views and populate them with them-and-us, either-or, practical vs. theoretical ghosts.

Perhaps those dualisms help explain why, though one of our Core Practices deals with aesthetics, we have not yet pushed our way past the art-as-frills mentality to what Greene calls "aesthetic engagements" in every content area we teach and in the deliberations of our networks. Those engagements "will help open the situations that require interpretation, will help disrupt the walls that obscure the spaces, the spheres of freedom to which educators might someday attend"[33]—in other words, address those issues and concerns outlined just above.

The unfulfilled portions of our vision are daunting, but we entertain the hope that the democracy, dialogues, and initiatives characteristic of Foxfire networks eventually will take place within school faculties, between schools and their communities, and among teachers in their professional communities. Given the momentum of policies and practices, and the prevalence of some contrary values and world views, we operate on the assumption that it will take at least two generations of Foxfire teachers, in conjunction with complementary organizations and programs, to secure that vision in reality. Foxfire-affiliated teacher networks are one crucial means to that end. They model, in a rough-hewn way, what teachers' professional lives could be and should be.

> If we are seriously interested in education for freedom as well as for the opening of cognitive perspectives, it is also important to find a way of developing a praxis of educational consequence that opens the spaces necessary for the remaking of a democratic society. For this to happen, there must be a new commitment to intelligence, a new fidelity in communication, a new regard for imagination. It would mean fresh and sometimes startling winds blowing through the classrooms of the nation. It would mean the granting of audibility to numerous voices seldom heard before and, at once, an involvement with all sorts of young people being provoked to make their own the multilinguality needed for structuring of contemporary experience and thematizing lived worlds.[34]

CONTRIBUTORS

In order of their contributions:

Hilton Smith is a secondary social studies teacher currently serving as Director of Foxfire's Teacher Outreach program.

Angela Allen, a member of the Crossties Network, teaches a self-contained all-male, all-black third grade at Whitefoord Elementary School in Atlanta.

Laurie Varner, a member of the Crossties Network, teaches first grade at Hendrix Drive Elementary, Forest Park, Georgia. She implements Foxfire by developing with her students individualized developmentally appropriate activities.

Jenny Wilder, the Teaching Associate for the Eastern Kentucky Teachers Network, is a social studies teacher in Jessimine County, Kentucky. In her work with the network, she works with Foxfire teachers at all grade levels and content levels.

Marylyn Wentworth is the coordinator of the Partnership Teachers Network, based at the University of Southern Maine. She serves as a consultant to several other programs with pedagogical orientations similar to Foxfire's.

Bob Jones is the coordinator for Soundfire [Puget Sound Education Consortium (PSEC) Foxfire Teachers Network]. He also serves as a consultant to the PSEC for school-wide restructuring. Bob is a experienced teacher for grades four through six.

Dottie Turnbull is the contact for the Louisville Area Foxfire Network (Kentucky). She teaches social studies at the Crosby Middle School in Louisville.

Melva Sue Priddy serves as the Chair of the Executive Committee of the Eastern Kentucky Teachers Network. She teaches language arts at George Rogers Clark High School, Winchester, Kentucky.

Ann Payne is the coordinator of MountainFire: West Virginia Foxfire Teacher Outreach Network. She taught in a variety of programs before agreeing to serve as coordinator.

Melody Starling is the contact for Sunfire, the Central Florida Teachers Network, in the Orlando, Florida, region. She is a lead teacher at Tuskawilla Middle School, Ovieda, Florida.

Jeff Sapp is a charter member of MountainFire: West Virginia Foxfire Teacher Outreach Network. He is currently a doctoral candidate at West Virginia's University's College of Education.

The Foxfire Approach:
Perspectives and Core Practices

Perspectives

This revision of what was entitled "Nine Core Practices" reflects the latest in our collective thinking about the principles and practices characteristic of the approach to instruction we pursue. The principles and practices are not scriptural; they are not oracular. They come from reflections and discussions on the results of classroom instruction. In time, we will refine them again to reflect the best of our thinking.

This approach to instruction is one of several promising approaches, some of which share many of the same principles. We've found that as each of us explores this approach in our classrooms, we broaden the base of experience from which we all work, often engaging other, resonant approaches and strategies. The approach never becomes a "recipe" for any teaching situation, nor a one-best-way teaching methodology that can be grasped through one-shot, in-service programs or teacher "handbooks."

In the contexts in which most of us work, few of us will be able to say that our instruction manifests all of these "core practices." Being able to assert that is not the point. The point is to constantly review our instructional practices to find ways to engage each core practice. For when that happens, we and our students experience the most elegant and powerful results this approach can deliver.

The goal of schooling—and of this approach to instruction—is a more effective and humane democratic society. Individual development through schooling is a means to that goal. Often given rhetorical approval while being ignored in practice, that goal should infuse every teaching strategy and classroom activity.

As students become more thoughtful participants in their own education, our goal must be to help them become increasingly able and willing to guide their own learning, fearlessly, for the rest of their lives, Through constant evaluation of experience, and examination and application of the curriculum, they approach a state of independence, of responsible behavior, and even, in the best of all worlds, of something called wisdom.

Core Practices

1) **All the work teachers and students do together must flow from student desire, student concerns.** It must be infused from the beginning with student choice, design, revision, execution, reflection and evaluation. Teachers, of course, are still responsible for assessing and ministering to their students' developmental needs.

   Most problems that arise during classroom activities must be solved in collaboration with students. When one asks, "Here's a situation that just came up. I don't know what to do about it. What should I do?" the teacher turns that question back to the class to wrestle with and solve, rather than simply answering it. Students are trusted continually, and all are led to the point where they embrace responsibility.

2) Therefore, **the role of the teacher must be that of collaborator and team leader and guide** rather than

boss. The teacher monitors the academic and social growth of every student, leading each into new areas of understanding and competence.

And the teacher's attitude toward students, toward the work of the class, and toward the content area being taught must model the attitudes expected of students—attitudes and values required to function thoughtfully and responsibly in a democratic society.

3) **The academic integrity of the work must be absolutely clear.** Each teacher should embrace state- or local-mandated skill content lists as "givens" to be engaged by the class, accomplish them to the level of mastery in the course of executing the class's plan, but go far beyond their normally narrow confines to discover the value and potential inherent in the content area being taught and its connections to other disciplines.

4) **The work is characterized by student action**, rather than passive receipt of processed information. Rather than students doing what they already know how to do, all must be led continually into new work and unfamiliar territory. Once skills are "won," they must be reapplied to new problems in new ways.

Because in such classrooms students are always operating at the very edge of their competence, it must also be made clear to them that the consequence of mistakes is not failure, but positive, constructive scrutiny of those mistakes by the rest of the class in an atmosphere where students will never be embarrassed.

5) A constant feature of the process **is its emphasis on peer teaching, small group work and teamwork**. Every student in the room is not only included, but needed, and in the end,

each student can identify his or her specific stamp upon the effort. In a classroom thus structured, discipline tends to take care of itself and ceases to be an issue.

6) **Connections between the classroom work and surrounding communities and the real world outside the classroom are clear.** The content of all courses is connected to the world in which the students live. For many students, the process will engage them for the first time in identifying and characterizing the communities in which they reside.

Whenever students research larger issues like changing climate patterns, or acid rain, or prejudice, or AIDS, they must "bring them home," identifying attitudes about and illustrations and implications of those issues in their own environments.

7) **There must be an audience beyond the teacher for student work.** It may be another individual, or a small group, or the community, but it must be an audience the students want to serve, or engage, or impress. The audience, in turn, must affirm that the work is important and is needed and is worth doing—and it should, indeed, *be* all of those.

8) As the year progresses, **new activities should spiral gracefully out of the old**, incorporating lessons learned from past experiences, building on skills and understandings that can now be amplified. Rather than a finished product being regarded as the conclusion of a series of activities, it should be regarded as the starting point for a new series.

The questions that should characterize each moment of closure or completion should be, "Now what?

(continued)

What do we know now, and know how to do now, that we didn't know when we started out together? How can we use those skills and that information in some new, more complex and interesting ways? What's next?"

9) As teachers, **we must acknowledge the worth of aesthetic experience**, model that attitude in our interactions with students, and resist the momentum of policies and practices that deprive students of the chance to use their imaginations. We should help students produce work that is aesthetically satisfying, and help them derive the principles we employ to create beautiful work.

Because they provide the greatest sense of completeness, of the whole, of richness—the most powerful experiences are aesthetic. From those experiences we develop our capacities to appreciate, to refine, to express, to enjoy, to break out of restrictive, unproductive modes of thought.

Scientific and artistic systems embody the same principles of the relationship of life to its surroundings, and both satisfy the same fundamental needs.—John Dewey

10) **Reflection**—some conscious, thoughtful time to stand apart from the work itself—is an essential activity that must take place at key points throughout the work. It is the activity that evokes insights and nurtures revisions in our plans. It is also the activity we are least accustomed to doing, and therefore the activity we will have to be the most rigorous in including, and for which we will have to help students develop skills.

11) **The work must include unstintingly honest, ongoing evaluation for skills and content, and changes in student attitude.** A variety of strategies should be employed, in combination with pre-and post-testing, ranging from simple tests of recall of simple facts through much more complex instruments involving student participation in the creation of demonstrations that answer the teacher challenge, "In what ways will you prove to me at the end of this program that you have mastered the objectives it has been designed to serve?"

Students should be trained to monitor their own progress and devise their own remediation plans, and they should be brought to the point where they can understand that the progress of each student is the concern of every student in the room.

NUTS AND BOLTS OF THE FOXFIRE TEACHER OUTREACH ORGANIZATION

Foxfire Teacher Outreach is a program of the Foxfire Fund, Inc., a 501(c)(3) educational entity. The responsibilities for governance rests with Foxfire's Board of Directors. Technically, Teacher Outreach and those networks still operating under Foxfire's 501(c)(3) are governed by that Board. The rest of the networks operate under the "governmental instrumentality" of their host institutions—colleges, universities, and school districts.

In actual operation, the coordinators of all the networks serve as the governing body for the Outreach operation. In 1990, when we realized we could no

longer meet around a large kitchen table, the coordinators agreed to the desig-
nation of a small group as an Executive Committee to assume responsibility for
short-term decisions and refining proposals for the whole group. The Teacher
Outreach staff (four folks in a two-person cabin) serves as a coordinating group
for the overall operation, and executes the oversight function for the Foxfire
Board. (Another dualistic source for occasional tensions.)

The first networks were funded almost entirely by Foxfire's original outreach grant. Later networks were added only when their host institutions provided for their funding. As of this writing, all the networks are to become
financially self-sufficient, through a combination of institutional support, grants,
and member dues.

Presently there are eleven networks and six "pending." For current information, including a list of the networks and pending sites with names and
addresses of the coordinators/contacts, sites and dates for courses and workshops, and guidelines for forming a Foxfire-affiliated network, contact Foxfire
Teacher Outreach, Mountain City, Georgia 30562.

NOTES

1. Maxine Greene holds the William F. Russell Chair in Foundations of Education at Teachers College, Columbia University. Best known for her work in the philosophy of education, her work cuts across philosophy, aesthetics education, literature,
and history. She applies her insights beyond academia, including serving as a consultant
to the Lincoln Center Institute for Performing Arts in Education in New York City.
The Dialectic of Freedom originated as a John Dewey lecture and was published in
1988 by Teachers College Press, New York.

2. Gene Ensminger and Harry Dangel, "The Foxfire Pedagogy: A Confluence of
Best Practices for Special Education," *Focus on Exceptional Children*, Vol. 24, No. 7
(March 1992).

3. Hilton Smith, et al., "Foxfire Teacher Networks," *Staff Development for Education in the 90's*, edited by Ann Liberman and Lynn Miller (Teachers College Press,
1991).

4. Greene, *The Dialectic of Freedom*, p. 14.

5. Ibid., p. xii.

6. Ibid., pp. 6-8, passim.

7. The Foxfire Approach: Perspectives and Core Practices (Rabun Gap, GA:
Foxfire, 1989), Attachment 2.

8. Greene, *The Dialectic of Freedom*, p. xi.

9. Ibid., p. 12.

10. Ibid., p. 14.

11. Ibid., p. 8.

12. Eliot Wigginton, "Foxfire Grows Up," *Harvard Educational Review* 59(1), (February 1989), p. 43.

13. Greene, T*he Dialectic of Freedom*, p. 12.

14. Ibid., p. 5.

15. Ibid., p. 9.

16. Junius Eddy and Hilton Smith, "Assessments of the Foxfire Approach in the Classrooms of Affiliated Teacher Networks, Part Five: Final Report," *Foxfire Teacher Outreach* (July 1991), p. 23.

17. Greene, *The Dialectic of Freedom*, p. 4.

18. Ibid., p. 5.

19. Ibid., p. 8.

20. Ibid., pp. 117-118.

21. John Dewey, *Experience and Education* (Macmillan Publishing Company, 1963).

22. Greene, *The Dialectic of Freedom*, p. 43.

23. Dewey, *Experience and Education*, p. 21.

24. Greene, *The Dialectic of Freedom*, p.28.

25. Ibid., p. 39.

26. Ibid., p. 39.

27. Ibid., p. 58.

28. Greene, *The Dialectic of Freedom*, p. 71.

29. Ibid., p. 71.

30. John Puckett, *Foxfire Reconsidered* (Urbana and Chicago: University of Illinois Press, 1989), p. 212.

31. Greene, *The Dialectic of Freedom*, p. 134.

32. Alan DeYoung, "Today, Kentucky, Tomorrow America? Linking the Foxfire Philosophy of Teaching to Contemporary School Reform," *The New American School: Alternative Concepts and Practices* (Newark, NJ: Ablex Publishers, 1992).

33. Greene, *The Dialectic of Freedom*, p. 133.

34. Ibid., p. 127.

Three

Doing Women's Studies
Possibilities and Challenges in Democratic Praxis

Cecilia Reynolds

> It would be a thousand pities if women wrote like men or lived like men or looked like men for if two sexes are quite inadequate, considering the vastness and variety of the world, how should we manage with only one? Ought not education to bring out and fortify the differences rather than the similarities?[1]

In many discussions about women and democracy the emphasis has been upon women's rights to the same activities, privileges and powers that men have traditionally held. An example of this is Mary Wollstonecraft's protest against "the gross sexism of the strategies in which women were not to participate as equals."[2] Democratic education has often been viewed as that which allows women and girls equal access to the same schooling experiences available to men and boys. Dewey's view of participatory democracy, according to Westbrook (1991), however, posits that democracy is "an ethical ideal" which "calls upon men and women to build communities in which the necessary opportunities and resources are available for every individual to realize his or her particular capacities and powers through participation in political, social and cultural life."[3]

An important opportunity for acting out such an ethical ideal currently presents itself in emergent Women's Studies programs in our colleges and universities. Drawing on my experiences as the Director of a Women's Studies program initiated in 1991 at Brock University in Ontario, this chapter describes how such programs provide possibilities for democratic praxis in schools. By that I mean Women's Studies programs are sites where theory and practice can combine to create praxis, "the customary practice or conduct"[4] which constitutes a democratic way of life "of free and enriching communion in which free social inquiry is indissolubly wedded to the art of full and moving communication."[5]

This opportunity for democratic praxis in Women's Studies programs, however, is limited by the location of such programs within institutional environments which are often hostile to many of the theories and practices which the programs' teachers and students entertain in their quest to realize their particular capacities and powers. Thus, the necessary full communication is frequently thwarted, particularly when it offers challenge to long-held beliefs and values, exposes tensions and contradictions in lived realities, gives evidence of continuing injustice, and/or experiments with new possibilities for everyday life.

This chapter also argues that participation in Women's Studies programs offers particularly valuable experiences for those who will become democratic teachers in our schools at a variety of levels. Unfortunately, little encouragement exists at present for education students to consider taking courses within the Women's Studies programs at our colleges and universities. Thus, important opportunities are currently being missed in terms of educational experiences for teachers which could develop knowledge, attitudes, skills, and the necessary incentives for them to sustain democratic praxis in their future teaching careers.

Women's Studies programs in our colleges and universities embrace notions of education as a liberating force but they also challenge "the liberating potential of perfectible reason."[6] Many feminist critiques target how "reason" in its traditional forms has assumed a separation of mind and body which is particularly problematic for women in our culture. Questions about what knowledge is and about who can know have led to questions about how full women's participation in the political, social, and cultural life of colleges and universities has been, even when they have been granted access to the hallowed halls of academe.

Women's Studies programs, such as the one at Brock, are usually designed in opposition to three longstanding academic traditions within universities: (1) restricted access, (2) discipline-based boundaries and (3) hierarchical structures of authority. In each of these areas, the experiences of students, teachers, and administrators within Women's Studies reveal identifiable challenges to the traditions, and possibilities for the realization of the ethical ideal of democratic praxis. While Women's Studies is the focus of this discussion, the implications of the analysis go beyond this example and raise questions about the prospects of democratic education in other sites; for example, teacher education programs designed to foster democracy.

Women's Studies, Academe, and Democracy

Histories of women at Canadian and other universities reveal that women have long been outsiders in the sacred grove of academe. Indeed, in 1900 only

10 percent of all college and university students in Canada were women and the 47 women professors made up only 5 percent of all faculty in Canada.[7] As we near the end of the Twentieth Century, women comprise 56 percent of all undergraduate enrollments, 48 percent of the country's masters students and 36 percent of all doctoral candidates.[8] In the professoriate, however, only 17.5 percent of all full-time faculty in Canada are female.[9]

When we consider certain aspects of women's participation as students and faculty, further questions arise about equity even when access exists. Studies reveal that female students are disproportionately found in part-time studies at both undergraduate and graduate levels. We also find that women faculty are clustered in non-tenure track positions and at lower ranks than their male colleagues. Traditional gendered patterns persist with regard to disciplines for students and faculty alike.[10] Recent qualitative studies in Canada[11] point to systematic and cultural factors which adversely affect women students and faculty. Thus, statistical and experiential data can be used to support the claim that universities in Canada, as elsewhere, continue to function as "guilds" which discriminate against women.[12]

Despite (or perhaps because of) all of this, over the last 20 years increasing numbers of universities have developed and implemented Women's Studies programs. These programs vary and have changed over time but all are tied to feminist thought and actions which insist that gender/sex is "fundamental to the ways we interact with each other."[13]

It is useful to identify three stages in the "re-emergence of feminism in Canada" since the 1970s.[14] The first stage was marked by the report of the Royal Commission on The Status of Women (1975) and focused on the elimination of sex differences and gender stereotypes. Research and political lobbying in this stage heralded the need for educational changes in textbooks, teacher and parental attitudes and policies, and procedures in schools at all levels which blocked the advancement of women into the highest levels of administration. The impact of such a push for change was felt sporadically across institutions and perhaps more strongly in elementary schools than in secondary or post-secondary institutions. Importantly, however, initiatives from the 1970s such as the establishment of feminist journals, research institutes, and funding programs, fostered an infrastructure for a developing scholarship on women.

The second phase in Canada, as elsewhere, focused on revaluing the female. In 1982 the Canadian Women's Studies Association was founded and from 1983 to 1985 five regional chairs in Women's Studies were funded by the Secretary of State. These Canadian developments in this and in the third phase which followed were linked to an international feminist critique within and across a growing number of traditional disciplines. Also, in societies around the world, women's groups were actively advocating social, economic, and political change.

In its third and most recent stage, feminism has come to recognize the diversity of perspectives needed to rethink and reform all areas of human interaction where individuals or groups are overtly or covertly oppressed. Moving from critique to construction, feminists of many different backgrounds and traditions have been grappling with myriad contradictions, the limitations of existing research methodologies and political strategies, and complex questions about knowledge itself. Global perspectives and local actions have been employed to foster social changes which include the diverse needs of such groups as native women, women with disabilities, French-speaking women, lesbians and immigrant women and girls.

In many respects, Women's Studies programs in Canada and elsewhere have developed and continue to operate in opposition to existing practices and structures within education. They hinge on what Cocks calls the "tension point between philosophy and poetry, abstract thought and concrete experience, culture and counterculture, objective and subjective force, domination and rebellion and last but not at all least masculine and feminine."[15] Some of these oppositions are preserved within Women's Studies, others are reconciled, dissolved, or broken into fragments. By examining three such tension points—restricted access, discipline-based boundaries and hierarchical structures of authority—we can increase our understandings concerning both the possibilities and challenges for democratic praxis which Women's Studies programs currently provide.

Restricted Access

As Novak[16] points out, in education we often employ a "doing to" metaphor which emphasizes such words as reinforcing, building, and motivating. That language is particularly noticeable in discussions about women in non-traditional fields such as engineering. In most Women's Studies programs, however, teaching is seen as a "doing with" enterprise emphasizing "choices, mutuality, and possibilities implicit in educational development as a social practice."[17] The intentionally inviting messages of feminist teachers in these programs work toward the inclusion of persons with diverse abilities and backgrounds, but they do so within institutions which historically have functioned to exclude not only women but many other "outsiders."

At perhaps a surface but importantly symbolic and visible level, Women's Studies and its related myriad feminist committees and individual activists have provided "the initial impetus for the development of equity programs"[18] in Canadian universities. Such programs include "groundwork data collection and analysis, policy review, and the establishment of goals and timetables for hiring and employee education"[19] concerning women but also pertaining to native Canadians, those of visible minority groups, non-traditional students (such as mature students or returning students) and students and employees with special needs.

Less visible but of equal importance is the construction of Women's Studies programs as sites for theoretic discourse and related political strategies for moving from the development of equity programs toward "meaningful and lasting transformations"[20] for women and others in academia. In these sites, questions such as, "Access to what?" and "Access at what costs?" can be repeatedly examined. Also, for members of many diverse groups, not only access to but their experiences within and the outcomes they realize need to be considered.

Like others who have tried to enact the principles of invitational education,[21] those in Women's Studies have encountered constraints that develop in practice. They have needed to reflect upon their own limited social and ideological positions and to consider how to "going beyond the individual classroom and publicly reconstructing school practices"[22] to reach out to and interact with those in the wider society.

Women's Studies came to most Canadian universities "through the work of a small number of enthusiasts. These academic feminists insisted that Women's Studies was a legitimate scholarly undertaking, entirely consistent with the mission of the university—the search for truth."[23] In our efforts to expand access for women and others within the university, however, women academics have sometimes not sufficiently examined their own rhetoric and contradictions, their own "partiality" as female scholars. Rooke warns us:

It is dubious practice to criticize the exclusive, arbitrary and partial nature of patriarchal structures yet continue to replicate them casually, opportunistically, cynically, or merely because they are familiar, comfortable, and convenient once we have gained admittance."[24]

One important challenge then in doing Women's Studies is, in the same instance, to establish it as a legitimate and respectable academic area of study which has important implications for and impact upon the everyday lives of a great diversity of women and to do so without restricting access only to those women who fit traditional structures in the university or college system. We must guard against inviting only some women and marginalizing others. If we use jargon or secret language understood only by insiders, Women's Studies can itself become a network of exclusion.[25] If we posit certain characteristics or dispositions as more favorable than others, we may succeed in our criticism of androcentrism by creating a similarly limiting gynocentric ideal.[26]

Women's Studies programs will need to meet this challenge in full knowledge that they do so as sub-units within institutions where authority structures are hierarchical and discipline-based boundaries exist.

Discipline-Based Boundaries

The organizational structure of most Canadian universities is closely tied to groupings of "disciplines" or "subjects." Often, these groupings are formalized as faculties or departments and are treated as administrative units. Communication, resource allocation, and other important activities occur according to such structures.

Traditional views of knowledge production posit that the intrinsic and pedagogic validity of new knowledge leads to the formation of a discipline which "matures" and becomes more "academic" over time.[27] Looking at the evolution of Science as a discipline in England from the nineteenth century, Layton defines three stages. The first stage hinges on relevance to the needs and interests of learners, and teachers of the new discipline bring "the missionary enthusiasms of pioneers to their tasks."[28] In the second stage, a tradition of scholarship emerges, teachers are drawn from a corps of trained specialists, and the "internal logic" of the subject influences the selection and organization of knowledge. In the final stage, teachers of the new discipline are a professional body and knowledge hinges on the judgments and practices of these "specialist scholars." At this stage, students must be initiated into the traditions of the discipline, a step which can create "a prelude to disenchantment."[29]

It is thought-provoking to consider such stages in relation to the development of Women's Studies programs. Such consideration urges us to move "beyond philosophical or macro-sociological analysis towards a detailed historical investigation of the motives and actions underlying the presentation and promotion of subjects and disciplines."[30] We would do well, then, to consider how Women's Studies programs have developed within our institutions. What actions have they taken to get established and why have they taken those particular actions?

It is relatively easy to see that because most Women's Studies programs have asserted the need for cross-disciplinary and inter-disciplinary study and scholarship, they have had to struggle for resources and legitimacy within institutions which are poorly designed for such activities. Students and faculty have had to deal with the realities of co-majors and cross-appointments which often mean heavier workloads, fewer opportunities for scholarships or publication and skepticism regarding vocational and career possibilities. One student reported:

> I often feel that I am discriminated against because of my choice to pursue Women's Studies. Derogatory remarks are made about Women's Studies and my participation in it. I have become a tangible target for the free-floating hostility which perpetuates sexism and racism.[31]

Within feminism, debate continues over separation and integration, about when it is important to pull away from men and discipline-linked knowledge production and maintenance and when it is beneficial to integrate with men and certain discipline-linked knowledge distribution channels.

The efforts of Women's Studies programs to find a place within the institution are complicated by strong tendencies within such structures for new areas to function only within the margins, outside the main business of the organization. Thus, a related challenge for Women's Studies programs is how to manage the need to co-habit, co-sponsor, cross-list, and collaborate with women and men housed in traditional disciplines or even those in other cross-disciplinary or inter-disciplinary programs, and how to avoid being marginalized, exploited, controlled or co-opted in the process.

That challenge is familiar to many women who consciously struggle to maintain both their identity and their relationality. With its emphasis on contextuatation and inter-relation, Women's Studies is particularly vulnerable to manipulation by dominant interest groups within the university. Linkages with other groups need to be carefully examined for their long-range benefits to the Women's Studies program and its members. Attempts at co-operation rather than competition are often interpreted by others as weakness. Those in the program need to be self-protective as well as co-operative. They often need to say "NO" in order to conserve their own integrity and limited resources even though others may view this as counter to their stated ideals. Their ability to do so, however, is limited by the hierarchical structures of authority within the institution and this creates a third tension point regarding the possibilities and challenges related to democratic praxis for those working within Women's Studies programs.

Hierarchical Structures of Authority

Ferguson points out that contemporary bureaucracy should be considered both as structure and process. It is not only a fairly stable arrangement of roles and assignments of tasks, it is also "a temporal ordering of human action that evolves out of certain historical conditions toward certain political ends."[32] As such an ongoing process, it must constantly be reproduced and any opposition must be located and suppressed.

Universities stand in the contradictory position of being bureaucracies in a number of ways while also being egalitarian and participatory organizations in other ways. Women's studies programs within universities generally strive to be democratic units in the larger whole. As such, they encounter a persistent set of problems or challenges met in most participatory organizations and they also serve as sites resistant to bureaucratic processes.

Among their challenges as participatory groups, members of Women's Studies programs are learning how to work collectively, make decisions with the participation of all members, and function co-operatively without the need for hierarchy. Examples of some strategies used are a rotation of leadership, an integration of social and organizational activities,[33] the formation of subcommittees for specific task completion, the use of newsletters which inform and allow for input, and the establishment of regular informal and interactive speaker series or forums.

Such strategies, however, are not without shortcomings. Principal among these is the time needed to work in this way and the limitations on available time due largely to bureaucratic processes within the larger organization. Also, being so used to bureaucracy, many individuals can become frustrated with what seem to be inefficient procedures. They may also fail to consider the possibility of challenging rules or they may fear the consequences of risking open confrontation.

Within Women's Studies classrooms, contradictions regarding authority often pertain to teachers and students alike. As Schniedewind[34] points out, the feminist values of community, communication, equality, and mutual nurturance should ideally be a part of the democratic processes in Women's Studies classrooms where participants come to know each other as people, speak honestly, take risks, and support each other. The realities are that students, so used to hierarchical structures and their manifestations, can and often do misinterpret the messages of feminist teachers. They sometimes doubt the expertise of the teacher and take advantage of new "freedoms."[35] In an effort to act in non-authoritative ways, teachers often try to conceal the fact that they do have final authority within the classroom.[36] Teachers and students alike must come to grips with the implications of the fact that their classrooms are sites where usual institutional practices legitimate existing systems of power and control.[37]

Sustaining classrooms as sites of resistance and possible change regarding usual practices, that is, sustaining them as sites of democratic praxis, presents the challenge of facing the "dialectical unity" between subject and object, consciousness and reality, thought and being[38] for *both* teachers and students. Thus, it is not sufficient to strive solely for consciousness raising, increased theoretical clarity, or an empowering sense of agency; there must also be constant and expansive investigations of realities, increased experimentation regarding practical applications of theories, and ongoing examination of shifts in the historical terrains upon which we may act as social agents.

Conclusions

In a pamphlet published in 1897, John Dewey stated that "education is a regulation of the process of coming to share in the social consciousness" and he also declared that "in the ideal school we have the reconciliation of the individualistic and the institutional ideals."[39] In this chapter, I have argued that while much attention has been paid to adjusting the process of education so that more women might come to share in social consciousness, greater scrutiny is required of our ideals regarding schools and of realities in those institutions if we wish to reconcile the needs of women (and many others) and the institutional ideals.

I have used my own experiences and those of others in the development and implementation of Women's Studies programs within universities in Canada as the basis for a discussion of possibilities and challenges regarding democratic praxis in schools. While my comments need not pertain only to Women's Studies programs or to Canadian universities, they are rooted in reported experiences from those sites. The discussion raises questions about praxis the "customary practice or conduct"[40] or as Lather defines it, "the self-creative activity through which we make the world . . . philosophy becoming practical."[41] What elements affect such activity or conduct? What happens when we try to change it? More particularly, what happens when we try to make it democratic, especially in terms of fostering "a way of life of free and enriching communion in which free social inquiry is indissolubly wedded to the art of full and moving communication"?[42]

Women's Studies programs are advantageous sites for such democracy largely because they strive to create for women, within colleges and universities, safe intellectual and physical spaces which foster a free and enriching communion between and among other women and a full and moving communication not only with other women but also with men, about aspects of their experiences which heretofore have been either silenced or marginalized in the traditional discourses of academe. The programs also foster permission, encouragement, legitimacy, and intellectual, economic, emotional, and physical support for free social inquiry connected to communication in which women's knowledges, questions, and approaches are deemed valuable and appropriate endeavors for students, teachers, and administrators within the program and beyond it in the larger society.

As has been outlined, this can be done by deliberately building an expandable infrastructure for the development of scholarship and activism related to women's lives. Democratic praxis can also be accomplished through the establishment of a visible and symbolic feminist presence within the organizational culture which sustains a continued emphasis on equity programs not only for women but also for members of other previously marginalized or excluded individuals within that organizational culture. Such praxis is also fostered by events sponsored and arranged by those in the Women's Studies program. Such events attempt to build community through conversations and allow others to share in the social consciousness of multiple feminisms as they continue to evolve historically.

Democratic praxis involves adherence to a belief in inter-disciplinary, trans-disciplinary and/or extra-disciplinary approaches to knowledge acquisition and development. Emphasis on connection and relevance is a part of academic life within a Women's Studies program. As well, praxis within the Women's

Studies program encompasses sustained efforts to run the program and teach the classes in adherence to collective, co-operative, and non-hierarchical models of human interaction. Questions of power and privilege are dealt with overtly; faculty, students, and administrators continually experiment in order to find more inclusive and egalitarian methods of getting things done. This search for better ways of being in the academy always include a cognizance of the need for better ways of being for both women and men, boys and girls in our larger society. But, while Women's Studies programs are advantageous sites for democracy, they are also sites where the customary practices and the philosophy on which they rest are often actively opposed within the university or college. That opposition comes largely because such programs posit an "alternative culture" to that traditionally found in academe and as such they offer "a broad based challenge to the given scheme of things."[43]

In this chapter, only three tension points in that opposition have been discussed and related possibilities and challenges identified. Such a narrow focus, however, clarifies the current stage of attempts by those within Women's Studies to reconcile the often contradictory ideals they hold as women and as members of the institution. The argument is made that students who participate in Women's Studies may be particularly well prepared for becoming democratic teachers because they have had to deal with each of the identified tension points between Women's Studies praxis and the structures of the institution.

The first tension point discussed has been that surrounding restricted access. We see a familiar battle here between notions of liberty and equality. The university, ostensibly, is an institution which fosters individual freedom and can assist us in "rising above the herd." On the other hand, it is also a place which fosters protection from "so much individual freedom that some people can rise up to exploit and oppress other people."[44] Abella reminds us of the difference between civil liberties and human rights. She argues that:

> There is a difference between treating people equally as we do in civil liberties and treating people as equals as we do in human rights. For purposes of the former, we treat everyone the same; for purposes of the latter, we treat them according to their differences.[45]

Abella goes on to comment critically upon a form of pluralism which posits "a variety of groups and a variety of views about them, all of perceived legitimacy and weight."[46] To date, most Women's Studies programs have been strongly linked with notions of equality, human rights, and pluralism. Inherent in such linkages, however, is a danger of holding a "naive understanding of its own situation."[47] This means that energies have often been directed at simplifying the role of Women's Studies programs within their institution so that the program can be defended. This defensive stance can mitigate against the necessary sustained self-inquiry and self-reflexive conversations which are necessary to continually work toward improving our attempts at realizing democratic praxis within such programs. In its oppositional stance, Women's Studies may indeed be foregoing an important opportunity to facilitate theoretic discourse and political action which questions pluralism and interrogates the dualisms of liberty and equality, or civil liberties and human rights. Also, in acting "against a regime of power," Cocks warns us that while we may be able to reverse "hegemonic values," those which have traditionally held power in academe, in so doing we may "maintain hegemonic classifications, however much (we) meant to negate them, through lacking a systematic way to break their hold."[48] More simply stated, the tension point of restricted access allows us to see the possibility of Women's Studies programs for important and expanded debate and action regarding these complex topics. It also illuminates the challenge of breaking away from hegemonic practices of exclusion and marginalization rather than simply reproducing them in a different but equally problematic way.

A second tension point discussed has been that of discipline-based boundaries. As a form of women's community, Women's Studies programs can help to "erode fixed feminine and masculine identities."[49] They present the possibility of exhibiting a legitimated "different moral law, different political commitment and a different living of everyday life."[50] The process of realizing such potential, however, is thwarted by the discipline-based boundaries within which such programs and communities must constitute themselves and attempt to grow. A major challenge is how they can do so in a manner which fosters not only their own identity but their relationships to others within the university structures and the wider society.

A third tension point discussed has been that of the hierarchical structure of authority within universities. Here, possibilities exist not only for a critique of such structure but for the creation of new egalitarian and participatory models. Importantly, such a tension point helps us see that Women's Studies programs can indeed erode the power structures currently in place. Women's Studies programs, however, must accept the challenge of refusing to "take the strength of that power at face value."[51] This applies not only to such programs as sub-units within the university but also in regard to democratic praxis within Women's Studies classrooms for both teachers and students.

Dewey saw education as a "regulation of the process of coming to share in the social consciousness."[52] It is an error, however, to believe that education alone will be sufficient to increase women's abilities to share in all forms of social consciousness. But we need to acknowledge the role of Women's Studies programs within colleges and universities around the world in fostering democratic praxis. As has been discussed here, many exciting possibilities present themselves in that regard at this juncture in history. Supported by ongoing analyses of the construction and maintenance of the ideals of schools and the individuals who exist within them, we can chart a path between fatalism and romanticism. We can even imagine moments when for a variety of possible reasons order becomes disorder, and entirely new desires, identities, ideas, and actions become explicitly possible and quite conceivably actual.[53]

NOTES

1. Virginia Woolf, *A Room of One's Own* (London: Triad Grafton Books, 1929), p. 95.

2. Mary O'Brien, "Political Ideology and Patriarchal Education," *Feminism and Education: A Canadian Perspective*, edited by Frieda Forman et al. (Toronto: OISE Press, 1990), p. 10.

3. Robert Westbrook, *John Dewey and American Democracy* (Ithaca: Cornell University Press, 1991), pp. xiv-xv.

4. *Webster's New Collegiate Dictionary* (Springfield, MA: G. C. Merriam Co., 1981), p. 896.

5. Op. cit. p. xviii.

6. O'Brien, p. 10.

7. Alison Prentice et al., *Canadian Women: A History* (Toronto: Harcourt Brace Jovanovich, 1988), p. 10.

8. Sandra Pyke, "Gender Issues in Graduate Education," Trevor, N.S. Lennom Memorial Lecture, The University of Calgary, 1991, p. 4.

9. Ibid., p. 9.

10. Ibid., p. 10.

11. Examples of such Canadian studies include Linda Briskin, "Feminist Pedagogy: Teaching and Learning Liberation." *Feminist Perspectives Feministes*. CRIAW #19, 1990, and Sharon Dempsey and Cecilia Reynolds, "The Internship: A Strategy for Fostering Equity and Excellence for Women in Canadian Universities." A paper delivered at the *Democracy in the University Conference*, Toronto, 1991.

12. Rose Sheinin, "The Charter of Rights and Freedoms: Its Relevance for Democracy in Higher Education in Canada." A paper delivered at the *Democracy in the University Conference*, Toronto, 1991.

13. Jane Gaskell and Arlene McLaren, *Women and Education: A Canadian Perspective* (Calgary, Alberta: Detselig, 1987), p. 3.

14. Ibid., p. 4.

15. Joan Cocks. *The Oppositional Imagination* (New York: Routledge, 1989), p. 1.

16. John Novak, "Advancing Constructive Education: A framework for Teacher Education," *Advances in Personal Construct Psychology* Vol. 1 (1990), pp. 233-255.

17. Ibid., p. 234.

18. Council of Ontario Universities Status of Women Committee. *Women's Studies Programs in Ontario Universities* (1989), p. 2.

19. Ibid., p. 2.

20. Patricia Rooke, "Re-ordering our Partiality: Reflections on Careerism and Feminist Commitment in Academia." *The Journal of Educational Thought* Vol. 23, No. 2 (1989), p. 107.

21. Novak, 1990, pp. 241-242.

22. Ibid., p. 241.

23. Margaret Gillett, *We Walked Very Warily: A History of Women at McGill* (Montreal: Eden Press, 1981), p. 47.

24. Rooke (1989), p. 117.

25. Ibid., p. 112.

26. Ibid., p. 114.

27. Joseph Ben-David and Randall Collins, "Social Factors in the Origins of a New Science: the Case of Psychology," *American Sociological Review* Vol. 31, No. 4 (1966), pp. 451-465.

28. Layton as referred to in Ivor Goodson, *School Subjects and Curriculum Change* (London: Croom Helm, 1983), p. 10.

29. Ibid., p. 10.

30. Ibid., p. 11.

31. Markita Fleming et al., "Gender power and silence in the classroom: Our experiences speak for themselves," *Lexicon* (March 1991), p. 10.

32. Kathy Ferguson, *The Feminist Case Against Bureaucracy.* (Philadelphia, PA: Temple University Press, 1984), p. 6.

33. Ibid., p. 207.

34. Nancy Schniedewind, "Feminist Values: Guidelines for Teaching Methodology in Women's Studies," *Learning Our Way: Essays in Feminist Education*, edited by Catherine Bench and Sandra Pollack (London: The Crossing Press, 1983).

35. Katherine Morgan, "The Perils and Paradoxes of Feminist Pedagogy," *Resources for Feminist Research* Vol. 16, No. 3 (1987).

36. Linda Briskin, "Feminist Pedagogy: Teaching and Learning Liberation." *Feminist Perspectives Feministes* (CRIAW #19, 1990).

37. Kathleen Weiler, *Women Teaching for Change: Gender, Class and Power* (South Hadley, MA: Bergin and Garvey Publishers, 1988), p. xi.

38. Ibid., p. 73.

39. Dewey as quoted in John Miller and Wayne Seller, *Curriculum Perspectives and Practice* (White Plains, NY: Longman, 1985), p. 76.

40. *Webster's* (1981), p. 896.

41. Patricia Lather, *Getting Smart: Feminist Research and Pedagogy With/in the Postmodern* (New York: Routledge, 1991), p. 11.

42. Robert Westbrook, *John Dewey and American Democracy* (Ithaca: Cornell University Press, 1991), p. xviii.

43. Cocks (1989), p. 218.

44. Jack Nelson et al., *Critical Issues in Education* (New York: McGraw-Hill, 1990), p. 24.

45. Rosalie Abella, "Equality and Human Rights in Canada: Coping with the New Isms," *University Affairs* (1991), p. 22.

46. Ibid., p. 22.

47. Cocks (1989), p. 218.

48. Ibid., p. 218.

49. Ibid., p. 215.

50. Ibid., p. 215.

51. Ibid., p. 216.

52. Dewey quoted in Miller and Seller, p. 76.

53. Cocks (1989), p. 221.

REFERENCES

Abella, R. (1991, June/July). Equality and Human Rights in Canada: Coping with the New Isms. *University Affairs*, pp. 21-22.

Ben-David, T., and Collins, R. (1966). Social Factors in the Origins of a New Science: The Case of Psychology. *American Sociological Review 31*(4).

Briskin, L. (1990). Feminist Pedagogy: Teaching and Learning Liberation. *Feminist perspectives feministes*. Canadian Research Institute for the Advancement of Women. No. 19.

Cocks, J. (1989). *The Oppositional Imagination: Feminism, Critique and Political Theory*. New York: Routledge.

Council of Ontario Universities Status of Women Committee (1989). *Women's Studies Programs in Ontario Universities*. Toronto, Ontario.

Dempsey, S., and Reynolds, C. (1991). *The Internship: A Strategy for Fostering Equity and Excellence for Women in Canadian Universities*. Paper delivered at the Conference Democracy in the University, Toronto.

Ferguson, K. (1984). *The Feminist Case Against Bureaucracy*. Philadelphia, PA: Temple University Press.

Fleming, M., Habib, N., Holly, T., Jones-Caldwell, S., Moules, M., Waserman, L., and Wehbi, S. (1991). Gender Power and Silence in the Classroom: Our Experiences Speak for Themselves. *Lexicon*, March.

Gaskell, J., and McLaren, A. (1987). *Women and Education: A Canadian Perspective*. Calgary, Alberta: Detselig Enterprises Ltd.

Gillett, M. (1981). *We Walked Very Warily: A History of Women at McGill*. London: Eden Press.

Gillett, M. (1991). Women in a Female Faculty. *McGill Journal of Education 26*(2).

Goodson, I. (1983). *School Subjects and Curriculum Change*. London: Croom Helm.

Lather, P. (1991). *Getting Smart: Feminist Research and Pedagogy With/in the Postmodern*. New York: Routledge.

Miller, J., and Seller, W. (1985). *Curriculum Perspectives and Practice*. White Plains, NY: Longman.

Morgan, K. (1987). The Perils and Paradoxes of Feminist Pedagogy. *Resources for Feminist Research 16*(3).

Nelson, J., Palonsky, S., and Carlson, K. (1990). *Critical Issues in Education*. New York: McGraw-Hill.

Novak, J. (1990). Advancing Constructive Education: A Framework for Teacher Education. *Advances in Personal Construct Psychology 1*, pp. 233-255.

O'Brien, M. (1990). Political Ideology and Patriarchal Education. *Feminism and Education: A Canadian Perspective*. F. Forman, M. O'Brien, J. Haddad, D. Hallman, and P. Masters (Eds.). Centre for Women's Studies in Education, Ontario Institute for Studies in Education.

Prentice, A., Bourne, P., Brandt, G., Light, B., Mitchinson, W., and Black, N. (1988). *Canadian Women: A History*. Toronto: Harcourt Brace Jovanovich.

Pyke, S. (1991). Gender Issues in Graduate Education. Trevor, N.S. Lennom Memorial Lecture, The University of Calgary.

Rooke, P. (1989). Re-ordering Our Partiality: Reflections on Careerism and Feminist Commitment in Academia. *The Journal of Educational Thought 23*(2).

Schniedewind, N. (1983). Feminist Values: Guidelines for Teaching Methodology in Women's Studies. *Learning Our Way: Essays in Feminist Education.* C. Bench and S. Pollack (Eds.). London: The Crossing Press.

Sheinen, R. (1991). The Charter of Rights and Freedoms: Its Relevance for Democracy in Higher Education in Canada. Paper presented at the Conference. *The University and Democracy*, Toronto, Ontario.

Webster's New Collegiate Dictionary. (1981). Springfield, MA: G. C. Merriam Co.

Weiler, K. (1988). *Women Teaching for Change: Gender, Class and Power.* South Hadley, MA: Bergin and Garvey Publishers Inc.

Woolf, V. (1929). *A Room of One's Own.* London: Triad Grafton Books.

Four

Democratic Empowerment and Secondary Teacher Education

Thomas E. Kelly

Introduction: Democratic Education and False Dichotomies

The purpose of this chapter is to propose a model of a secondary teacher education program (STEP) dedicated to the democratic empowerment of pre-service teachers and their future pupils. Because I seek to communicate with a broad audience interested in teacher education, not just with those for whom the notion of a democratic education has an intuitively clear or salutary connotation, I want to state at the outset what I do not and do mean by the term "democratic empowerment."

In the hopes of minimizing misinterpretation, and to respect those whose association with the term leaves them skeptical and impatient, I will start with what I see it isn't. To me, democratic empowerment of prospective secondary teachers does NOT mean any of the following: a disregard of academic content or a dismissal of significant facts and concepts; a lowering of authentic academic standards; an obsession with process or protecting students' self-esteem at all costs; a categorical disrespect for authority; a laissez-faire surrender of governing authority to those too immature and incompetent to use it responsibly; or a subtle or heavy-handed indoctrination into radical leftist politics. To the extent these descriptions characterize a practice labeled democratic, they represent to me a corruption of democratic education. In softer terms, they may reflect a misguided understanding and/or a temporary failure to strike a dynamic (and always difficult) balance between competing values in particular settings.

In fact, far from rejecting intellectual rigor, academic substance, disciplined interaction and fairminded analysis, I hope to demonstrate that the proposed democratic STEP draws from the best of the dominant reform traditions in teacher education, i.e., the academic, the social efficiency, the developmental and the social reconstructionist.[1] At the same time, it attempts to avoid some of the problems of these competing visions. In other words, I hope to show that democratic education is profoundly integrating in spirit and practice, not in a mindlessly eclectic way, but in a stance deeply compassionate and principled.

The perspectives I offer in this chapter are guided by my belief that education and teaching in a democracy should seek to diminish individuals' original limiting states of existence—ignorance, incompetence, egocentrism and dependence—by enhancing their approximate opposites: the deep understanding of self, others, and the world; and the commitment and ability to negotiate and share power for mutual fulfillment as respectful equals in just and caring communities. Embedded in this vision is a core set of dynamics around which a democratic STEP might be organized and to which it would devote sustained attention. These interactive dynamics include issues of authority/power, knowledge/truth, conflict, community, diversity, justice, public advocacy and service, and self- and institutional renewal.

Overview of Chapter

The chapter will proceed in the following way. After briefly situating these dynamics in the context of democracy, I will discuss, in broad strokes, several sets of scholarship which in turn: a) emphasize the centrality of the schools' civic mission in a democracy, b) reveal the inevitable multidimensionality and interrelationships of teaching and learning, the student and the curriculum, the school and society, and c) indicate how democratic practices take into account this complexity and can make a positive difference in multidimensional development of secondary school students. I then elaborate on these practices and rationale, identifying a number of roles that democratic STEPs should seek to nurture in teachers. In the final section, I outline a series of specific features which might characterize a democratic STEP.

Democratic Education: A Glimpse at Defining Dynamics

I mentioned a number of key dynamics I associate with democracy. Let me briefly elaborate. It is understandable that issues of authority, power, and institutional renewal should be a primary focus for education in a democratic society: a society whose very birth pronounced revolt against pre-existing, arbitrary, and distant power; whose rhetoric proclaims government of, by, and for the people, equality under the law, and inalienable rights of self-determination; and whose suffrage (and its presumption of legitimate personal wisdom) is, at least formally, if belatedly, independent of race, gender, or class. Forged into our national psyche and written into our national constitution is a healthy suspicion of centralized power and hierarchial authority. We, the people, the official authorities over our own lives, only surrender that authority pragmatically and provisionally. Reflected in the consent principle, our nominal leaders serve us, not the reverse. When they abuse their power and formal authority; when, indeed, they are insubordinate to us and principle, it is our right, "the Right of the People to . . . institute new Government."

The claim to being an authority in and over one's own life is problematic, however. In an epistemological sense it raises questions of knowledge and ideological distortion, self-understanding and self-deception, truth and false consciousness. Do I really know the truth about myself, others, social reality? Is my perspective merely my egocentric, ethnocentric bias? Has it been shaped by forces of which I am not aware? Raising and pursuing these questions are themselves democratic acts. They pose an ever-needed challenge to the certainty of received wisdom; and they presume and potentially expand an arena for free and critical inquiry.

In an ethical sense, the claim to being an authority over one's life raises questions of acting as freely as one prefers while fulfilling potentially competing responsibilities to others. Put differently, the ethical questions involve respecting and negotiating individual liberty and diversity within a framework of community. The Statue of Liberty, the Balance Scales of Justice, and the inscription "E Plurabus Unum," are paramount symbols which capture these essential democratic themes or inherent tensions.

Teaching: Inevitably Far More Than the Academic

I take very seriously several sets of scholarly projects which relate to the means and meaning of democratic empowerment. One is the scholarship from individuals of diverse political persuasions who argue that schools in a democracy should intentionally cultivate in students, *regardless* of students' political ideology, the understandings, dispositions and capacities to act effectively as citizens.[2] These scholars and practitioners argue that democracy is not merely a topic to be studied, but foremost a daily experience to be reflectively lived and collaboratively refined. Doing so involves the development of sophisticated, lifelong intellectual and participatory capacities. These empowering attributes include knowledge of formal and informal political-legal processes, the ability to develop informed and reasoned ethical positions on controversial issues, the capacity to gather support for one's advocated position, and the sense of efficacy and commitment to confront and resolve various "psycho-philosophical" dilemmas associated with citizen action.[3] To fulfill schools' compelling civic mission in a democracy, all teachers need to be deliberately educated to serve as exemplars and leaders in this endeavor.

The Implicit Curriculum and Constructivism

A second set of scholarship reveals why the task of democratic education cannot be confined solely to social studies educators. Scholarship addressing the hidden, latent, or implicit curriculum has demonstrated that schools and teachers engage in practices which regularly generate unintended and often disempowering impacts on students. These outcomes can adversely affect such significant domains as students' future aspirations, sense of efficacy, and conceptions of legitimate knowledge, work, authority, conflict, and citizen activity.[4]

The importance of this scholarship for teacher educators is substantial. It says that learning, while not always conscious, is always and unavoidably multidimensional. Students are continually being exposed to messages with potent civic, social, epistemological, and personal implications. These learnings may or may not be supportive of the academic agenda.

To maximize communicating constructive and compatible messages, teachers need systematically to consider a cluster of dimensions within which dynamics salient to democratic dispositions and capacities interact. These dimensions include the voices and values incorporated and silenced within the curriculum, the assumptions about learning implied in instructional and evaluative practices, social relations and the locus of decision-making within the classroom, academic groupings and the structure of the school day, and the relationship between school and the broader community. To concentrate almost exclusively on academic content, as some well-intentioned critics would have teachers and teacher educators do,[5] while seemingly possessing the virtues of focus and feasibility, appears too narrow-minded in light of the potency of the implicit curriculum.

Thus, in a democracy, responsible preparation of secondary teachers involves systematic attention to a complex, holistic conception of teaching and learning. As we seek to attend to our responsibilities, several other sets of scholarly resources provide essential assistance.

One is the scholarship in the cognitive sciences which tells us that what students learn in classrooms is not only a function of *external* messages sent to them through either the intended or the implicit curriculum. It is also a function of the existing perspectives or beliefs that they bring with them to the teaching-learning encounter. As research in attribution theory, locus of control theory, and intellectual, social and moral development indicates,[6] individuals construct meaning, and their pre-existing perspectives mediate that construction in ways that can deepen, distort, or dismiss the messages of the intended curriculum. If we are seriously interested in understanding and influencing what teacher education students are actually learning in our classrooms, attention to their entering beliefs relevant to course goals and processes is essential. In a very significant, Deweyian sense, students themselves are a central curricular dimension, and polarizing conceptions of the student and the curriculum, in effect, represents another instance of a misguided false dichotomy.[7]

Intersecting this literature is scholarship on students' motivation to learn. In an informative summary, Brophy[8] centerpieces the expectancy X value theory of motivation. This theory states that individuals will tend to exert reasonable effort to achieve a particular goal if they perceive two sets of conditions operating: 1) they think they can succeed in the given task (the expectancy factor); and 2) they give sufficient priority to succeeding in the task (the value factor). The first condition directs teachers' attention to two related areas: teaching practical performance skills vital to success and instrumental to forming a solid sense of efficacy; and, as noted above, processing students' past experiences and their derived meanings—vital factors which can mediate current conceptions of efficacy and the perceived value of any skill development.

The value factor in this theory further undermines the tenability of a narrow subject matter orientation to classroom teaching and learning. What individuals value is mediated by a host of factors, many of which are external to the classroom, including, for example, social-economic class, family dynamics, gender, race, religion, popular culture, and the peer group. Working through the beliefs and behaviors of students, these mediating influences function as an ever-present curriculum subtext whose potency to affect learning varies in complex ways, at times invisible and at times identifiable and patterned. The outrage that seems to characterize many social reconstructionists[9] in part reflects their view that school people don't take into sufficient account these powerful but less overt factors. As a result, the latter continually misrecognize problems and blame victims. For their part, school people may be skeptical about the critique, believing it is overly deterministic in its implied (if not explicit) deemphasis of student and home responsibility or teacher-school efficacy. They may also feel overwhelmed by its call for teachers to take concurrent corrective action on seemingly every front imaginable.

Teaching—Democratic Experiences Can Make a Positive Impact

The affirmative message of research is that teachers need not feel powerless amidst these external and potentially overwhelming forces. Teachers can and do make constructive differences in the lives of diverse students. In all areas over which teachers have some control (e.g., curricular, instructional, managerial, and evaluative practices, and role relationships with students), classroom-related experiences can positively affect students' beliefs and behaviors and their motivation to learn.[10]

Of particular relevance is scholarship on adolescent development and the secondary school experience. A comprehensive review of experiential edu-

cation programs[11] revealed that the relationship most instrumental to multidimensional adolescent social development was one characterized by collegial
mentorship. As mentors, adults were seen by adolescents as possessing valued
expertise. As colleagues, adults treated adolescents with mutuality and multidimensionality. Mutuality involves adults' belief that adolescents can make
useful contribution to the learning process. Teachers show genuine respect for
students' knowledge and interests, manifested in a nonimpositional, nonpa-
tronizing, invitational style of interaction. Multidimensionality involves relating to others in an authentic, non-posturing way. Interaction is characterized by
engagement at diverse levels of experience between people seen as individuals,
not mere role incumbents.

Adults who convey a collegial attitude toward youth see it as natural
and appropriate to share their personal feelings and beliefs on relevant matters.
As a consequence, youth tend to feel entrusted and empowered. Treated as
colleagues, youth begin to see themselves as more adult.

Research from the National Center on Effective Secondary Schools[12]
adds to our picture of selected empowering practices. When students experience
a sense of ownership over their work, when they are engaged in responsible
tasks which have real life consequences for others, when students are involved
in sustained cooperative work with diverse peers, and when adults provide
timely guidance, self-esteem and meaningful competence are enhanced.

A final body of scholarship I want to mention is that associated with
cultivating a caring, collaborative, productive community.[13] This work has
highlighted the synergistic power of creating a community culture within which
support, challenge, and critique interact to significantly increase academic,
personal, social, and moral development of community members. Using the
concepts of Frank Smith,[14] as individuals are invited into a club and come to
identify with its members, they learn a lot, quickly, informally, holistically.
The challenge for teacher educators is to make that club as inviting as possible.
Implied above and elaborated below, the attractiveness of the invitation will
depend upon its responsiveness to the common and diverse interests of prospective members, that is, to its capacity to respect individuality within community.

Realizing Democratic Teacher Education:
A Repertoire of Roles

In the previous two sections I have highlighted an array of scholarship and
research that speak to the need for a multidimensional perspective on responsible preparation of secondary teachers in a democracy. I want to briefly
describe several roles which might serve to summarize and extend the preced-
ing commentary, and lead into the forthcoming section on program implications.

Subject Matter Scholars and Renaissance Learners

As emerging subject matter scholars, members of democratic STEPs know and love their discipline in depth. To the outsider they may appear as miracle workers or eccentrics, for they see elegant order amidst apparent chaos, differentiate the significant from the trivial, and transform isolated facts into coherent concepts and compelling generalizations. At root, though, they exemplify the vitality of the mind, focused and fascinated.

As Renaissance learners, they also seek breadth and integration across disciplinary boundaries. Their self-chosen pursuit of mastery in science, math, language, literature, history, or physical education, while attuning them to the aesthetics and interconnections within their own subject, has also served to challenge a parochial outlook on life. Possessing standards of excellence and an empowering grasp of the Gestalt within one discipline, they seek analogues in other fields. With an inquisitive mind and a tolerance for ambiguity, Renaissance learners exemplify and appreciate the benefits of a liberal education.

Reflective Students of Teaching, Learning, and Themselves

In democratic STEPs prospective teachers will direct their inquisitiveness and quest for sophisticated understanding toward studying another complex and multidimensional subject: the interaction of teaching and learning. Grounded in Dewey's[15] distinction between "reflective action" (the active, persistent, and careful consideration of any belief in light of the grounds that support it and the consequences to which it leads) and "routine action" (that which is guided essentially by habit, external authority, and circumstance), these reflective practitioners take on a scientific perspective about teaching, learning and their own experience. Without prematurely dismissing or authorizing their own experience, peers' experience or the results of research, they closely examine each in light of the others, seeking general principles, qualifying conditions and illustrative cases.

Research and others' experience, for example, may help reveal to prospective teachers that distinctive principles apply to teaching different content matter,[16] or that their personal "apprenticeship of observation"[17] in K-12+ classrooms has left them with misperceptions about what is generally true or possible in the teaching encounter.[18] As a case in point, given the historical and contemporary predominance of frontal teaching strategies in secondary schools and colleges,[19] it is quite likely that prospective secondary teachers possess constricted perspectives about the possibilities of democratic classroom experiences.

On the other hand, autobiographical analysis might help identify limitations of research findings. Even if research on other teaching settings is theo-

retically grounded, methodologically rigorous, and demographically similar
to one's own, it does not necessarily capture fully the potential uniqueness of
one's own context and experience. What such research does provide are powerful hypotheses to be thoughtfully tested, not rules and strategies to be unques-
tioningly applied. In other words, it stimulates—not supplants—rational analysis, speaking *to* teachers but not *for* them. Reflective students of teaching and
learning come to know this vital difference.[20]

Philosophers of the Problematic

Democratic teachers let multiple voices speak to them. They are particularly
interested in perspectives which speak to dynamics that frustrate and fulfill
the promises of democracy itself, in and out of schools. Thus, they seek to
understand the complex interplay between knowledge, culture, power, economy, schooling, and distributive justice as they impact teachers' work settings
and along lines of race, class, and gender.

　　　Their quest for understanding these dynamics will necessarily bring them
in contact with the leftist critiques of schooling.[21] As with other competing
interpretations, democratic teachers will not view these critiques unproblemat-
ically. They will recognize, however, that an authoritative understanding of
the contextual constraints and potentials of their own role as teachers demands
that they understand these critiques and take them seriously.

　　　More generally, as philosophers of the problematic, teachers develop
the ability to distinguish the known from the unknown, the obligatory from
the permissible, the precise from the ambiguous. Further, they seek to apply
general principles in the domains of ethics and epistemology to concrete cases
where facts, meanings, and priorities can be difficult, albeit crucial, to determine. Guided experience in clarifying their personal positions on controversial
issues will provide democratic teachers with potentially important capacities
conducive to effective political advocacy and educative pedagogy.

Nurturers of Democratic Dialogue

Identifying the problematic within the taken-for-granted, and clarifying one's
own position on that problematic, are substantial personal achievements. But
just as knowing one's content does not automatically translate into knowing
how to teach it, so too is coming to understand issues not necessarily equivalent
to knowing how to help others actively engage in similar processes of critical
examination. To transform those achievements into contributions to others
involves teachers developing a complex set of skills and sensitivities associated
with facilitating caring and critical dialogue on controversial issues.[22] These

include establishing a climate where trust, openmindedness, and dissent can flourish, insuring that a best case fair hearing for all competing points of views is presented, identifying common and contrasting perspectives, opening up the teacher's views for critique, and examining concrete personal action and obstacles implied in students' preferred stances.

My experience over the last ten years indicates that the development of talented discussion leaders demands multiple opportunities and systematic guidance. It is by no means automatic. Without focused attention, teachers, including those sympathetic with the reconstructionist perspective, tend to be overwhelmed by the complex dynamics involved in addressing controversial issues. Some avoid discussions altogether. Others distort the process by creating a quasi-lecture within a shallow and often heavy-handed question-answer format. In effect, negligence and/or indoctrination replace critical and caring inquiry. As a result, both conventional ideas and their critiques, each of which should be problematized (not preached), escape the sustained scrutiny instrumental to informed decision-making.

Compassionate Colleague[23]

Skilled discussion technique, thoughtfully applied, is crucial to ensuring that the experience of confronting controversial issues endemic to democratic living is an educative, not a mis-educative one. It is, however, not sufficient; effective discussions of controversial issues provoke conflict and vulnerability at the intellectual and emotional levels. For adolescents to feel optimally comfortable to engage in this kind of meaningful dialogue, they will need to experience the norm setter—the teacher—in certain salutary ways. I use the term "compassionate colleague" to capture a mode of being in relationship with others I believe to be most broadly educative and mutually fulfilling.

Compassionate colleagues interact with students in honest, empathic, invitational, and collaborative ways. They forthrightly share their own feelings, needs, and precious values, and seek to understand those dimensions in students. In both words and actions, they communicate by request, not demand; power *with*, not power *over*. As much as possible and especially in cases of student-teacher disagreement, teachers will be "heavy listeners," successfully conveying this essential message to students:

> As much as I believe strongly in this matter, I am fundamentally open to your influence. I know I do not know it all. I am as committed to respecting and meeting your needs as I am to my own. As you consider my request, one based on my needs and values, I want you to know that as important to me as the request itself is a genuine willingness to honor it because you appreciate its value. Emphatically, I do not want

you to comply out of fear, guilt, shame, or other similar motive, because I strongly suspect that doing so will rob you of your sense of autonomy, leave you preoccupied in potentially destructive ways with this loss, and, overall, decrease your desire to contribute to the welfare of others.

Let me explain the statement about potentially destructive preoccupation. If your compliance is rooted in any of the motives indicated, you may be encouraged to believe that I was responsible for your behavior, when this is almost never the case. This belief and its opposite—that others are responsible for your behavior or that you are responsible for others' behavior—are at the core of domination and oppression and serve as festering grounds for violence. For all our sakes, I do not want that motive or misconception to contaminate or characterize our relationship.

There is another vital part of this message that needs to be sent. It speaks to the false dichotomy between authoritarianism and permissiveness, or, put differently, between "you must do what I say/demand" and "you may do anything you please." The essence of this message is this:

> I need also to make something very clear. I do not want you to confuse my desire for a respectful, warm, freeing relationship with my willingness to be a victim or to let others be victims. If, for example, your behavior is physically or verbally abusive, I may need to use force to stop your continued abuse. I need for you to understand that any such force is protective, not punitive. It will be exercised with the greatest care and restraint, and accompanied with my sincere attempt to understand from you the needs and feelings involved in your behavior. I never intend to punish or harm you because I realize it does you a profound disservice, pollutes our relationship, and is generally counterproductive; that is, you will be less not more likely to act willingly in compassionate ways.

> I want to be sure you understand what I am saying. Could you please tell me what you heard me say?

While compassionate collegiality is certainly challenging, I believe it represents the most transformative mode of interacting with others. Because our relationship with students is such a powerful dimension in what we actually teach them, this element of a STEP program needs careful attention. Thus, despite multiple forces in society which conspire to discourage honest, empathic, invitational and collaborative relationship,[24] democratic STEPs will embody a commitment to promote compassionate collegiality through self-reflexivity, personal example, and public critique.

Co-Creators of Democratic Classrooms

When considering classroom experience, five dimensions are paramount. These relate to teacher-student role relationships, management, curriculum, instruction, and evaluation. I use the term co-creators of democratic classrooms to capture the elements of collaborative authorship and engagement I see as central to democratic experience. I have just described the ideal role-relationship in terms of a compassionate colleague. In that description, a management practice was implied. Let me briefly elaborate on that practice.

Catalysts of Collaboration. The conventional view of classroom management is authoritarian or teacher-directed. The teachers' role is to establish and enforce the rules and students are to comply with them. In democratic STEPs and classrooms, management is seen as an issue of collective, not exclusively teacher, governance; and as a fundamental, not incidental, part of the intentional curriculum. Democratic teachers take on the challenge of being catalysts of collaboration. They seek from the outset to co-create with students a shared set of class goals, policies, and procedures for making decisions and resolving conflict. This attempt at co-creation embodies the quest for a caring and self-renewing classroom community, one intending to maximize mastery achievement, meaningful engagement, and responsible choices for students. This lived commitment to sharing power and forming a collegial "we" identity is, for the democratic educator, a paramount curriculum message.[25]

It should be re-emphasized that this deliberate intent to distribute power and decision-making is both principled and qualified. Democratic STEPs help teachers exercise the use of protective force judiciously, to insure rights to safety and an orderly environment. When individual and collective self-regulation of students' behavior falters, responsible teachers intervene with two kinds of strengths: the force of their institutional position, and the compassion of their educated character. Beyond preserving the necessary rights, the purpose of the intervention is to help students reconsider their choices in light of their responsibilities, and assume greater constructive authority over their actions.

Learner-Sensitive Multiculturalists. As democratic teachers examine a school's formal curriculum within their subject area, that is, the learning goals that are explicitly pursued and the materials that are actually used, they are sensitive to a number of issues. One relates to the goals that are prescribed for students. Beyond their clarity, do they focus exclusively on the academic, or do they reflect a more compelling multidimensional conception of the teaching-learning encounter? Do they include a learner-centered and constructivist conception of student authority and authorship? Do the curriculum guidelines somewhere encourage teachers to assess what students already know and want to know vis-à-vis the curriculum content, so as to maximize challenge and self-directed engagement and minimize needless redundancy and boredom? Are students explicitly encouraged to develop their own learning goals in relation to the curriculum studied?

In terms of the actual materials used, democratically oriented teachers will seek to create educative balance in several ways: to include relevant voices and diverse perspectives, and to provide curricular choice for students in cases where achieving desirable learning goals lends itself to optional content.

Psychologizing Pedagogue. At the instructional level, democratic practice calls for mastery achievement for all through meaningful engagement and sensitive attention to diversity in the intellectual, psychological, social, and moral domains. Teachers may promote a number of practices. A suggestive sample of practices follows:

- psychologizing pedagogy;[26] that is, framing instructional purposes in terms that students can grasp as clearly important to them, and applying learning consistently to their lives through analogies connected to central dimensions of their lives: personal aspirations; peer, work and family issues; popular cultural phenomena (e.g., television shows, sports, and music); developmental desires for autonomy, mastery, community, and social contribution.

- including students regularly as teaching resources to explain concepts and achieve instructional purposes.

- enlisting students' imaginative involvement through story telling.[27]

- engaging students in a consideration of the moral implications of subject matter, including attention to issues of gender, race, and social class.

- promoting projects with advocacy-related applications to real problems in students' lives and communities.

- using diverse learning formats to accommodate differences in student abilities, pace, learning style.

- structuring heterogeneous, cooperative learning groups.[28]

- involving all students in active construction of knowledge and values.

Done well, psychologized instruction dynamically integrates the content of the curriculum with the interests and experiences of the learner. It hooks and stretches the learner in educative, often satisfying ways.

Authentic Evaluator. To enhance students' meaningful engagement in the evaluation sphere, democratic educators may exemplify the following types of practices:

- promoting individual student goal setting and ongoing self-assessment of academic achievement and responsible classroom participation

- designing thoughtful "authentic" evaluation exhibitions,[29] ones that, in contrast to standardized testing or conventional objective tests, both connect to the curriculum taught and involve concrete and synthesizing application of the curriculum to a real life, non-school related task

- involving students in the composition of these evaluation exhibitions

- showing commitment to student mastery through policies on retaking exams or exhibitions and performing supplementary or "extra-credit" activities

- involving students in regular opportunities for constructive critique of class dynamics and decisions, through class meetings, immediate debriefing of experiences, weekly advisory feedback groups, anonymous survey responses, suggestion boxes, etc.

Public Advocates for Justice

Democratic STEPs not only nurture teachers who act as compassionate colleagues and catalysts of student collaboration within the classroom, they also cultivate individuals who seek to address barriers to justice within the multiple spheres of their lives—the STEP, university, local schools, state organizations, local and national communities.[30] Integrating the intellectual, pedagogic, and participatory capacities associated with the roles described above, these teachers channel their outrage at social injustice and empathy for its victims into concrete, collaborative action designed to improve public policies and the quality of people's lives. Public advocacy is thus a logical extension of democratic teachers' commitment to the welfare of people in their totality.

Program Features

In this section I want to give more concrete form to the rationale and roles I have articulated above. I do so by describing particular program features which would be characteristic of a democratic STEP. Some derive from firsthand experience, others from examples in the professional literature, still others from my vision of the desirable and possible. All of this is currently being considered by members of the John Carroll University Education Department where I work. Let me briefly provide some context.

John Carroll is a small Jesuit liberal arts university located in the Cleveland suburbs. Its Education Department has traditionally emphasized the integration of elementary and secondary students. Its current program emphasizes four strands: The Teacher as Person, Foundations, Child Study, and High Focus Methods. After an introductory course, secondary students take courses in Educational Issues, Educational Psychology, General Methods, Problem Solving and Conflict Resolution, Reading in the Content Area, Multicultural Education, and Special Methods in the Content Area. Student teaching and a concurrent seminar complete their program.

To overcome secondary students' expressed sense of isolation and to provide a more powerful cohesive theme to the STEP,[31] several of my departmental colleagues and I are considering a number of STEP revisions. The revisions are designed to create a caring, challenging, and just community where prospective secondary teachers feel intellectually stretched, a sense of belonging, responsibility to others, ownership in the governing policies and practices, personal efficacy, and commitment to constructive change in all aspects of their lives. The following features are designed to promote these conditions.

1. *Regular Monthly Meetings of the Whole.*

The function of these meetings would be educative (speakers and panel discussions on educational issues), political (airing of grievances, considering changes in practices), recreational and festive (participation in games, movies, potluck dinners), and ceremonial (presentation of awards for achievement and improvement, formal initiation of new program members).

2. *Program Advisory Groups.*

On a rotating basis, STEP students would be selected to serve on an advisory body, representative by subject area.

3. *Course Advisory Groups.*

Perhaps also on a rotating basis, class representatives would meet with instructor(s) approximately once a month to assess course progress and discuss refinements. These meetings would complement processes of constructive critique regularly solicited by STEP faculty at the conclusion of class meetings (i.e., What went well today? How might our experience together be more fulfilling?) The meetings of both program and course advisory groups would serve multiple purposes: to exemplify and promote compassionate collegiality, democratic dialogue, and reflective practice; to uncover any unintentional incongruities between goals and practices; and to co-create more responsive educative experiences.

4. *Interdisciplinary Community Peer Tutoring.*

Majors in the different content areas would be encouraged to tutor other STEP members experiencing difficulty in a content area. Awards might be given to those cadres of tutors whose major STEP members demonstrated the most achievement and improvement. Beyond "remedial" tutoring, majors in interdisciplinary groupings would periodically meet to share their genuine enthusiasm for their content. These meetings might be organized around catchy themes like "The Neat and the Novel" or "Dazzling Untold Stories." In all, these experiences could provide multiple benefits: engender a sense of pride and collective responsibility; strengthen subject matter mastery through the constructivist act of explaining it to others; nurture the Renaissance learner identity; and enhance awareness of effective teaching skills for both tutor and student, especially as norms of compassionate collegiality and pedagogic self-reflexivity become pervasively modeled and integrated throughout STEP experiences.

5. *Community Peer Advising/Support.*

Prospective secondary students in the introductory course would be linked with an upperclass peer advisor within their discipline. These peer advisors would perform several services: help orient new students to STEP values, expectations and resources; nurture a sense of identity and belonging to the STEP community; and provide timely and sensitive peer support. Performance of this latter service will be enhanced because STEP members will be educated in basic counseling communication skills and sensitivities instrumental to compassionate collegiality. Introduced in the first Education course, the sensitivities of compassionate collegiality will be concentrated on in the Problem Solving and Conflict Resolution course and continuously modeled, applied, and examined in all aspects of the STEP experience.

6. *Cooperative Learning Experiences.*

STEP members will continually be involved in course projects where successful achievement and grade evaluation require collaborative planning and responsible cooperative execution. The nature of possible projects are multiple: team teaching, planning a debate on different philosophies of teaching and learning, preparing a paired textbook analysis or organizing a group presentation on aspects of adolescent development, multicultural education, interdisciplinary curriculum, or the role of parents and the larger society in secondary classrooms. These activities would involve a reflective critique of the collaborative process itself, focusing on key variables influencing success such as the teacher's role and group composition issues. It would also compare the experience to the results of research reported in professional publications, to more individualistic and competitive learning structures, and to other collaborative projects personally experienced by STEP members. Beyond providing opportunities for developing compassionate collegiality and reflective insight about a particular pedagogy, these projects are intended to foster enhanced academic learning and more positive group affiliation, positive outcomes consistently reported in the research on cooperative learning.

7. Negotiating Authority and Conflict.

Effective teachers need to feel efficacious. Because democratic living at its root raises questions of authority and conflict, and because young, prospective teachers often feel powerless and confused when confronting authority or conflict, democratic STEPs need to focus on these dynamics in explicit and careful ways.

Through readings, case studies, and personal autobiography, STEP members will identify sources, resources, and concerns associated with being and becoming an authority. Epistemologically, issues of truth and indeterminacy will be examined as prospective teachers explore what it means to know their subject matter. Interpersonally, concepts of compassionate collegiality, collaborative and invitational power (power with), and coercive power (power over), as well as their implications for teaching, will be carefully explored.[32]

Initiated in the beginning course, the focus on dynamics of authority and conflict becomes central in the Problem Solving and Conflict Resolution course, the second course in the Teacher as Person strand. In this course students examine their entering perspectives around interpersonal conflict, and work to integrate the skills and sensitivities associated with compassionate collegiality. In particular, through readings, video, role play, or interaction with actual secondary students from partner schools,[33] they confront a set of conflicts in five categories: student-student, student-teacher, teacher-teacher, teacher-parent, and teacher-superior. Conflicts are selected by class members based on the latter's actual experience or anxious anticipation, by the course instructor based on the conflicts' frequency of appearance or importance, and by recommendation from secondary students or cooperating teachers as ones resolved problematically. Prospective teachers are also presented with literature on peer mediation and asked to facilitate that process, either as a role play or with volunteer secondary students. This activity helps them address a central concept in democratic classroom governance (i.e., students' response-abilities in resolving their own conflicts).

To approach authentic evaluation and to encourage extensive integration of compassionate collegiality principles, the final exam in this course is two-fold: a written outline response to five self-chosen conflict cases, explaining principles and approaches to resolution, and a performance exhibition resolving one conflict either in a role play or with actual secondary students. That conflict may be drawn from a hat, chosen by the student or selected by the course instructor in light of the prospective teacher's developmental needs.

8. Multicultural Experiences.

A recent demographic study of teacher education candidates[34] indicates that prospective teachers tend to be white, monolingual, from small town or suburban communities, and inclined to teach in traditional middle-class schools with "average" (not handicapped or gifted) youth. Only 15 percent wanted to teach in the inner city where inequalities and cultural diversity are very apparent. On the one hand, a desire to teach the middle group may be construed as good news because it is students in this middle group who are frequently neglected in secondary schools.[35] However, given the projected imminent increase in the multicultural population, a democratically minded STEP must be committed to overcoming the cultural insulation of its members.

STEPs can enhance multicultural sensitivity and efficacy in a number of ways: a required course on the topic, sensitizing curricular materials in all courses, multicultural professors and speakers, required field experience in a range of multicultural settings at both the early and student teaching level. Besides schools, settings might also include museums, housing projects, churches, adolescents' homes, service agencies, and successful work establishments. To permit understanding the impact and interaction of various factors on people's lives, experiences which cut across race, ethnicity, and social class, as well as gender, need to be included.

In all, what's sought here is empathic insight, that is, a complement of intellectual and emotional understanding. This understanding might best be cultivated by a combination of academic content, compassionate listening, and first-hand encounters with multicultural individuals and settings. With assistance from the first two sources, the latter can provide previously sheltered individuals with "shocks that edify." Democratically minded STEPs try to ensure that for promising future teachers, these shocks lead to enlightenment and enhanced professional commitment rather than to intimidation and a quest for heightened insulation.

9. Public Service and Advocacy.

As implied above, the path from exposure to empathy is not an inevitable one. Nor does exposure to injustice necessarily evoke outrage and a commitment to help rectify that injustice. It is because it is not inevitable but so very important that reconstructionists passionately believe a fundamental goal of both liberal arts and teacher education is to nurture that commitment.

The STEP being proposed here takes this commitment seriously. Reflected in its multidimensional and holistic view of individuals and their environment, democratically minded STEPs recognize that the classroom lives of adolescents are not independent of their lives outside school. If students are victims of substantial abuse or neglect, whether by identifiable people or by structural forces, their basic needs will not have been met, and their essential well-being is endangered. Inevitably, their school performance will be adversely affected. Because they relate to students as compassionate colleagues, democratically minded teachers may be especially attentive to injustices their students experience and will seek to empower students to take effective action.

It is perhaps not difficult to sense how the reconstructionist perspective can be overwhelming, given the profound injustice it sees, and the interdependence of multilayered forces it perceives as causal. The position taken here is that democratically minded secondary teachers are, by definition, advocates for students' welfare and STEPs should help them become good ones. This means helping prospective secondary teachers do at least two tasks: make that which is problematic more visible and understandable, and then act effectively on the implications of what they see. To these ends, STEP students need to be conversant with insightful critiques of schools' roles in society and with progressive models of school restructuring, ones which feature such elements as successful school-community partnerships, community service projects and greater attention to what Jane Roland Martin calls the reproductive processes of society.[36]

To focus sharply on both the society and the advocacy dimensions of this agenda, democratic STEPs would endorse and, if necessary, co-create an additional course, interdisciplinary in nature, with a required service component in a local agency devoted to the underserved. The course would examine proposed causes and promising solutions to pressing social issues which impact the lives of adolescents and their families (for example, AIDS, poverty, homelessness, teen pregnancy, health care, environmental decay, violence, racism, sexism). It would also explicitly address issues of advocacy in the context of one of the course's culminating projects—some form of public advocacy by class participants. Another culminating project would be a synthesizing assessment of the service and advocacy experiences, and their particular implications for teaching in the secondary school. A final project would be an assessment of the quality of democratic class discussions.

10. *Other Community and Public Contributions.*

With strong guidance and encouragement, STEP members would be expected to generate knowledge about teaching and then "go public" in their roles as reflective practitioners of teaching and co-creators of democratic classrooms. Projects might include participation as speaker or panel member at a monthly meeting; making self-designed curriculum units available to community members and local school teachers; presenting these units at local and national conferences; talking to local PTA and Future Teachers of America; coordinating/working on a computer bulletin board; writing for the secondary program newsletter; participating with faculty in research and publication efforts; creating videotapes of particular democratic practices attempted during student teaching. While not every STEP member is expected to participate in each activity, all would be expected to demonstrate initiative and ability in many of these domains. The particular domains and the degree of involvement would be a matter of some negotiation. As STEP members offer helpful service to others, they fulfill a central developmental need by enhancing their identity as capable professionals.

11. *Experiences in Ethical Decision-Making.*

STEP members will be involved in issues-oriented coursework in the liberal core, learning about theories of male and female moral development, leading discussions on controversial value issues, confronting psycho-philosophical issues associated with political advocacy, and maintaining a journal around the theme of living morally in an immoral world.[37] These experiences are designed to foster the skills and sensitivities to perceive, reason, and act in principled moral ways; to understand obstacles to doing so; and, as teachers, to be able to nurture comparable skills and sensitivities in their students.

Conclusion

The democratic STEP sketched above is based on the view that an enriched community environment will enable students to meet the demanding performance expectations placed on them. These expectations flow from the commitment to educate people in subject matter and citizenship. Because the dynamics associated with this commitment are so multidimensional and interrelated, a rigorous program, one that also entails joy and community, is imperative. Focusing on sophisticated intellectual, dispositional, and participatory capacities, the proposed STEP will strive self-reflexively to exemplify the very qualities it seeks to foster. It is my hope that graduates of this STEP experience will be better empowered than usual to co-create with their future colleagues (i.e., students, fellow teachers, parents, administrators) classrooms and schools which thrive as thoughtful and caring democratic communities. All of us deserve nothing less.

NOTES

1. See Liston and Zeichner (1991) for an informative description of these dominant traditions.

2. Battistoni (1985), Giroux (1983), Goble and Brooks (1983), Guttmann (1987), Newmann (1975), Will (1983), Wood (1992).

3. See Newmann (1975, p. 92-103) for a description of significant dilemmas associated with political action.

4. Anyon (1980), Apple (1979), Apple and Weis (1983), Brophy (1979), Goodlad (1984), Rosenbaum (1976).

5. Liston and Zeichner (1991, esp. p. 5-13) provide a useful historical summary of the academic tradition in teacher education. Kramer (1991) offers a contemporary voice in support of increased academic focus and rigor in teacher education. Her perspective draws on her tour and provocative profile of 15 teacher preparation programs throughout the United States.

6. Weiner (1984), DeCharms (1968), Piaget (1929), Perry (1968), Selman (1976), Gilligan (1982), Kohlberg (1983).

7. Dewey (1902/1956).

8. Brophy (1987).

9. The social reconstructionist critique of schooling has numerous articulate spokespeople. Contemporary representatives include Berlak (1986), Beyer (1988), Giroux and McLaren (1987), Sears (1985), Shor (1987), and Wood (1992). Liston and Zeichner (1991, p. 26-34) provide historical perspective and description of current practices which embody the social reconstructionist agenda in teacher education.

10. Aceland (1976), Veldman and Brophy (1974).

11. Conrad and Hedin (1981).

12. Newmann (1990-1991), Kelly (1989b).

13. Berman (1990), Johnson and Johnson (1984), Noddings (1984), Oliver and Newmann (1967).

14. Smith (1992).

15. Dewey (1933).

16. Shulman (1986, 1987).

17. Lortie (1975).

18. Feiman-Nemser and Buchmann (1985).

19. Boyer (1987), Cuban (1984), Goodlad (1984).

20. Smyth (1989).

21. The leftist critique of schooling, including neo-marxist and feminist writings, while voluminous and significant, tends to be ignored, especially in teacher education programs which emphasize the academic and social-efficiency perspectives. Selected examples of these perspectives not indicated in Note 9 above include Apple (1982), Bowles and Gintis (1976), Culley and Portuges (1985), Freire (1970), McLaren (1989), Weis (1988).

22. Kelly (1986, 1989a, 1992).

23. My ideas about compassionate communication have been influenced by Marshall Rosenberg. While he has written about his approach (Rosenberg, 1983), the best introduction to his ideas may be through audio and videotapes available from the Center for Nonviolent Communication, 3326 East Overlook Rd., Cleveland, OH 44118-2116. The Center also has a resource list available to the public.

24. Selected obstacles to compassionate collegiality are elaborated in Kelly (1992).

25. Berman (1990).

26. Dewey (1902/1956).

27. Storytelling has long been understood to be a memorable mode of communicating important information and values. Egan (1986) makes a powerful case for storytelling as a central pedogogical strategy in all disciplines. While his explicit focus is on the elementary curriculum, his thesis has significant implications for secondary educators.

28. Slavin (1985) and Newmann and Thompson (1987) review research and issues related to cooperative learning in the secondary school. Heterogeneous cooperative learning strategies have been advocated as alternatives to selected undesirable effects of ability grouping and tracking (see Oakes, 1985 and Goodlad, 1984). To address the various concerns that advocates of tracking and ability grouping raise, and to provide rich support for Goodlad and Oakes' perspectives, more in-depth case studies of these heterogeneous groupings would be very informative.

29. Sizer (1984, 1992), Wiggins (1989).

30. See Liston and Zeichner (1991, ch. 7) for an elaboration of different professional contexts within which teachers might advocate for greater justice.

31. Based on extensive review of the nation's teacher preparation institutions, Goodlad (1990) urges significantly greater internal coherence within teacher education programs.

32. Kreisberg (1992), Purkey and Novak (1988).

33. Goodlad (1990) recommends that teacher education programs develop intensive partnerships with local school systems to enhance the authentic quality and coherence of teacher preparation.

34. Zimpher (1989).

35. Powell, Farrar, and Cohen (1985).

36. By reproductive processes, Martin (1987) means not only conception and birth but "rearing children to maturity, caring for the sick, feeding people, etc." (p. 407). Conrad and Hedin (1989) and Kendall and Associates (1990) provide multiple perspectives on service learning projects. Various restructuring efforts are categorized in

helpful bibliographic form by the National Center on Effective Secondary Schools (1990). The Center's address is: School of Education, Wisconsin Center for Education Research, University of Wisconsin-Madison, 1025 W. Johnson Street, Madison, Wisconsin 53706.

37. Bill Ayers has indicated to me that the theme of living morally in an immoral world is one that he and Herbert Kohl are currently addressing in the lives of classroom teachers.

REFERENCES

Aceland, H. (1976). Stability of Teacher Effectiveness: A Replication. *Journal of Educational Research 69*: pp. 289-292.

Anyon, J. (1980). Social Class and the Hidden Curriculum of Work. *Journal of Education 162*: pp. 67-92.

Apple, M. (1979). *Ideology and Curriculum*. London: Routledge and Kegan Paul.

————. (1982). *Education and Power*. New York: Routledge and Kegan Paul.

Apple, M., and Weis, L. (Eds.). (1983). *Ideology and Practice in Schooling*. Philadelphia, PA: Temple University Press.

Battistoni, R. (1985). *Public Schooling and the Education of Democratic Citizens*. Jackson, MS: University Press of Mississippi.

Berlak, A. (1986). Teaching for Outrage and Empathy in the Liberal Arts. Paper presented at the Conference on Curriculum Theory and Practice Bergamo Center, Dayton, OH.

Berman, S. (1990). The Real Ropes Course: The Development of Social Consciousness. *Educating for Social Responsibility 1*(1): pp. 1-18

Beyer, L. (1988). *Knowing and Acting: Inquiry, Ideology and Educational Studies*. London: Falmer Press.

Boyer, E. (1987). *College: The Undergraduate Experience in America*. New York: Harper and Row.

Brophy, J. (1979). Teacher Behavior and its Effects. *Journal of Educational Psychology 71*: pp. 733-750.

————. October, 1987. Synthesis of Research on Strategies for Motivating Students to Learn. *Educational Leadership*, pp. 40-48.

Bowles, S., and Gintis, H. (1976). *Schooling in Capitalist America*. New York: Basic Books.

Conrad, D., and Hedin, D. (1981). *Executive Summary of Experimental Education Evaluation Project*. Minnesota: Center for Youth Development and Research.

———. (1989). *High School Community Service: A Review of Research and Programs*. Madison, WI: National Center on Effective Secondary Schools.

Cuban, L. (1984). *How Teachers Taught: Constancy and Change in American Classrooms 1890-1980*. New York: Longman.

Culley, M., and Portuges, C. (Eds.). (1985). *Gendered Subjects: The Dynamics of Feminist Teaching*. London: Routledge and Kegan Paul.

DeCharms, R. (1968). *Personal Causation*. New York: Academic Press.

Dewey, J. (1902 and 1956). *The Child and the Curriculum/The School and Society*. Chicago: The University of Chicago Press.

Dewey, J. (1933). *How We Think: A Restatement of the Relation of Reflective Thinking to the Educative Process*. Chicago: Henry Regnery.

Egan, K. (1986). *Teaching as Story Telling: An Alternative Approach to Teaching and Curriculum in the Elementary School*. Chicago: The University of Chicago Press.

Feiman-Nemser, S., and Buchmann, M. (1985). Pitfalls of Experience in Teacher Preparation. *Teachers College Record 87*(1): pp. 53-65.

Freire, P. (1970). *Pedagogy of the Oppressed*. New York: Continuum.

Gilligan, C. (1982). *In a Different Voice: Psychological Theory and Women's Development*. Cambridge: Harvard University Press.

Giroux, H. (1983). *Theory and Resistance in Education: A Pedagogy for the Opposition*. South Hadley, MA: Bergin and Garvey.

Giroux, H., and McLarden, P. (1987). Teacher Education and the Politics of Engagement: The Case for Democratic Schooling. in *Teaching, Teachers, and Teacher Education*, edited by M. Okazawa-Ray, J. Anderson, and R. Traver. Cambridge, MA: Harvard Educational Review Reprint, pp. 157-182.

Goble, F., and Brooks, B. (1983). *The Case for Character Education*. Ottawa, IL: Green Hill Publishers.

Goodlad, J. (1984). *A Place Called School*. New York: McGraw-Hill.

———. (1990). *Teachers for Our Nation's Schools*. San Francisco: Jossey-Bass Publishers.

Gutmann, A. (1987). *Democratic Education*. Princeton: Princeton University Press.

Johnson, D., Johnson, R., Holubec, E., and Roy, P. (1984). *Circles of Learning: Cooperation in the Classroom*. Washington, DC: Association for Supervision and Curriculum Development.

Kelly, T. (1986). Discussing Controversial Issues: Four Perspectives on the Teacher's Role. *Theory and Research in Social Education 14*(2): pp. 113-138.

―――. (1989a). Leading Discussions on Controversial Issues. *Social Education 53*(6): pp. 368-370.

―――. (1989b). Education for Public Citizenship through Community Projects. *Democracy and Education 3*(4): pp. 3-11.

―――. (1992). Beyond Silence and Partisan Shrieking: Diversity, Compassion and the Nurturance of Democratic Dialogue. Paper presented at the Annual Institute for Democracy in Education Summer Conference, Athens, OH.

Kendall, J., and Associates (Eds.). (1990). *Combining Service and Learning: A Resource Book for Community and Public Service.* (2 vols.) Raleigh, NC: National Society for Internships and Experiential Education.

Kohlberg, L. (1983). *Essays on Moral Development, vol 2. The Psychology of Moral Development.* San Francisco: Harper and Row.

Kramer, R. (1991). *Ed School Follies.* New York: The Free Press.

Kreisberg, S. (1992). *Transforming Power: Domination, Empowerment and Education.* Albany, NY: State University of New York Press.

Liston, D., and Zeichner, K. (1991). *Teacher Education and the Social Conditions of Schooling.* New York: Routledge.

Lortie, D. (1975). *School Teacher: A Sociological Study.* Chicago: University of Chicago Press.

Martin, J. (1987). Reforming Teacher Education, Rethinking Liberal Education. *Teachers College Record 88*(3): pp. 406-410.

McLaren, P. (1989). *Life in Schools: An Introduction to Critical Pedagogy in the Foundations of Education.* White Plains, NY: Longman.

National Center on Effective Secondary Schools. (1990). *Bibliography of Research Related to Secondary Education.* Madison, WI: National Center on Effective Secondary Schools.

Newmann, F. (1975). *Education for Citizen Action.* Berkeley: McCutchan Publishing Co.

―――. (Winter, 1990-1991). Authentic Work and Student Engagement. *National Center on Effective Secondary Schools Newsletter 5*(3): pp. 2-3.

Newmann, F., and Oliver, D. (1967). Education and Community. *Harvard Educational Review 37*: pp. 61-106.

Newmann, F., and Thompson, J. (1987). *Effects of Cooperative Learning on Achievement in Secondary Schools: A Summary of Research.* Madison, WI: The National Center on Effective Secondary Schools.

Noddings, N. (1984). *Caring: A Feminine Approach to Ethics and Moral Education.* Berkeley: University of California Press.

Oakes, J. (1985). *Keeping Track: How Schools Structure Inequality.* New Haven: Yale University Press.

Perry, W. (1968). *Forms of Intellectual and Ethical Development in the College Years.* New York: Holt, Rinehart and Winston.

Piaget, J. (1929). *The Child's Conception of the World.* London: Routledge.

Powell, A., Farrar, E., and Cohen, D. (1985). *The Shopping Mall High School: Winners and Losers in the Educational Marketplace.* Boston: Houghton Mifflin Company.

Purkey, W., and Novak, J. (1988). *Education by Invitation Only.* Bloomington, IN: Phi Delta Kappa Educational Foundation Fastback.

Rosenbaum, J. (1986). *Making Inequality.* New York: Wiley.

Rosenberg, M. (1983). *A Model for Non-Violent Communication.* Philadelphia, PA: New Society Publishers.

Sears, J. (1985). Rethinking Teacher Education: Dare We Work Toward a New Social Order? *Journal of Curriculum Theorizing* 6(2): pp. 24-79.

Selman, R. (1976). Social-Cognitive Understanding: A Guide to Educational and Clinical Practice. In T. Lickona (Ed.) *Moral Development and Behavior.* New York: Holt, Rinehart and Winston, pp. 299-316.

Shor, I. (1987). Equality is Excellence: Transforming Teacher Education and the Labor Process. In *Teaching, Teachers, and Teacher Education,* edited by M. Okazawa-Rey, J. Anderson, and R. Traver. Cambridge, MA: Harvard Educational Review Reprint, pp. 183-203.

Shulman, L. (1986). Those Who Understand: Knowledge Growth in Teaching. *Educational Researcher* 15(2): pp. 4-14.

———. (1987). Knowledge and Teaching: Foundations of the New Reform. *Harvard Educational Review* 57(1): pp. 1-22.

Sizer, T. (1984). *Horace's Compromise: The Dilemma of the American High School.* Boston: Houghton Mifflin Company.

———. (1992). *Horace's School.* Boston: Houghton Mifflin Company.

Slavin, R. (1985). *Cooperative Learning.* New York: Plenum.

Smith, F. (1992). Learning to Read: The Never-Ending Debate. *Phi Delta Kappan* 73(6): pp. 432-441.

Smyth, J. (1989). Developing and Sustaining Critical Reflection in Teacher Education. *Journal of Teacher Education* 40(2): pp. 2-9.

Veldman, D., and Brophy, J. (1974). Measuring Teacher Effects on Pupil Achievement. *Journal of Educational Psychology 66*: pp. 319-324.

Weiner, B. (1984). Principles for a Theory of Student Motivation and Their Application with in Attributional Framework. In R. Ames and C. Ames (Eds.) *Research on Motivation in Education: Student Motivation: Vol. 1*. New York: Academic Press, pp. 15-38.

Weis, L. (Ed.) (1988). *Class, Race and Gender in American Education*. Albany, NY: State University of New York.

Wiggins, G. (1989). Teaching to the (Authentic) Test. *Educational Leadership 46*(7): pp. 41-47.

Will, G. (1983). *Statecraft as Soulcraft: What Government Does*. New York: Simon and Schuster.

Wood, G. (1992). *Schools that Work: America's Most Innovative Public Education Programs*. New York: Dutton.

Zimpher, N. (1989). The RATE Project: A Profile of Teacher Education Students. *Journal of Teacher Education 40*(6): pp. 27-40.

Five

Teaching for Democracy
Preparing Teachers to Teach Democratically

Keith Hillkirk

For the past three years a group of faculty and students at Ohio University has been conducting an experiment. Together they are seeking to learn how to provide a teacher with preparation experience that focuses on what they believe to be the original and true mission of public schools in this country: preparation for democratic citizenship. This chapter will tell the story of that experiment by looking first at the rationale for the program and then examining its birth and evolution.

Program Rationale

Bullough[1] has forcefully argued that we as a nation have forgotten the origins and intentions of public schooling. He points out that one of the forefathers of American public education, Thomas Jefferson, saw a clear link between democratic government and education. For the American people to govern themselves and avoid falling back into the despotic traditions they had so recently escaped, Jefferson recognized the necessity of a knowledgeable and educated citizenry. This belief in the connection between democracy and education led Jefferson to champion public commitment to schooling.

More recently, Bullough contends, we have moved away from this commitment to public education for democracy and towards a conception of schooling as nothing more than preparation for the work world. Such a concept is exemplified by recent calls for vouchers and applying marketplace competitive values to public schooling. What we are thus in danger of losing is what a long tradition of American educators have argued should be the essential focus and purpose of public schools: a civic education that seeks to "serve the general welfare of a democratic society."[2]

The Teacher Education for Civic Responsibility (TECR) Program was prompted by the shared belief of a group of faculty members that we have indeed strayed from our society's intention to serve the public good by educating all American children for democratic citizenship. As the Program Mission Statement states:

> No nation in recorded history has ever made the promise that America makes to its citizens—a free public education to every citizen, regardless of race, creed, gender, or handicapping condition. We have made this promise because, as Jefferson first put it, public education makes democracy possible. This commitment requires that public schools be sites of democratic education. Thus, at a minimum, teachers and schools that take their civic mission seriously work to insure that every student:
>
> - can read, write, listen, and compute in ways that enable one to understand the issues that confront us as citizens;
>
> - values the fundamental precepts of democratic life, including equity, community, and personal liberty;
>
> - has a willingness to participate publicly in the name of the common good;
>
> - believes that one's contribution makes a difference, that one has the right and obligation to contribute, and that we have a duty to honor the contributions of all our neighbors; and
>
> - has an awareness that there are a variety of ways to order social life and that it is the right of citizens to choose freely between multiple social options.[3]

To develop the above characteristics and commitments, along with the knowledge and skills necessary for further education and the world of work, the program deems it essential that teachers continually examine their practices, curriculum, and the entire school experience in relation to young people's development as citizens. Hence the TECR Program has been framed around the civic mission of teachers in educating their students about the rights and responsibilities of citizenship in a democracy.

Program Design and Inception

The initial cohort group of TECR students entered the program in the fall of 1989. Their interest had been sparked by a series of presentations and invitations to apply during freshmen orientation. Applicants were interviewed by faculty members; 11 were selected on the basis of their perceived interest and potential in becoming teachers committed to creating a classroom that fosters democratic habits such as self-discipline, mutual respect, and cooperation. Since the original group, three additional groups have entered the program, bringing program enrollment to 67 students.

TECR students experience a teacher-education curriculum which in some ways reflects traditional preparation:

1. The first year is largely devoted to fulfilling university requirements of general education in liberal arts. In some cases, as explained below, these requirements are met through liberal arts courses which have been specifically designed to reflect program emphasis on connections between democracy and education.

2. Elementary, secondary, and special education students must meet state certification requirements for academic credits in subjects they will teach.

However, their preparation experience fundamentally differs from the traditional program in ways that are intended to reflect the TECR Program's focus on the civic role of the teacher in preparing their students for democratic responsibility and participation. As indicated in Table 5.1 and explained below, six major distinctions may be identified between the traditional and the TECR experience.

Liberal Arts Core

As mentioned above, all university students are required to fulfill General Education distribution requirements by taking courses in humanities, mathematics and science, comparative arts and literature, communications, and social sciences. Where possible, TECR faculty have consulted with faculty in other colleges who have developed courses which frame study of the liberal arts around notions of public responsibility and democratic government. In other cases, already existing courses have been identified which are particularly relevant to program goals. These courses begin during the freshman year and culminate with the Tier 111 requirement that all seniors take an interdisciplinary course which emphasizes the interrelationships between artificially separated bodies of knowledge.

One example of such a liberal arts course that is required for all TECR students is Political Science 102, which focuses upon the respective roles that government and the private sector play in responding to societal problems such as unemployment and homelessness. Students are challenged to examine the

Table 5.1 Differences Between TECR and Traditional Teacher Preparation

TECR	TRADITIONAL PREPARATION
1. Liberal arts core courses selected and developed for their relevance to citizenship in a democracy	Individual student course selections
2. Cohort grouping	Students enroll and take courses as individuals
3. In-depth program focus on cooperative learning and project-centered teaching and techniques for creating and maintaining a classroom democracy	"Smorgasbord" approach to teaching models and strategies
4. Field experience at all grade levels for all TECR students; opportunity to return to work with teacher who becomes chosen mentor	Field experience only at level of certification
5. Field work in model classrooms and schools	Field assignments based upon classroom availability and chance
6. Intensive university and public school faculty collaboration regarding course development, teaching, field placements, etc.	Sporadic faculty collaboration

ways that citizens in a democracy can better understand the origins and causes of such problems, as well as to consider the cost and benefits of alternative solutions. Another required liberal arts course examines the historical interaction of technology and society, including the various ways that technologies have affected and continued to affect our private and public lives. Examples of topics that are studied include biotechnology and its implications for human freedom; technology, the law and public order; and the problems and possibilities of cable television.

Student Enrollment in TECR Courses

Within the traditional program elementary, secondary, and special education pre-service teachers follow different course sequences. Rarely do they find opportunities to interact with one another, particularly in relation to their professional preparation.

In contrast, TECR students enter the program as part of a cohort group which moves through the preparation experience together. In a number of courses, within and outside the College of Education, students from all three areas take courses together. They are thus able to gain insight into students of differing ages and ability levels through the shared experiences of their peers. These enriching experiences are augmented by changes in the structure and content of the TECR curriculum itself.

The TECR Curriculum

Working collaboratively, the TECR faculty designed a sequence of education courses which are intended to introduce and develop pedagogical understandings, commitments, and skills that will enable preservice students to create and nurture democratic environments within their classrooms.

Freshman Year. The Professional Education course sequence begins in the spring of the freshman year, when first-year TECR students enroll in "Democracy and Education." In this course students inquire into and explore the writings and ideas of people like Jefferson, Madison, and Dewey. Students are challenged and expected to reflect critically on their own schooling experience, particularly in relation to the ways that their own understandings and commitments to democratic participation were enabled or hindered.

As in other courses within the professional sequence, students and instructor continually compare and contrast theory and practice in the ways that the formation and evolution of public schools in this country have achieved or veered from their avowed intentions. Students carefully examine and consider the factory model of schooling[4] which has dominated the structure of American public schools throughout this century and also consider alternative ways of organizing classrooms and schools which are more reflective of participatory democracy. As explained below, this initial exploration of the underlying purposes and outcomes of schooling is accompanied by a field experience which exposes students to elementary, middle school, and secondary classrooms.

Sophomore Year. During their sophomore year, students begin focused study of learners and the complex relationship between teaching and learning. Unlike the traditional program, where elementary, secondary, and special education students focus on the developmental characteristics and needs of the particular students they will teach, TECR students study child and adolescent development from birth through young adulthood in the year-long course "Childhood in America." Once again this course is accompanied by regular opportunities to observe and interact with students and teachers in public school classrooms. Each student also observes and studies a particular child or adolescent over a three-to-six-month period, to gain further insight into the dynamics of development.

In addition to their study of human development, second-year students also begin their study of the teaching act itself. "Teaching Techniques for the Democratic Classroom" explores the nature of the teacher/student relationship and the challenges of creating a classroom atmosphere that moves away from teacher dominance and control.

In this introductory methods course, particular attention is given to two models of teaching: explicit teaching[5] and cooperative learning.[6] These models were selected for focused study and practice because of their emphasis on student participation and active involvement in classroom learning.

Explicit teaching provides an effective strategy for direct instruction in skills and sequential subject matter that was derived from research in elementary and secondary classrooms. It emphasizes the need and benefits of ongoing communication between teacher and students through its focus on guided practice and feedback, two explicit teaching functions which are characteristic of any effective teacher/learner interaction. Students prepare and teach two explicit teaching lessons during the course, one in the university classroom and the other in their field experience classroom. Both lessons are videotaped and carefully analyzed in relation to the student's effectiveness in applying the explicit teaching functions.

The second model of teaching, cooperative learning, is used in a variety of ways during the course. Students experience cooperative group work repeatedly and join the instructor in reflecting upon alternative ways of structuring groups, assignments, and roles. Cooperative learning was selected for emphasis during this course and a second course in pedagogy for four reasons:

1. Cooperative learning emphasizes student ownership and participation in their own learning, two qualities which are highly consistent with the TECR Program's goals of promoting active and responsible citizenship.

2. The particular model of cooperative learning used in the TECR Program was developed by Johnson, Johnson, and Holubec.[7] It is structured around five essential components: positive interdependence, individual accountability, group processing, face-to-face interaction, and cooperative skills. Each of these components reflects specific qualities and skills critical to a democratic classroom atmosphere and, more generally, participatory democratic government.

3. Classroom research on cooperative learning has consistently demonstrated its effectiveness in enhancing both academic achievement and social skill development.[8] In numerous studies which have compared competitive, individualistic, and cooperative learning environments, cooperative learning's effectiveness has been indicated for students of all ages and abilities.

4. Finally, cooperative learning is emphasized because it enhances the learning and teaching experience of students and instructors within the program itself. The qualities which students need to develop and refine for themselves and which will enable them to work effectively within challenging school and classroom environments are consistently modeled and practiced.

A third education course that students take during their second year, "Learning from Non-western Culture," focuses attention on African and Asian cultures and examines alternative educational and schooling traditions. This course is offered concurrent to the introductory methods course with the intention that students be challenged to think and relate to other cultures' educational conceptions and practices and become sensitive to our increasingly pluralistic society and world.

An example of curriculum correlation between these two courses is the World Hunger Day Project. For the past two years, TECR students have organized and implemented a Hunger Day in a middle school the first year, and an elementary school more recently. This experience provides a complex organizational and teaching challenge as the TECR students have prepared and served three different types of meals to public school students: 1) an elite group eats a meal typical for many U.S. families that includes meat, vegetables, and starch; 2) a somewhat larger group receives vegetables and starch; 3) the majority eats a simple meal of rice and water, which is a typical diet for millions of hungry people around the world.

TECR students are responsible for organization and food preparation, as well as overall educational planning for Hunger Day, which ensures that students grasp the symbolic "point" of the experience. Hunger Day thus teaches valuable lessons to all involved.

Junior Year. During their third year, TECR students continue their study of the underlying connections between public responsibility, democratic government, and public schools, as well as their development of teaching skills to expand and enhance their instructional repertoire.

In "Advanced Teaching Techniques for the Democratic Classroom," they further develop their understandings and skills related to explicit teaching and cooperative learning. In addition, attention is given to a number of other teaching models which again emphasize student ownership and involvement in their own learning and the teacher's role as facilitator of student learning. These models include inquiry learning, project-centered learning, and group discussion. As with other courses described above, a field experience that allows students to apply and reflect daily upon the connections between theory and practice accompanies this course.

Focus on practical skill development continues in "Curriculum Design for the Democratic Classroom." Students design and develop learning materials and activities which reflect program emphasis on experiential learning. They read and apply the work of noted theorists of democratic education like James, Dewey, and Kirkpatrick while examining historic and modern applications of their ideas in programs such as Foxfire, whole language, the integrated day, and the Project Method. Each student in this course develops a teaching unit in consultation with an inservice teacher (in most cases a teacher they have known and worked with for the previous two years).

Senior Year. The first cohort group of TECR students entered student teaching during the winter quarter of the 1992-1993 academic year. Each student was placed with a cooperating teacher who is familiar with and committed to program goals and philosophy. Prior to, and following, student teaching, each student enrolled in a pre- and post-student-teaching practicum that involves weekly work and time spent in the classroom with the teacher who mentors his/her student teaching experience. Regularly scheduled seminars with a university supervisor are also held throughout the senior year—before, during, and after student teaching.

Field Experiences

TECR field experiences differ from the traditional program in a number of ways. As mentioned, elementary, secondary, and special education students move through the program as cohort groups. Beginning their first year, students are provided with practical experience in elementary, middle school, and secondary classrooms. Not only do these experiences expose them to developmental characteristics of children of various ages, but students also gain from opportunities to observe teachers as they plan and teach to meet the needs of different age levels.

Additionally, because public school and university faculty have closely collaborated in the development and inception of this program, more creative and flexible practicum assignments have been made possible. All students have had opportunities to observe and learn in different classrooms and schools; some have also requested and enjoyed the opportunity to return to work with previously visited classrooms and teachers.

Visits to Model Schools and Programs

During the Christmas/New Year vacation in 1990 and '91, TECR students and faculty made special trips to schools and programs that provided unique examples of the application of program principals. In 1990 students visited Chicago and Milwaukee schools to observe and study thematic and whole language approaches to the teaching of reading and writing, as well as a bilingual school that has adopted site-based management.

In 1991 students and faculty traveled to New York City, where they spent four days visiting Central Park East Community School, a member of the Coalition of Essential Schools. Central Park East faculty and students are committed to a school experience that integrates academic disciplines and is jointly owned and shared by students, their families, and the school faculty and staff. Both groups returned from these visits with concrete and creative examples of ways that classrooms and schools can be organized to reject the factory model of schooling in favor of a more responsive and participatory learning environment.

Faculty Collaboration

The sixth and perhaps most significant distinction that sets the program apart from the traditional teacher preparation program is the intensive faculty collaboration that began with the informal conversation that sparked the idea of framing a program around the civic mission of the teacher. As the program continues into its fourth year, so does this collaboration.

Six faculty members within the College of Education meet bi-weekly to manage and oversee the program. This group has developed and taught the professional course sequence described above. They also work closely with public school teachers and other university faculty in designing and arranging field experiences for students.

In many ways the shared vision and commitment of these faculty members have contributed to the design and initiation of the TECR Program. They represent teaching experience at six major universities in different states. A common starting point for each of them was a desire to create a program that provided a focused emphasis on democratic and experiential education throughout the pre-service teacher's preparation—as opposed to what in some places has become a smorgasbord of course offerings in pedagogy and psychology, at times with contradictory emphases and themes.

Student and Faculty Perceptions to Date

Student and faculty perceptions of the program as it completes its fourth year are quite positive. Early in the program's third year, students and faculty were asked to complete an anonymous questionnaire to evaluate program effectiveness to date. Of the 23 who responded, 13 indicated they were very satisfied with the program, nine indicated satisfaction, and one stated they were somewhat satisfied. None indicated that they were not satisfied with the program.

The following major strengths were identified repeatedly:

1. *Field Work:* Fourteen respondents indicated that the emphasis on field
   experiences beginning during the first year has been a significant plus
   for the program. Students stressed that they highly value opportunities
   to see connections between theory and practice. The following comments reflect student perceptions of the value of the field component:

   > "Getting into the schools our freshman year was great! I
   > knew after spring quarter that I was *definitely* in the right major."
   > "The field work is definitely at the top of the list for the
   > Program's strengths."
   > "I also like the field work. It lets me see, (sic) what we
   > have discussed in class, (sic) in action. The things we discuss
   > are proven. It's often difficult to understand a concept unless
   > you see it with your own eyes."

2. *Models of Practice:* Eight students specifically highlighted the value
   of the emphasis on experiential learning. Student viewpoints were
   expressed in a variety of ways:

   > "Other classes don't let us learn from each other as this
   > program does—what a good way to learn."
   > "Another important aspect is that we learn from doing.
   > We don't sit, take notes, and get lectured. We get to go into
   > the field, write about what we see and feel, and teach one
   > another about our readings and experiences."
   > "The hands-on examples and roll (sic) play make me
   > really understand the concepts that are being taught."
   > "We teach how we were taught. The program is very con-
   > ducive to the development of innovative minds and creative
   > teaching styles because we are being taught in innovative ways
   > ourselves."

   Another student observation spoke not only about the TECR program but also the disenfranchisement that students often feel.

   > "We are treated as intelligent individuals instead of just
   > plain students. What we learn in class is what we need to know,
   > not only for teaching, but for our lives. We aren't given 'use-
   > less' information that we swallow and never use."

3. *Cohort Grouping:* Seven students expressed positive regard for the
   strong sense of group identity and cohesion they have developed
   through the cohort grouping of elementary, secondary, and special
   education preservice teachers.

"The other people in the class have become my best friends."

"We all want to help one another understand. We've learned to work together and share our experiences in order to benefit the whole group. This is due to the fact that we're in a small class atmosphere and we have many of our classes together."

"The program, which has proved to me that democratic teaching nurtures creative minds more so than traditional methods, is constructed around a 'close-knit' group of students who deal with each other in close, personal ways—this has important benefits which believe are important when dealing with a class. We teach how we were taught."

A majority of student respondents indicated one major problem as well, one that appears to be related to the program's newness. Students described frustration with their role as "guinea pigs" in breaking new ground and indicated that they sometimes feel uneasy when courses that they are taking, and which are being taught for the first time, do not appear in the official university bulletin. It is anticipated that as the program grows in numbers, becomes better known, and is described in detail in the university bulletin, this problem will dissipate.

It is also important to note that, as indicated above, student acceptance into the program follows a formal application and interview by program faculty. When students are accepted into the program, they are informed that their continuation depends upon mutual agreement between themselves and the faculty that both they and the program benefit from their participation. During the program's first three years, four students have chosen to leave the program. Two decided to transfer to other institutions, one of whom has since returned to the university and rejoined TECR. The other two students, following careful consultation with program faculty, decided that they would be better served by the traditional program.

A Look to the Future

What lies ahead for the Teacher Education for Civic Responsibility Program? As indicated above, students and faculty are pleased and excited by the program's first three years. With full recognition that the ultimate indicator of program success will be the classroom effectiveness of its graduates, we look forward to the first cohort group's graduation in June 1993. The gradual growth in admissions (from 11 the first year, to 15 the second, to the 26 students who were admitted in the program's third year) indicates increased student awareness and interest.

A number of program courses were moved to public school settings for the 1992 spring quarter. This move enabled cooperating teachers to gain clearer understanding of the TECR curriculum and facilitated collaboration between public school and university faculty. Three of the education courses in the program are now being taught by public school educators in their schools. Support for making these moves appears to be a reflection of the interest and enthusiasm of public school administrators and teachers.

Conclusion

This chapter opened by describing the Teacher Education for Civic Responsibility Program as an experiment. Those of us on the "inside" of the experiment know that it is far from over. Much remains to be learned about effective ways of preparing teachers who are knowledgeable, skilled, and committed to creating more responsive, open, and ultimately more democratic learning environments for their students.

At the same time, feedback from TECR students and instructors indicates that their experiences to date have enabled them to consider possibilities for teaching and learning and the teacher/learner relationship that are new and exciting. As Freire has observed, "knowledge emerges only through invention and re-invention, through the restless, impatient, continuing, hopeful inquiry men pursue in the world, with the world, and with each other."[9] If Freire is right, perhaps the point is not that the experiment be completed, but that it continue.

NOTES

1. Robert V. Bullough, Jr., *The Forgotten Dream of American Public Education* (Ames, IA: Iowa State University Press, 1988), Chap. 1.

2. R. Freeman Butts, *The Revival of Civic Learning: A Rationale for Citizenship Education in American Schools* (Phi Delta Kappa Educational Foundation, 1980), p. 114.

3. *Proposal to the Faculty of Curriculum and Instruction for an Emphasis within the K-12 Teacher Education Program: The Teacher Education for Civic Responsibility Program* (Ohio University College of Education), p. 2.

4. Bullough, p. viii.

5. Barak V. Rosenshine (April 1986). Synthesis of Research on Explicit Teaching. *Educational Leadership 43*(7): pp. 60-69.

6. David W. Johnson, Roger T. Johnson, and Edythe Johnson Holubec, *Cooperation in the Classroom*, rev. ed. (Edina, MN: Interaction Book Company, 1991).

7. *Ibid.*, pp. 1:8-1:13.

8. David W. Johnson and Roger T. Johnson, *Cooperation and Competition: Theory and Research* (Edina, MN: INteraction Book Company, 1989).

9. Paulo Freire, *Pedagogy of the Oppressed* (New York: Continuum, 1970), p. 58.

Six

Deliberately Developing
Democratic Teachers in a Year

Barbara McEwan

It cannot be doubted that in the United States the instruction of the people powerfully contributed to the support of the democratic republic; and such must always be the case, I believe, where the instruction which enlightens the understanding is not separated from the moral education which amends the heart.

Alexis de Tocqueville, 1848

Civility toward others manifested through tolerance of words, thoughts, and actions that are different from our own is, for many, the essence of coexisting in a democratic society. Similarly, instructing each succeeding generation in ways of living from day to day within the precepts of civility and tolerance to guide personal interactions is a commonly perceived mission of democratic education. However, bringing de Tocqueville's vision of moral education to life can prove to be a challenge because often the ideals exist without a structure for shaping them into reality. Democratic living is most effectively passed on to children by providing them with an understanding of how their human rights are always balanced with citizenship responsibilities. Accordingly, it is vitally important that those who teach children have an opportunity to experience firsthand the freedom and choices that delineate the role of citizen in a democracy.

My colleagues and I firmly believe that democratic education can best be ensured by empowering students at all levels. Genuine empowerment occurs when students are provided with the opportunity to make significant choices about the structure of their school day while also learning about the expectations society holds. In order for that empowerment to occur, teachers first must come to understand what it means to be personally empowered themselves.

Although college classes do not often employ strategies that allow students to make decisions concerning their own learning, teacher education programs should make every effort to provide pre-service teachers with choices and to encourage personal responsibility in order to create a model for democratic teaching which they might employ when they have their own classrooms. If future teachers never have an opportunity to personally experience the balance of individual rights and group responsibilities, it seems reasonable to suppose they might not be able to impart this information to their students in a way that is meaningful and lasting.

Empowering pre-service teachers with the opportunity to make significant decisions about their own learning so that they might empower their students often involves creating a sense of dis-equilibrium in the way pre-service teachers think about education in general and students in particular. Altering preconceived ideas about schools and schooling requires that time be spent reflecting upon pre-service course work and field-based practicums. However, the Professional Teacher Education program at Oregon State University was designed as a one-year teacher-training experience. Reflection time is severely limited in such a concentrated experience and can easily get lost in the crush of everything else that must get done. Nevertheless, creating reflective teachers remains, for my colleagues and myself, a primary focus for our efforts.

Creating a Framework for Democratic Teacher Training

When the newly hired staff was brought in to implement a fifth-year elementary education program at Oregon State University (Corvallis, Oregon), we began our task by agreeing that our goal was to foster in our students a sense that their profession is integral to sustaining a viable democracy. For this ideal to become reality, my colleagues and I agreed our first task would be to write a philosophy statement which would serve as a guide to us and to our partnership schools in our mutual effort to train Master of Arts in Teaching (M.A.T.) candidates.

We began with the premise that public schools exist to foster democracy and as such should be models of equitable educational practices. The statement evolved out of a shared writing experience, one of many democratic teaching strategies we intended to pass on to our students.

> The College of Education at Oregon State University is creating within the Department of Curriculum and Instruction a new five-year program for Elementary Education designed to culminate in a Master of Arts in Teaching degree. Our goal will be to educate and encourage teachers to create and sustain schools that help prepare students for successful community living. This program will be founded on the belief that education is a process which facili-

tates individual growth from dependence to independence within a social context exemplifying principles of equality, freedom, responsibility, and mutual respect enabling students to achieve to the best of their abilities. In short, the philosophy of this program affirms that the central purpose of education is to contribute to a more literate, participatory and, therefore, more equitable society.

                                                    McEwan and Winograd, 1990

Once the preamble was crafted, we began to clarify the process of how we would identify and select those schools with which we would form our partnerships.

Selecting Schools

Our first priority was to identify several elementary schools engaged in democratic education, defined by us as practicing such strategies as Whole Language, cooperative learning, authentic assessment, and other techniques that ensure equitable learning opportunities in classrooms. We also focused on an examination of their discipline strategies to determine if they represented a consistent approach designed to treat all students fairly. We were particularly interested in those schools that had established or were in the process of developing techniques that encourage every individual to achieve at his or her highest possible level. In addition, we shared a commitment to find schools that have culturally and/or economically diverse student populations.

We recognized from the beginning that the preamble to our philosophy statement would remain theory and not practice if we did not make the effort to work with public schools that were currently operating in concert with the goals of our program and with which we shared a common vision of the nature of public education. With our pre-service students spending most of their time in our various partner schools, a shared philosophy between the site schools and the university was a crucial element for the success of the program. Accordingly, the decision was made to share our statement with public schools in the area and solicit their responses to our vision.

When we tried to anticipate the manner in which schools might respond to and match the goals of our program, it became clear that more delineation of our philosophy was necessary. A series of belief statements that would further define and add depth to our preamble was therefore created.

- **We believe that our pre-service teachers and teacher education program must strive to achieve the highest standard of academic excellence.**

This standard is based on a commitment to scholarship by both teacher educators and pre-service teachers. Scholarship entails a conception of the teacher as both learned and a learner, as a reader and writer, as a problem poser and problem solver, and, finally, as a critical and creative thinker.

- **We believe that educators at Oregon State University and in the public schools must work together to develop and implement the teacher education program.**

  This partnership ensures both university and public schools share and promote concepts, purpose, means, and a sense of mission in the education of pre-service teachers. Therefore, we will actively recruit and form partnerships with school administrators and teachers who engage in collaborative practices among themselves and in partnership with our College of Education.

- **We believe in fostering teaching aimed at improving educational opportunities for every student.**

  Oregon State University's design for teacher education endorses the concept that learning emerges most effectively from social activity and promotes pedagogy which reflects this interactive perspective. Examples of this pedagogy include collaborative reading and writing communities, cooperative learning techniques, integrated curriculum, and humane discipline strategies.

- **We believe that teacher education must be specifically oriented toward understanding and addressing the needs of students identified as being at risk.**

  Our program is committed to the study of at-risk students and educational practice that is aimed at improving their lives. We believe that the increasing numbers of at-risk students who live in the margins of our communities represent one of the most compelling issues facing education today. At-risk students typically face difficulties in integrating themselves into the life of the school communities. The challenge for our teachers is to develop strategies that effectively help these students form significant relationships with their peers and educators, thereby facilitating their integration into school life.

- **We believe educators must have the knowledge and inclination to develop and critique educational practice and theory.**

  Our program will educate teachers who have the skills to bring a critical perspective to educational research as well as produce action research themselves. We believe that this view of teacher as reflective and critical professional bodes well for teacher effectiveness and student learning.

- **We believe teacher education programs must work with local schools to make a significant contribution to the urgent needs of restructuring.**

  As we move toward the twenty-first century, we must unite, college to schools, schools to college, in order to create educational options that serve the needs of all students. Our students will be the resources that enable the creation of dynamic schools structures.

- **We believe in the development of an appreciation and responsibility toward the immediate school community and the larger communities of each educator's and student's region, nation, and world.**

  Our program will educate teachers to understand and appreciate the relationship between the school and its families and community. The effectiveness of schools depends on the quality of involvement in classrooms of parents and guardians as well as other adult members of the community. Site schools will be encouraged to use the expertise and interests of adults in their communities to enhance the education of students.

- **We believe the concept of tolerance is critical to the creation of an equitable classroom environment at every level of education.**

  Our program will prepare teachers who understand, value, and affirm differences among students according to their learning styles, cultural background, gender, ability, social class, and interests. Our teachers will be knowledgeable, creative, and critical regarding pedagogical strategies which address these differences. Site schools will reflect and practice tolerance for the valuing of individual differences among students.

"Our program is designed to contribute the following innovations tour teacher education program:

1. Partnership schools, part of our Educational Excellence in Practice program, that reflect our educational philosophy and will work with us as a team to educate our pre-service teachers.
2. Intern teachers on site in the partnership schools for a full school year.
3. On-site delivery of course material to be team taught by college faculty and school-based educators.
4. Limited enrollment in the Master's of Arts in Teaching degree program to ensure the highest quality students becoming elementary teachers.

5. A clear focus on the idea that both college and schools are ultimately serving the welfare of each child in each classroom with which we work."

Winograd and McEwan, 1990

The entire document went out to several area schools, along with an invitation which asked principals to tell us about their belief statements and what they perceived to be the commonalities between our approaches to education. We also requested that schools submit a copy of their parent/student handbooks, so that we might be able to better understand the school climate they sought to maintain.

Some schools that had initially expressed interest in working with us chose not to respond to the application, some submitted cursory information, and other schools mailed in elaborate and detailed documentation of their educational goals and outcomes. After reading through the materials we received, we requested on-site visits in 17 schools.

Armed with checklists that covered everything from seating arrangements to the amount of printed material available in the classrooms as well as interview questions for faculty and administrators, we separately or in teams visited each school. As we conducted our visits, it became apparent that we needed to add one more descriptor to the list of qualifications for a site school.

The state of Oregon currently is going through enormous growth and change in terms of its approach to public school education. The schools we ultimately selected to work with are all in the process of creating more democratic environments through invitational curriculum strategies such as those described above as well as integrative curriculum, developmentally appropriate non-graded primary classrooms, team approaches to intermediate grade level teaching, and an increasing movement toward site-based management.

Given all of the innovations that are currently taking place in many schools, we added the criteria of identifying sites that were enmeshed in the change process, rather than those that might perceive themselves to be finished products. Our faculty felt that our students would only benefit from watching the pleasures as well as the agonies of a school staff working together to adapt and alter old patterns. We ultimately selected nine schools with whom we felt we could form viable partnerships for the first year of our program.

Selecting the Students

Our next task was to turn our focus to the process of selecting students. Again, we relied on the philosophy statement for guidance. We developed a three-tiered standard for screening candidates into the M.A.T. degree. First, we had some state- and university-imposed criteria which we used for the initial screening process. The university's graduate school requires a specific standard for grade point averages (G.P.A.s) for admittance to any program and Teachers' Standards and Practices Committee, Oregon's certifying agency, has established certification criteria that include particular scores on the National Teacher's Examination.

Oregon State University's Professional Teacher Education Coordinators' Committee, consisting of representatives from our several secondary programs as well as elementary education, decided that the scores designated as acceptable by the state's certifying agency would serve as entry scores for all our programs. If the students submitting applications met the basic requirements for grade point average and test scores, they moved on to the second round of consideration.

The elementary education portion of the Professional Teacher Education program worked closely with the other programs to develop the next two steps in the admission process. We requested that prospective candidates submit transcripts, a statement of why they want to be teachers, letters of reference, and a resume. We screened the applicant pool to assess their degree of experience in working with children as well as review their course preparation and/or comparable life experience. Since we received as many applications from individuals who were choosing to make mid-life career changes as we did from those who were about to graduate from an undergraduate college program, we developed an equitable system to assess skill competencies as opposed to coursework.

The education faculty participated in the development of application forms that listed subject area competencies such as History, Mathematics, Science, Speech Communication, Human Development, and Science. Undergraduate candidates could demonstrate competencies in these areas by listing coursework. Candidates who were transitioning into education from another career could list their life experiences as well. For instance, one individual listed her work as a speaker for The Boy Scouts of America under the heading of Speech Communications. This was considered to be a viable alternative to a course on Public Speaking.

Because we were in the first year of our program and our initial applicant pool was small, we invited all those who submitted paperwork and met the first standard of G.P.A. and test scores to participate in the third step of the acceptance process: the interview and writing sample. This year our applicant pool was larger so the three-step process was much more selective.

Prior to being interviewed, candidates for the first year of our program were invited to produce a writing sample in response to a common prompt on a set day and time under our supervision. Students were given 75 minutes to respond to one of two statements; the first was a quotation by Jerome Bruner and the second option was to record their thoughts to a quote by a veteran teacher commenting on the value of teacher education programs. Students could bring nothing but a pencil to the writing session.

Because previously submitted materials might have been generated by other people, it was explained to our candidates that it was important to determine their ability to spell and write meaningful sentences free of grammatical errors. This process was not as reliable as we might have wished. Because some of our candidates were residing out of state, they were given the writing prompt over the phone and asked to Fax their writing sample back to us within one and a quarter hours. However, we were still faced with the uncertainty of who might have actually done the writing, and had to trust that the candidates would follow directions.

Interviews proved to be a much more successful process. We conducted them in the various site-schools, each with a team consisting of a school principal, a member of the college's education faculty, and a classroom teacher. In our site-based managed schools our candidates were often interviewed by the principal, university faculty, and several teachers. The number of teachers on an interview team was left to the discretion of the administrator and his or her staff. Alternative phone interviews for those who were out-of-state were also arranged and, with the use of conference calls, were similarly conducted by teams.

Evaluation criteria for the interviews were established that would reflect the democratic principles of our program. Working together with principals from our site schools, we developed questions that we felt would accurately assess a candidate's strengths, weaknesses and his or her ability to think through problems.

1. Tell us about yourself and your experiences working with children.

2. What personal strengths and qualities do you have that would enable you to be an effective teacher?

3. What are some things that you feel you would have to work on to be the teacher you want to be?

4. How would you handle a child who refuses to cooperate?

5. Why are you choosing education as your profession?

6. Do you have any questions of us?

We relied heavily on the principals from our selected site schools for their input in developing these questions, as they have to assess prospective employees on a regular basis and therefore have much more expertise in this area than do most of our college faculty.

After we had developed the questions, we established assessment criteria for the quality of the responses. We paid particular attention to developing evaluation standards that would not be discriminatory. For instance, we chose not to include eye contact as part of the assessment, knowing that there are some cultures that view eye contact as disrespectful.

Our completed list reads as follows:

INTERVIEW EVALUATIONS

Rate the interviewee on a scale of 1 to 4, with 4 being the highest.

Dress and Appearance:
A score of 4 would indicate that the interviewee dressed in a professional manner and was neat and clean in appearance.

Responses:
A score of 4 would indicate that the interviewee considered his or her answers before speaking, demonstrated a knowledge of the subject being discussed, and was able to see both sides of a question.

Communication:
A score of 4 would indicate that the interviewee used no obvious grammatical weaknesses, the interviewee paced his or her answers, and that the sentences were complete.

Personality:
A score of 4 would indicate that the interviewee was enthusiastic, interacted well, listened carefully, had a pleasant demeanor.

Knowing that the attributes we sought in candidates could not be quantified, we relied on our best professional judgment to determine the rankings. We used the same questions in order to establish consistency among the various interview teams. Candidates were scheduled every half hour, with 20 minutes devoted to the interview and 10 minutes set aside for the interview team to discuss and rank the candidate they had just questioned. When we finished, we had selected a cohort of 50 students, our target number, and then we selected a waiting list of five.

Placements: Matching Students, Teachers, and Schools

Typically, teacher education programs in the past have placed students where they can, as they can. Under the old system at Oregon State University, students were assigned to classrooms for a period of time on a basis that could only be described as random. In an effort to begin teaching our students about personal power through genuine choices, we chose to approach this process from a different perspective. After soliciting support from our Assistant Dean, Lance

Haddon, the administrator in charge of field placement, and our Dean, Wayne Haverson, we held a "placement fair" in the spring to welcome our new students and introduce them to representatives from each of the partner schools. Each school gave a short presentation about its curricular goals, students, and staff. Students had an opportunity to mingle with building representatives and sign up to visit those schools that were of interest to them.

While this seemed like a good idea as it was being planned, two problems quickly surfaced. The students who were from out of state could not participate and so were closed out of this very important step. On the other hand, the prospective mentor teachers who attended described the event as being too much like a fraternity or sorority "rush" and they were uncomfortable with what became a competitive atmosphere as students swarmed to sign up for some schools while paying little attention to others.

Out-of-state students primarily arranged their own placements over the phone by speaking with principals and prospective mentor teachers. In a few instances the university faculty made their placements, but in most cases these proved to not be as successful as those arranged by the students themselves. It was one of the first indicators that this program would work best when the university resisted the temptation to make unilateral decisions.

This year the reception and placement process took on a new look. We invited a teacher-representative from each partner school to help us formulate next year's placement process. We invited next year's cohort to meet with this year's students to discuss their placement options. After chatting with the current cohort, next year's students signed up to visit two or three schools rather than randomly roaming through all of them.

In order to help our students choose their fall placements, mentor teachers were asked to fill out a form that described their curriculum and discipline strategies as well as a statement of their expectations for the student-intern. Students will not be placed with mentors until they have spent time in the classrooms and have been interviewed by the mentor. As with last year's process, the placement will be considered done when it is one of mutual agreement.

In the first year of our program, we decided that the placements would be for one full academic year. Our rationale was that this would give student interns a chance to watch one group of children for an entire year with some opportunities to observe other grade levels as time would allow. In retrospect, it was incredibly naive to think that full-year placements would work for all 50 students. In most cases the placements were very successful; when relationships were strained, the problems could be ironed out with some mediation on the part of university supervisors and building principals. But when the working relationship broke down, our partnerships were severely strained.

Most teachers and principals viewed the full-year placement as a solid commitment akin to a marriage, which was a descriptor I heard in more than one partner school. At the university, while we understood the perspective of the partner schools, we were also working to protect the rights of students who were paying to receive training and only had one year in which to achieve levels of mastery that would serve as springboards to successful careers. When a student's placement was changed, the ultimate decision was made by the university personnel and the unilateral aspect of such decisions did severe damage to the trust we were working so hard to establish.

In an effort to respond to the problems and correct them, we decided that in the future we will make use of a two-pronged approach. First, we have established guidelines that will be followed in all cases when there is a problem between a mentor and intern. Second, we will identify 25 more sites than we will have students for next year. Rotation will be encouraged as a standard part of the program. A student intern might select to remain in one class for the entire year, but that decision will be optional. We will emphasize the value of seeing more than one grade level.

While rotation among classrooms clearly has its drawbacks, the altered expectation of not being in one classroom for a full year should alleviate the mutual pain and embarrassment that occurred this year when placements were dissolved. The plan to identify 75 prospective placements for 50 students has been met with widespread approval from the mentor teachers.

In addition, principals have offered to become more personally involved in conflicts between mentors and students when they do arise. During the past year I found that the objective perspective of a building principal could often bring clarity to issues that, at first, appeared hopelessly muddied. In short, next year we will be expanding on the definition of what a university-school partnership is all about.

Becoming a Teacher from June to June

When the actual program began, we added a third member to our faculty. The elementary education faculty combines to make a unique team in that we have the expertise among us to cover most areas of a standard teacher education program. Ken Winograd's area of expertise is whole language, with particular attention to integrating writing with the development of math story problems. Karen Higgins has worked extensively in the area of teaching math as problem-solving as well as having specialized knowledge of authentic assessment strategies. My own research is in the area of classroom discipline in general and in particular the model titled *Judicious Discipline* (Gathercoal, 1990). I have also taught social studies methods for a number of years.

More importantly, the three of us share a common commitment to model the concepts we teach, which at times can be easier said than done. But developing a program with a consistent perspective of education has been the glue that has helped us work together smoothly even during bumpy times.

The Program

The Professional Teacher Education program has been designed to run a full calendar year beginning with summer term and ending the following year at the end of spring term. The summer term consists of course work designed to raise the students' level of awareness as to the issues they will be facing in the schools, and provide them with an understanding of the foundations of education, as well as give them a measure of insight into the psychology of children, a working knowledge of civil rights issues as applied to public school students, and some instruction in curriculum design and classroom discipline.

The courses were deliberately structured to introduce students to the concept that information delivery can occur in an integrative fashion. One example of this was the use of the book *Among Schoolchildren* (Kidder, 1989). Ken Winograd used the book in his course titled "Developmental Reading" as a way to introduce specific techniques in the teaching of reading. Karen Higgins and I used the same book in our course titled "The Diverse Learner" as a means of analyzing classroom climates.

At the end of the summer there was another opportunity to have our student experience integrative education. A foundations course titled "Students, Teachers, Schools, and Communities" and taught by Forrest Gathercoal culminated in "The Ideal School Project." Drawing upon all their summer courses as well as their life experiences, teams of elementary and secondary students worked together to create the cognitive, affective, and physical environments that would be most conducive to the success of young people in a public school. Elementary education faculty attended the presentations of the projects to observe the manner in which our students incorporated other class content into their projects.

The faculty shared a common goal of wanting to submerge our students into the world of education. Summer term was and will continue to be an intense introduction to the teaching profession. At the end of our first summer, one small group in the elementary education cohort printed badges that read "M.A.T. Student, Personal Life On Hold."

The student-interns began working in their site school placement on the day their mentor teachers returned to school to begin the academic year. They spent the entire month of September with their mentors observing how classes were set up and how the atmosphere in a classroom is created. During this time they also pursued a variety of special projects, working one-on-one or in small groups with university faculty. One group observed and recorded strategies modeled by mentor teachers for establishing classroom discipline in the beginning of the year, a second group studied miscue analysis, a third group worked on a project having to do with teaching math as a problem-solving activity. The projects kept the university faculty closely connected with our students through small-group meetings designed to assess their progress.

During fall and winter terms our student-interns divided their time between their placement responsibilities and coursework on campus. They were in the schools three days a week and back on campus for two days. The division of time has been a very controversial issue in our program. In the past, time divided between placements and course work was handled by splitting the day between the college and the classroom. Students would spend the morning in their placements and return to campus for their after-noon classes. This was a very unsatisfactory arrangement because by the afternoon they were tired and had little energy for their classes. In addition to this problem, the new Professional Teacher Education program works with partner schools located 45 minutes to one hour away from Oregon State University, so the option of returning in the afternoon does not exist in this program.

A major objection to the three day/two day split has been that the mentors and interns must plan for the upcoming week on Wednesdays and that the interns never see the full week during those terms. One solution that is being explored for next year might be blocks of time in the schools and blocks of time back on campus. For instance, students might stay in the schools for two weeks and then return to campus for the same period of time.

Although the division of our interns' time between campus and school led to tensions between the university and its public school partners, most of the issues were calmly resolved through group process. Members of the Oregon State University Education faculty met regularly with our partner schools' principals. These meetings were more than information sessions but in the spirit of partnership empowerment, they were also opportunities to air con-cerns, review options and work together to find solutions to concerns.

Winter term was configured in the same way as fall term. During spring term the student-interns were in their site school placements full time, only returning to campus for a weekly seminar scheduled late in the afternoon.

College Classes

Coursework in the program reflected the commitment our faculty has made to the democratic curriculum and discipline strategies that have been cited above. Although the courses had specific numbers and credit hours assigned to them, in actual fact the lines of distinction between them were deliberately blurred. Our primary objective was to present information that students could immedi-ately apply in their practicum settings. The subject matter consisted of instruc-tion in democratic practices such as how to design integrated curriculum and how to maintain a classroom environment that would allow all students to have their individual learning styles addressed and special needs met. In addi-tion our pre-service interns received instruction in how to conduct applied research while teaching. The theme of democratic education ran through every course presented in our program, all of which reflected a consistent, student-centered approach to instruction.

Class Meetings

In the curriculum of the program there are unique features designed to build a sense of personal empowerment by providing opportunities for genuine choice, model the concept of democratic learning processes that focus on ensuring equal educational experiences, and provide time for personal reflection. At the beginning of summer term we included in our schedule a variety of activities that would permit all of these program features to occur. Class meetings designed to encourage student input into the program and a chance for them to suggest changes were scheduled as a regular part of the elementary education summer program. Karen Higgins, Ken Winograd, and I sat in on the meetings as well as a fourth faculty member, Tom Evans, who initially guided the action research projects that will be discussed later in this chapter. Although pieces of undecided business in the program were deliberately left undecided so that our students could help us resolve them, we found that this use of class meetings quickly became a self-defeating process.

Personal empowerment through the ability to make decisions about one's education, as stated earlier, is often a new concept to students. They do not enter a program with the typical expectation that anyone will ask them for input into the structure of their learning experience. They are usually told when to show up and what to do, no questions asked. As a result, giving our students options seemed to create dissonance in them and they became unsure of how to handle the power they were given. As a result, we found that the class meetings were dissolving into gripe sessions and that little business was getting done.

Even worse, we discovered ourselves to be drawn into discussions about the nature of the program during times designated for instruction. We were feeling frustrated by the tone the exchanges were taking and some of the students expressed their dismay over the same concerns. At that point we decided to limit class meetings to periodic discussions based around general issues. We eliminated asking our students to make decisions about the program's basic structure. While we maintained our commitment to providing our students with a sense of empowerment, we sought alternative means of accomplishing this goal.

Interestingly, I shared my concerns about the problems we encountered with a principal who was in the process of developing a site-based managed school. She informed me that her faculty had engaged in much the same sort of behavior as their level of professional empowerment increased. We speculated together that perhaps when individuals experience an unfamiliar level of power there is fear as well as exhilaration. The fear our students and her faculty may have been feeling revealed itself in power struggles. Understanding this, we were much better prepared to deal with those issues as they occurred during the year.

Once we determined that class meetings would be a time for sharing information and thoughts, the experience became much more useful to the communication process within a cohort of 50 people. The university faculty share the belief that class meetings contribute significantly to a democratic classroom environment because it allows for shared input and open discussion. As such, it is a strategy with which we want our students to feel comfortable. Knowing the benefits that result from an open forum, we ironed out the problems and now feel that the class meetings are a very positive aspect of our program.

Given everything we now know, we will not discontinue class meetings but we will provide more structure for them in the future, using them as a time to adjust and amend the program. The class meetings themselves have proved very valuable during the year as a time set aside for us to share information and exchange views. It is now an accepted practice with which we all feel comfortable. Democratic practices are neither easy nor smooth, and all of us now view the difficulties experienced in the initial class meetings as a natural growth process from which we all learned.

Journal Writing

Journal writing was, from the beginning, a requirement of the program. We encouraged students to use their journals to vent frustrations, share their successes, and generally process their professional growth. This proved to be highly successful for some of our students but just a task to be completed to others. Journals also became a vehicle through which students shared very personal aspects of their lives, providing the university faculty with meaningful insight into their perceptions of themselves as future teachers. The journals contributed to our goal of empowering our students; when individual students expressed a personal request in an entry for some special consideration, we did our best to meet their needs.

I have used journal writing before in the classes I have taught. I always find that the first round of entries are sparse and, for the most part, superficial. My practice has always been to write lengthy comments, questions, and thoughts back to the students in the margins of their entries. When students find that their journals are indeed being read, they are much more likely to use the journal as it was intended and write passages that are reflective and personally more revealing.

In my experience, successful journal writing depends to an enormous extent upon the level of trust developed between the writer and the reader.

Confidentiality and thoughtfully written responses are crucial to creating an atmosphere that would encourage the quality of entries we hope to see generated by our student interns. However, difficulties arose just for the reason that many of our students were deeply engaged in the process. They would write lengthy passages that, oddly enough, included phrases such as "I have no time for this damn journal."

Two of us shared the task of reading the journals and so the writers who spent time processing their experiences represented a significant commitment of our time in order to write appropriate responses. In an effort to gain a measure of control over this process, we requested that students limit their entries to topics dealing directly with their courses or field experiences and that they write at least two entries a week. However, the imposed structure was met with resistance if not outright hostility. After one or two weeks of reading entries that complained about journal writing in general, we abandoned the activity for the remainder of the year.

Despite the problems that arose from the journals, their value far outweighed the negative aspects. We remain committed to the activity because we want our students to use journal writing in their own classes. There are few more effective means of communicating one-on-one with every student in a class than through a personal correspondence in a journal. A serendipitous substitute for the journals arose from what at first appeared an unlikely source.

Video Cohorts

While we were eliminating journal writing, we were also developing a new instructional design that would help students reflect upon their developing abilities as teachers. We formed them into six groups of what were called "video cohorts," with roughly eight students per group. My two colleagues and I supervised two groups each and divided our time between them. The groups met in members' homes. Every other week four students were responsible for preparing a videotape of their teaching to share with the rest of the group over a total of four sessions. The tape-makers were also required to submit a one-page reflection paper covering the lesson on the tape and what they had learned from their cohort. The tapes and the papers were reviewed by the faculty member supervising that particular group.

Before the interns began sharing their tapes, we had a large class meeting to discuss the process. We particularly focused on what might or might not be perceived as helpful comments and constructive feedback. We talked about the issues of risk-taking and how that might be facilitated in the groups. Then we helped them schedule their first meetings, at which time each group would decide whose videotape would be shown when and how their own group interactions would work. This was a highly successful process. Everyone involved learned a great deal about teaching, and the feedback was very useful to those who made tapes.

I believe that this reflective process filled the gap left by the journal writing. It provided a time for interns to share their personal insights about teaching with a faculty member and receive specific feedback. Next year we will probably use the journal writing during the summer portion of the program so that we might get to know the students better. After that, the journal-writing process will be replaced with the videotapes and papers. This year, spring term has no structure for this type of personal interaction and a creative alternative should be developed so that next year no communication void will exist.

Conducting Action Research

The major element that distinguishes our program from most teacher education programs is the emphasis on action research. During the initial summer term our students were introduced to the concept of conducting action research as part of the normal routine of a classroom teacher. The research project is closely tied to our goal of creating democratic teachers. Training our students to investigate the needs of their students rather than dismissing concerns without taking time to consider their source, we believe, helps them focus more effectively on each individual learner.

At first, the idea of identifying a research topic, conducting the research, and reporting their findings seemed an overwhelming task to most of them. When the students went out to their placements at the beginning of the school year many of them felt at a loss to know how they should begin carrying out their research projects. Topics they thought they would research did not seem to fit their situations or did not work out. It took the majority of our students a few months to identify a topic with which they could feel comfortable.

During winter term the cohort was divided into four smaller research groups loosely based around similarities in their research topics. Each group was supervised by one faculty member with similar research interests. The smaller research groups met on a regular basis to discuss their progress. Their projects culminated in a research symposium organized by Tom Evans and Ken Winograd. Based on the conference style of the American Educational Research Association, students presented their findings in groups of three or four during simultaneous conference sessions. In most cases they had discovered some significant findings on topics ranging from what attributes contribute to a successful mentor teacher/student intern placement (Bailey, 1992) to the ways in which curriculum design and grade level contribute to decisions about classroom seating arrangements (Bauer and Phillipsen, 1992). Most gratifying to the faculty is our knowledge that the students will continue in the role of action researchers when they have their own classrooms.

Assessing the Students

The democratic curriculum strategies that were taught and modeled included alternative strategies for assessment. Assessment strategies that are based on academic understanding of subject matter and that avoid economic, gender, or ethnic bias are essential elements of democratic education. Student-interns were taught how to conduct authentic assessment through observation as well as helping their students develop portfolios. The elementary education faculty was committed to practicing these same concepts as we assessed our students' performance levels. Their overall success in the program was assessed in three different ways: practicum observations, presentation of their research projects, and assembling and defending their professional portfolios during two-hour oral examinations.

The field supervision responsibilities were divided among the elementary education faculty and graduate teaching assistants. We visited students for informal as well as formal observations, in each case providing them with written feedback. Evaluation forms had been developed by the program coordinators but it became clear very quickly that these forms were difficult to use effectively with the interactive classroom environments in which our students were placed. Supervisors often did not have an opportunity to see a standard lesson being taught. More often, our student-interns had their pupils involved in learning center activities, small group explorations, silent reading, or a "choice" period during which children were all engaged in a variety of activities. Since we had deliberately sought out such classrooms as ideal settings for our students to learn the democratic educational practices cited above, the evaluation forms became a source of tension between mentor-teachers and the university. Mentors were frustrated by a form that had little to do with their approach to classroom organization.

The elementary education faculty realized we would have to change the forms used for intern assessment if we were to accurately assess the performance of our students in these innovative settings. We are currently rewriting the evaluation forms, working together with a group of mentor-teachers to develop a tool that more accurately reflects the open-ended activities supervisors observe during their classroom visits.

The research projects were assessed during the symposium presentations. A completed research project contained a statement of the problem, a description of the setting in which the research was conducted, the research design, the findings of the study, and any appendices that would further clarify the study. The printed project was bound and a copy was submitted to the supervising faculty member of each student's research cohort. Those projects will serve as guidelines for our future student interns. Students retained one copy of their study as part of the third assessment tool, the portfolio.

Since the Professional Teacher Education program culminates in a Master of Arts in Teaching degree, a graduate-level exit process had to be set in place for this program. It was decided that each student would complete a two-hour oral examination as opposed to a written exam. The elementary education faculty decided to place the focus of the oral examinations on a presentation and defense of each student's professional portfolio. We encouraged students to consider the portfolio from two perspectives. First, they were given suggestions as to the pieces of information they might include that would represent their professional growth over the course of the entire academic year. Special projects, videotapes, lesson plans, and units were either required or recommended to be included. Second, we reminded students that once the portfolio was assembled, it would be of immeasurable value to them as they interviewed for faculty positions for the following year.

The portfolios that were presented exemplified their work and professional promise as no other measurement could. Students devoted a great deal of time not only to the content of the items included but their visual presentation as well. Time, effort, and thought were evident in the manner in which these portfolios were assembled. They effectively reflected the professional growth experienced in our students during the time they were in our program.

Where Are We Headed?

Our continual focus on creating and sustaining a democratic teacher-education program is leading us to further decentralize the decision-making processes with which we are engaged. We recently brought together mentor-teachers representing each of our current partnership schools to discuss their perceptions of our program and what needs to be altered in order to improve upon what we are currently doing.

We began with a brainstorming session of ideas and suggestions for next year. Because our mentor-teachers have their own perspective of our program, their input was invaluable. They provided us with solid suggestions for improving our placement process and strengthening the avenues for communication between the university and the schools. It was agreed that the meetings would continue on a regular basis, and their suggestions are currently being drafted into proposals for changes in our program.

While one objective for forming this committee was to improve the lines of communication and another was to gain greater benefit from the expertise in our partner schools, a third objective is also being met. Members of elementary education faculty have all been classroom teachers for a number of years and in a variety of school settings. However, except for two or three, our mentor-teachers have never had experience as teacher-educators working in a university setting. It has become increasingly clear to us that if we are ever to have true give-and-take partnerships, we need to provide the mentors with opportunities to understand our workplace environment and our professional demands.

Too often over the past year, our inability to visit site schools regularly was interpreted as a lack of interest. What we hope to help mentor-teachers understand are the very real demands of university standards for research, teaching, and service. While we are all teachers, our job descriptions are very different from those of our program's mentors and it is this difference which has, at times, strained the partnership. Working closely with the mentors to alter and improve our program has helped this situation immeasurably.

The newly formed committee has also contributed to teacher empowerment, which we find exciting. I personally saw an example of this shortly after our first meeting with mentors. It has been our practice over the past year to regularly meet in each site school with the mentor teachers, principal, and interns. Each elementary education faculty member covers three or four schools and we schedule a meeting with each one approximately every six weeks.

In the past, I led the meetings by proposing an agenda and opening up discussion to the members of the site school team for their input and suggestions on whatever matters were being brought before them. However, I experienced a very different site school meeting within a few days of the initial committee gathering. I was prepared to lead the agenda as usual when the mentor-teacher who represented her school on the committee took over the meeting, presented her agenda, and led the discussion. Previously she had been relatively quiet during the site meetings but this time she was assertive and clearly presented the issues her team had agreed to discuss. I was impressed with the fact that our meetings on campus were accomplishing exactly what we hoped, an expansion of the partnership concept.

In a similar vein, toward the end of the academic year, we brought our current cohort together with next year's student-interns. The elementary education faculty played a low-key role in the exchanges. Rather than leading the process, we encouraged the students to meet casually with one another and provided an opportunity for our present cohort to experience the role of mentor. We made no effort to limit the discussions other than to remind our current student-interns of professional courtesy that should be extended to their mentors. It was gratifying to see our current students acting in the role of being teachers of teachers. Personally, it represented for me an important step towards their sense of personal and professional growth.

Some Concluding Thoughts

During the 1990-1991 academic year, just prior to the first year of our new Elementary Education program, Oregon State University experienced an upheaval as a result of a state-wide ballot initiative to limit property taxes: Ballot Measure Five. Within two weeks of the measure's passage, teacher-education programs throughout the state were severely hit by budget cuts. One outcome of those cuts was the closing of the College of Education at Oregon State University. The elementary education program will now be part of the School of Education and housed in the newly configured College of Home Economics and Education.

The College of Home Economics has always housed the Early Childhood Education program. Now elementary education will join with early childhood as well as extending into a middle-level grade program as well. The new configuration will unite our programs along a continuum of developmental stages and, as such, will better prepare our student-interns to meet the needs of the children they will serve.

Looking back over the year, I would say that our program has been successful not only in preparing teachers who can design and effectively teach invitational curriculum strategies, but it also has provided them with an opportunity to experience a variety of strategies for incorporating democratic concepts into daily classroom interactions. Our student-interns have studied and practiced a number of methods for teaching and managing children, all of which reflect a consistent belief that the purpose of public school education is to create citizens who understand their role in our greater society and are capable of independent, critical thinking.

REFERENCES

Bailey, Sue. (1992). Mentor/intern relationships. Unpublished study.

Bauer, Sandra, and Gwen Phillipsen. (1992). Determining classroom seating arrangements. Unpublished study.

Gathercoal, Forrest. (1990). *Judicious Discipline* (Sacramento: Caddo Gap Press).

Kider, Tracy. (1989). *Among Schoolchildren* (New York: Avon).

Seven

An Institute for Independence Through Action, Process, and Theory

J. Cynthia McDermott

The Action for Responsibility Institute (hereafter "ARI") at California State University, Dominguez Hills (hereafter "CSUDH") was established for the purpose of training teachers and allied school personnel in the promotion of independence and participation in sustained democratic process among students and their peers in their respective communities. Dr. William Glasser instructed a group of approximately 85 participants (approximately half of whom were elementary school teachers, with the rest being principals, counselors, social workers, nurses, peer tutors, and substitute teachers), drawn from Los Angeles Unified School District and Compton Unified School District, in the principles of community building and control theory, and in developing a child-centered, need-satisfying educational environment. Further study included community building processes with Cooperative Adventures and implementing the training in various school settings in the Greater Los Angeles school community.

This was funded by two grants from the U.S. Department of Education, Drug-Free Schools and Communities Fund, awarded to the CSUDH School of Education.

Independence: The Mission of Education

Hopelessness and despair pervade the ambiance of classrooms and retard the educational development of children wherever there is poverty in this country, and among the places where this is true are the inner-city communities of South Central Los Angeles and Compton—two communities which stand out in the otherwise prosperous and trend-setting region of Southern California. In such an atmosphere, children fail to learn how to mobilize their personal power and instead tend to become passively dependent upon authority figures and others to take care of them, make their decisions for them, determine their destinies for them. Academically they become chronic underachievers, as a pattern of passivity takes hold and depression sets in (often for life).

Much evidence exists which demonstrates the lack of independence held by members and participants in the educational community throughout America. Often it is not discussed in seminars or written about in professional journals, but is simply observed by administrators and participants in the day-to-day routine of school operation. For example, in most elementary schools, rows of students in silent lines continue to travel from one part of the campus to another, bringing to mind military camp or prison. A high premium is placed on conformity, on acceptance of regimentation, on "keeping your mouth shut" that resembles a form of slavery. Such premiums eventually result in disillusionment, loss of hope, and apathy, with the very spirit and integrity of the child being killed.

> To obey, we perform. We work. We do our homework. We put in overtime. We conform. A life of compliance is a life of denial. We deny our feelings. Obedience has its cost: the destruction of the self. To be good is to be a slave, unfree.
>
> Starhawk, *Truth or Dare*,
> San Francisco: Harper Collins, 1987, p. 81

A more graphic example commonly occurs in the area of teaching subjects which involve student creativity. In elementary school art classes, for example, it is not uncommon for teachers to teach art by requiring all the children in the class to draw a given object the same way and to color it the same color. Children in such classes are sometimes even penalized in some way, usually by getting a scolding from the teacher in front of the other students, if they dare to color the leaves of a tree orange, for instance, instead of green.

Children under the thumb of such teachers thus have no opportunity to express themselves through art, or even to discover, much less celebrate and develop, their own talents, whatever they are. As a consequence, in order to maintain their self-esteem and avoid "getting into trouble," they are duty-bound to follow the teacher's instructions to the letter. Rather than take initiative and decide for themselves what they want to draw, how they want to draw it, and what color it should be, their independence is squelched by a teacher whose primary need is to control his/her class rather than to appreciate individuality among students and foster its growth, and their independence, in a natural way. In so doing, the over-controlling teacher unwittingly lays the foundation for developing "people pleaser" personalities—dependent, often fearful students who take no risks and develop no independent decision-making skills. Such is the nature of traditional education in America, and it has existed for centuries. Sadly, the same pattern can be found today, even in spite of the women's movement and relaxation of some other cultural and educational traditions and formalities.

Typically, students are systematically discouraged early on of taking initiative, of acting on their own. They are denied the opportunity to give input with regard to matters which affect them or to make decisions about such matters. Instead they are told that they are "too young" to make such decisions, or don't know enough to state an opinion worthy of even being heard by adults, much less gain adult respect. As a consequence, they fail to acquire the essential civic skills necessary for active, reflective, and conscious participation in the very democratic process which is supposed to be their birthright granted to them by the U.S. Constitution. These skills are particularly important for students who are "at risk"—that is, already disenfranchised because of socioeconomic status, poverty, class, language difference, or cultural background.

This deprivation and failure to develop civic skills affects not only the students. Teachers who are themselves defined and treated as under-class suffer similar deprivation, often having experienced the very kinds of denial of opportunity for personal growth described above. As teachers, they teach what they know, passing on their own deprivation to their students, who then become destined, unless they make a concerted effort as adults not to do so, to pass on what they have learned to their own children. And so the cycle continues from generation to generation, resulting in a system which fosters competition, emphasizes products such as test scores over process, and discourages community.

The Action for Responsibility Institute

Recognizing the effects of stifled independent thinking and behavior on the individual and the community, CSUDH School of Education faculty members submitted two grant proposals to the U.S. Department of Education for the purpose of establishing a training devoted to the promotion of independence and personal responsibility among individuals—teachers and students—teaching them the skills necessary for full participation in the democratic process. It was further theorized that once given such skills, such individuals would be able to function fully in society and would have no need to use drugs.

We named this training the Action for Responsibility Institute and set as its goals the following:

1. Educating trainees to understand the differences between a classroom in which students are encouraged to exercise independent thinking, as opposed to one in which they are not so encouraged;

2. Helping trainees feel more comfortable taking risks, voicing opinions and positions, and exercising their own options (sometimes called empowerment);

3. Presenting trainees with a theoretical model to support new action; and

4. Giving trainees specific skills in creating democratic, responsible classrooms.

ARI was a dream. a plan to help a few teachers and support personnel look at classroom and school practices through a new lens. It was based on a synthesis of several theories, most notably the works of William Glasser and Scott Peck, and the process of Mondragon. Together their contributions create a new order which describes an individual as someone who 1) behaves to satisfy basic needs; 2) chooses behaviors which will satisfy those needs from among alternatives; 3) is by nature altruistic; 4) can choose moral responses; 5) can learn to see the good of the group before individual goals; and 6) is willing to commit to beliefs and take responsibility for his or her actions. The individual envisioned by the above theorists is a responsible, caring person and a lifelong learner who is willing to act when necessary, able to take risks, and, as we argued in the grant application, would therefore not take drugs.

Selection of Trainees and the Training

Once the grants were funded, volunteers were sought. Altogether, 85 people consisting of elementary school teachers and principals from the Compton Unified School District and support personnel (counselors and police officers) from the Los Angeles Unified School District were selected to participate in this 45-hour project. Our participants became our colleagues and had nothing else in common other than their employment with their respective school districts. As individuals, they varied as broadly from one another as our Greater Los Angeles communities. We worked to model a community.

The process began with two days of lecture by Dr. William Glasser, who explained Control Theory and how to implement it in classrooms. Students were required to read *The Quality School* prior to the lectures. After the theoretical model had been explained, participants spent several days in simulation activities called "Cooperative Adventures." These are a series of increasingly complex and difficult physical, mental, and emotional challenges (similar in some ways to Outward Bound and Adventure Ropes courses) presented to groups in such a way that success can only be achieved through communication and cooperation. At the conclusion of the training, participants were expected to spend 15 hours practicing what they had learned.

The Cooperative Adventures phase of the training included a number of low-risk, introductory adventures designed to enable the participants to develop sufficient trust in one another to work in teams, with each individual taking responsibility for his contribution to the team's efforts and goals. Gradually a sense of community and mutual interdependence developed so that the participants could connect their Cooperative Adventures experiences with the needs of their students and with the Control Theory model.

The Contribution of William Glasser's Control Theory

The theoretical foundation for ARI was provided mostly by the work of William Glasser. In his book *Control Theory*, published in 1984, Glasser propounded a belief that was completely opposite from any that had preceded him. He explained that the one thing that is common to all humans is that they behave and that they can choose how they wish to behave. What behavior they *choose* ideally is designed to meet one or more of their four basic psychological needs: fun, freedom, power, and love and belonging. Nothing or nobody can MAKE people behave in any given way. Tokens, grades, or threats cannot force students to be respectful of one another, nor do these things enable them to be more empathic. People do what they do because it is important to them— that is, it is need-satisfying.

By contrast, traditional American education since its inception has been based on the stimulus-response (S-R) model, which, over time, teaches children to conform as a result of pressure or coercion. It is this pressure or coercion that leads us away from individual responsibility and continues to create passive, angry, non-risk-taking students (and later, teachers). Glasser's thinking provides the psychological support necessary to propel our work as democratic educators.

Individuals who work to create a need-satisfying community allow us to see Control Theory in practice in a real environment beyond the school. When such communities come together, there is a recognition of engaging in useful tasks which are need-satisfying. Community is important because (as we defined it) a democracy is a place in which individuals can be successful together, where collective vision and strength can gather to enhance the work of the individual, and where competition and coercion are not draining the energy of individuals. It was our hope that by teaching our ARI trainees Glasser's approach, they would begin to understand that an educational atmosphere in which the four needs (fun, freedom, power, and love and belonging) were being met would result in trust, cooperation, and successful accomplishment of educational goals, and ultimately a community of learners.

Glasser recommends that a school or classroom which practices a Control Theory approach encourage high quality in everything that is done. Quality should be talked about and children should self-evaluate their work, since they are taught that they are ultimately most accountable to themselves. The curriculum should be useful and teach life skills, but never through the use of fear or coercion. Children in such schools are thus taught to take responsibility for their actions, and have no need to blame others for their own misdeeds or mistakes. Such phrases as "Jose made me hit him" would not occur, since no one can "make" anyone else do anything.

Glasser relates a story that illustrates the working of his non-stimulus-response model. A friend of Glasser's, who is a professor of criminology, did not believe in Control Theory until he attended a conference in Las Vegas and was robbed. A criminal followed him to his hotel room, pointed a gun at him, and demanded his wallet. The professor said no. He told the robber that the robber could have his cash, which he took out of his wallet and put on the floor, but not his credit cards or driver's license. The robber took the money and left. Later the professor explained that he now understood Control Theory: When threatened with the strongest possible stimulus, he chose to respond the way he wanted. The incident pointed out that no one and nothing can make us do anything.

We chose to teach Cooperative Adventures because the techniques demonstrate the four psychological needs of Control Theory, and therefore model new behaviors. Glasser argues that behavior can be taught, and if students do not know the positive behaviors we want, it is a moral imperative to teach them. Students have hierarchical competitive models of behavior emblazoned in their behaving system. We all do! We know how to shield our worksheets from the eyes of our classmates because we were taught to do that. We also know hundreds of stories of people who have succeeded at the expense of others: the spelling bee champion, the football hero, the cheerleading queen, etc. What we know little about are the models of a community working together to solve a problem, or even to have fun.

Once we had completed the training in Cooperative Adventures, our next challenge was to infuse Cooperative Adventures into the participants' classrooms to create communities in which students and teachers are encouraged to think and act independently and responsibly, and thus are able to satisfy their individual needs. We needed to further explain community and used the following model.

The Need for A Sense of and Equilibrio

Building community changes ecology and moves people beyond hopelessness and passivity. This process is called "equilibrio." The concept of equilibrio is the mortar that binds together the large and ever-growing cooperative social system known as Mondragon in the Basque area of Spain. What is significant about this model to our work in schools is that these cooperatives place community at the center of their work as they produce products in a noncompetitive way. The product is not their reason for existence or for their working together. More than 40 years old, these nearly 200 co-ops have succeeded because of a solidarity at their core in which members reframe and discuss what works on an ongoing basis, with all members encouraged to participate equally. The operative dynamics include democracy and self-management, personal and collective risk-taking, a community-centered nature, earnings related only to a person's own work, ability, and will to make social choices that continue to hold back the destructive nature of industrialism, and—most important—equilibrio.

In the introduction to *We Build the Road as We Travel* (Philadelphia: New Society Press, 1991), Morrison defines equilibrio.

> This means not just equilibrium of balance, but also implies harmony, poise, calmness, and composure. Equilibrio is a vital process that harmonizes and balances a diverse and growing community of interests: those of the individual and the co-op, the particular co-op and the co-op system, and the co-op system and the community and environment. (p. 4)

In other words, a caring community is one that centers first on the development, sustenance, and health of the community itself. In that environment, every member of the community can feel safe and trusted, and trusting. The community provides the empowerment and the escape from hopelessness. Together, a community can achieve anything. This community is what a democratic, consensus-driven ecology must be about.

This sense of a living, breathing, evolving dynamic is the antithesis of a community fixed on accomplishment for the sake of the product. Even actions such as a barnraising or building houses for Habitat for Humanity create only the illusion of community, but do provide important first steps in developing community. Not until the environment of the group goes beyond the product and focuses on the acceptance and inclusion of all members will equilibrio be achieved. Most of us have few lived experiences of equilibrio and consensus-building because equilibrio requires practice, time, and reflection. It also requires commitment and the willingness to release our own control to that of the group. The democratic pursuit of equilibrio is a healing art deeply rooted in the ethics of a caring community (Gilligan, 1982). It requires that the participants allow the healing to happen through a social contract.

A community that is viewed as organic fosters the elements needed for survival because as it lives and evolves, a social transformation is created that provides both personal and communal freedom. Thus, a disempowered, product-oriented, hopeless classroom can be transformed into an organic community that not only transforms education but the larger society as well.

Other Models for Community

A powerful model for understanding the stages of the birth of community action is drawn by M. Scott Peck in *The Different Drum: Community Making and Peace* (New York: Simon & Schuster, 1987). Peck describes four stages of community-making, each of which is necessary to reach the essence of equilibrio.

Stage One: Pseudo Community. This stage occurs when everyone is polite and seemingly concerned about everyone else. People are friendly and perhaps even hug and show affection, but they deny individual differences and avoid conflict at all costs. Much polite behavior is in evidence, and people nod and smile even if they disagree with one another. These behaviors are safely exhibited as individuals focus outwardly toward a product to achieve, rather than looking for a definition of community. This stage is marked by an absence of emotional depth.

Stage Two: Chaos. In this stage, individuals try to fix the group and stay in personal control. There is much unproductive arguing. Individual differences are recognized, and stronger and louder members try to persuade and even convert those who are different. Conflicts occur, but no attempt to resolve them is in evidence. Each individual is trying to maintain his or her own control over the group, rather than use individual control to strengthen the group.

Stage Three: Emptiness. This stage requires individuals to "empty themselves of barriers to communication." This vital stage is the step to community in which the group then recognizes its need to change and become risk-takers. This stage is about trusting the group and admitting failures.

Stage Four: Community. This stage is what Mondragon defines as equilibrio. The community's work is the development and sustenance of the community—that is, the task and the process, not the creation of a thing or the happiness of the individual. This final stage is characterized by a sense of peacefulness and tranquility. This is not to say that conflict does not occur. Conflict must occur and be resolved because true community requires dialogue, reflection, and change. What occurs is a shared empowerment that comes from the collective strength of the community.

Pseudo Communities

Several strategies are adopted and operational in many elementary schools which purport to create child-centered, democratic, project-oriented classrooms. One is known as Cooperative Learning, which is a system supposedly designed to help students learn from one another, increase their knowledge base, and support one another emotionally. Such goals can transform the classroom and how it operates to affect the individuals within it on a day-to-day basis. Several definitions of Cooperative Learning have been modeled by various authors and systems.

Strategies of Cooperative Learning have been taught to and implemented by teachers in many of our service districts. Ironically, Cooperative Learning often turns out to be very competitive and works successfully against any sense of community or tribe. Students continue to be unkind to one another, competitive, judgmental, and angry. When they are unsuccessful academically or perform poorly in some other way, they are set up in an immoral fashion to see themselves as bad students or bad people. The success of one group comes at the expense of all the others. Individuals are, by nature, altruistic, and this non-altruistic behavior works to increase the students' sense of their lack of control and lack of power (Kohn, 1990). What exists is not a new process, but another way to group students within the old paradigm of getting a good product. Classrooms which do not provide time for students to learn how to be kind and work through a process of building community deliberately undermine the opportunity for community.

Stories From the Field

Our colleagues returned to the children in their classrooms enthusiastic about creating change in their relationships. Some told us that what they had experienced and learned had in fact forever changed their lives and the way they viewed education. A few skeptics in the group, however, wondered if they really had the skills to implement what could potentially create radical change. Several scenarios occurred.

A few colleagues attempted one or two Adventures and met with old behaviors sometimes more strongly evidenced than before. For example, in one sixth grade class students were unsuccessfully following this challenge: "Form six groups of approximately equal size that are mixed." After 45 minutes of great discomfort for the teacher, the challenge had not been met. Why was that?

It seemed clear that these students lacked the necessary practice that would enable them to talk with one another, to trust one another's opinions and ideas, and to take a risk and try something new. The teacher was also without those behaviors in the classroom. The result? The teacher chose to tell the students how to solve the problem, thus regaining control and releasing the students from any responsibility they had in solving the challenge. The teacher's habit of teaching by telling was too enticing. The students were now farther away from empowerment than they had been before. Their opportunity to experience community in its highest form had been taken from them as the teacher struggled to keep her power. She believed that she had solved the problem and enabled the students to feel better when in fact she had damaged them even more. As she described it, her class became even more difficult to manage, and she became convinced that our training could only work with certain kinds of students who already had self-control and creative problem-solving skills. Although the teacher in this case wanted the children to be responsible and caring, the risk of moving out of the way and allowing this to happen was too great. A deeper understanding of why an enabling behavior creates the robots we watched failing to complete a seemingly simple task was needed.

The class described above was a failure, but it makes the point that change does not come easily. In the main, however, the opportunity to move from process to understanding to process changed learning environments for students. In one third grade classroom, recess was a very difficult daily event; fights occurred, with name calling and intimidation, resulting in frustration and anger for everyone involved. After several weeks of community building the students asked to have a class discussion about recess. The students recognized that they had little power to change things on the playground. Because they felt unsafe, the class decided to hold recess in the classroom, and to practice and make up new Adventures. Curious students dropped in to visit, increasing the class population at every recess. The teacher reported that her class realized that they could change the recess behavior, and began conducting Adventures at recess for anyone who wanted to join and who was willing to follow the rules.

The training was implemented in other ways as well, some of which are still in operation. Peer tutors work after school with elementary students to discuss making choices and changing behavior. One junior high tutor reported that if everyone could have the opportunity to experience the trust and decision-making he experienced, the world would be a satisfying place for all people. This young man had been a serious behavior problem in school and was named to be a tutor almost by mistake. Nevertheless, his leadership skills blossomed, and he is now the type of role model we want for all of our "at-risk" students. He has experienced a new sense of power at school, improved his grades, and gained respect from students and teachers alike, and a newly found self-respect as well.

Counselors use the training in group situations with children, encouraging them to work through their problems and concerns in a trusting environment where other students cooperatively suggested behavior changes. One principal is using the Adventures during recess to create a focus for otherwise undirected time. In general, from every quarter, our colleagues are teaching students to understand their own behaviors, to understand that what they do is a choice, and to model new behaviors in a lead management style with Cooperative Adventures.

Relationship to Drug Use Prevention and At-Risk Status

The creation of a pro-active, non-behaviorist, caring classroom community is lifesaving for our children. Statistics reporting that children become drug users and potential abusers as early as fifth grade (typically age 10) are probably missing their mark by several years. The truth is more likely that the problem begins earlier. A more radical view might suggest that eating potato chips, candy, and drinking soda is its own form of abuse, since it leads to unhealthy eating habits, disease, and early death—perpetuating the idea that there is no reason to take care of "myself." What will change these behaviors?

The literature is not as clear as intuition. Children choose behaviors that they have seen carried out by people they like, that are need-satisfying, and that keep them respected by their cohorts. Gang behavior is an excellent example. In gangs, the members are listened to, so they have power; being "Home Boys," gives them a feeling of belonging and significance. They behave in ways they interpret create freedom and they have fun. They work together to tag the community and to protect one another. They swear a trust to each other and take risks constantly. But what is missing in gangs is a sense that individuals, by their choice of behaviors, can influence whether their community becomes life-affirming or self-destructive, and therein lies the reason that gangs are unhealthy. Gang members must act according to the rules of the gang; if they don't, they may be killed. There is no individual responsibility in gangs, no sense of a positive community. Gang behaviors, in fact, are part of the hopelessness that settles daily, chronically, over poverty-stricken communities. It is that same hopelessness—of not getting one's psychological needs met—that leads to the excessive use of substances, which in time produces addictions. To counteract the powerfully unhealthy effects of gang memberships, new behaviors which provide for the same needs must be taught. The classroom must be changed, for as it stands currently, it not only contributes to these psychologically and physically detrimental behaviors, but in fact promotes and teaches them. In that sense, the school, the curriculum, and the disempowering nature of the classroom are killing our children. The drug seller and the gang chief are simply taking advantage of what the educational community so blindly provides—the robots of the sixth grade class, students who have no opportunity to think for themselves, to take responsibility for themselves.

What Could Have Been Better?

The training gave all participants the opportunity to learn ways to create independence in students. But of course, since people vary in their ability to absorb this kind of new experience, individuals experienced independence at varying times and at various levels of intensity. Some were ready to empty themselves early in the process, while others never did and probably remained in the pseudo-community stage during the entire course of the training. More time was needed to talk about the four different stages as outlined by Peck. However, it is also true that, unlike the Mondragon co-ops, our participants did not join us so they could learn to build a community. Although they were with us voluntarily, their reason for attending could have been one of any number of possibilities. We learned as we created our community that being as forthright, as "up-front," as possible and allowing our participants to pass when they needed to, created respect and safety. We invited participants to engage in a kind of training which would help them lead-manage their classrooms. Inviting them to create a community would have been a more appropriate invitation.

Funding for the training was for one year only; thus, no allowance was made for systematic follow-up training. However, all participants became members of the Southern California Institute for Democracy in Education (IDE), and monthly meetings have occurred since the training—providing a form of follow-up, though not as extensive as we would have preferred. Our colleagues know we are only a phone call away, and many are continuing students at the University and visit the IDE office when on campus. Finding more funding as a community would have been a wonderful project to explore while we were together; and certainly, should this project be undertaken again, it would be advisable to obtain sufficient funding to cover follow-up, if at all possible.

Initially we thought that training an entire school staff would be the best plan, but the logistics of doing so rendered it impossible to undertake at that time. On most sites, however, each participant has a buddy for the purpose of providing encouragement while the participant steps into new territory. It has been found that at several sites, colleagues are enticing others with the community-building concept and passing it on. With recent budget cuts, some staff have been moved. Support will be needed for those teachers moving to new sites without any other trained Institute teachers.

Time is always a critical factor. A greater commitment from each district to provide planning, follow-up, and support time would increase success. Faced with destructive and deep budget deficits and cuts in California, districts are assuming a business-as-basics approach to the management of both money and time. "Bare bones" budget conditions appear to be a long-term condition that will be with us for the foreseeable future, but site principals who have seen the success of the training are committed to supporting the process.

To the pessimist, Los Angeles appears to be sinking quickly. The social uprising of Spring 1992 demonstrates that people feel they are not part of the community, have no voice in what happens to the community or to themselves, and thus no power to bring about desired changes. Teachers often feel the same way, and not all of them have the support, wherewithal, or established skills to take children into the community to experience democracy. Many of our schools must be concerned with drive-by shootings, shrinking funds, an increased student load, and greater demands for services with fewer resources than ever before. Some schools function under a model of instruction which requires particular skills to be taught at particular times in quiet rooms. There is a critical shortage of teachers, which has given rise to emergency hiring practices and the granting of temporary contracts; teachers under these contracts who are interested in a caring community environment are often unwilling to jeopardize their jobs in order to achieve the conditions needed for optimal learning opportunity. But within these constraints, processes must develop that can provide for change in a way that keeps everyone safe.

Next Steps

Schools are communities, but unlike Mondragon or a barn-raising or the creation of housing for Habitat for Humanity, they are forced communities. Students are required to be there and are placed in rooms with other children whose only commonality is their age. A given student may be the teacher's pet or the teacher's scapegoat. The work might be too difficult for some students and too easy for others; few options exist if the match is to the child's or the teacher's disadvantage. Teachers and principals often assume an all-powerful, omnipotent attitude, leaving both students and parents disenfranchised.

Administrators and teachers within individual schools must take stock of the many ways in which students are disempowered, and work to create a climate and a culture which restores empowerment to them. One caring classroom cannot change the climate of a school. We are continuing to work with two of the schools where several Institute participants teach and where there is administrative support, and believe that in time, change can be brought about. We recognize that not everyone is ready for community, and achieving change will be slower in some schools than in others.

Creating a community is fun, empowering, frightening, exciting, and remarkable. Many varied and interesting tales were told during the time the Institute met, and we hear new stories every day. It seems appropriate to end with a story which we believe illustrates the significance of the Action for Responsibility Institute.

Once, perhaps not so long ago, there were four village merchants who were good friends. They knew everyone in the village and they worked hard. One was a baker, one sold plants and flowers, another made pottery, and the fourth sold food. One day, during their shared noon meal, one of the merchants had an idea.

"Wouldn't it be glorious if we had one day off a year—maybe our birthday—when we would be free to sit with our friends and talk!?"

The other merchants agreed, but realized that it would never happen. They were poor people who lived in a poor village, and they needed to work all

the time. Sadly, they said their goodbyes and returned to their shops. That
night, one merchant reflected on the conversation and decided to do something. He knew that soon the potter would be having a birthday. On the day of
the potter's birthday, very early in the morning, the caring merchant went to the
potter's shop and did all of the potter's chores. That afternoon, the potter was
gloriously happy and quite amazed that such excellent fortune had befallen
him; after all, he was only a poor and humble villager.

"Imagine!" he exclaimed, his eyes wide with amazement. "All of my
chores were finished before I got to my shop. It must be magic!" The caring
merchant never said a word.

Several months later, it was time for the baker's birthday. The caring
merchant again accomplished the baker's chores early in the morning and
never let on about what he had done during their lunch conversation. Once
again, the celebrating merchant, the baker, described the shock and joy she
felt upon discovering the wonderful gift. Months passed, and again the merchant provided his gift of caring and love, this time to the last of the merchants, the plant seller.

Months afterward, the caring merchant arrived at his business one morning to discover that not only all of his chores had been done, but there were simple gifts of bread, flowers, and a beautiful vase. The merchant sat down and
began rocking and rocking. Tears streamed out of his eyes. The gift of giving to
friends was important, but when all of the community worked together, it was
magnificent. A community working together is truly a wonderful and empowering experience.

What is so familiar about this tale is the heroic nature of the protagonist:
One person's efforts to change the world through empathic, beyond the call of
duty effort. But the story evokes an even deeper vision: a vision of a community—a village, if you will—in which individuals work together to overcome
the daily difficulties, frustrations, and hardships associated with a less-than-
comfortable life. A community is also a place where momentous events are celebrated and recreated.

What is missing for students across the nation, and particularly for
those struggling with problems brought on by racism, classism, and poverty,
are positive models which can help individuals feel they can belong and
contribute to the community in a meaningful way, while learning within a
supportive framework to be their own person, and to have a voice and create
change. We must struggle to create the desire and need to change the school
environment, which is inherently exclusive. Children know they have no
power, and building a partially inclusive classroom can be dangerous. Without the Mondragon elements, a fabricated, manipulative inclusiveness
teaches children that it is not safe to take a risk. It is not safe to move
through the stages of community building, beyond pseudo-community, without risk-taking.

Conclusion

The Teacher Preparation Program at California State University, Dominguez Hills has many partnerships with the 20 school districts in our service area. In the development of those contracts, the following principle guides our thinking:

When we hold hands, we can reach twice as far.

The village merchants in the story told above understood this idea. Our colleagues experienced it. With a bit more practice, our students and teachers will extend those community bonds to heights and depths and breadths we have yet to imagine. We envision a world made up of communities which practice the democratic principles of consensus, inspiring and empowering people, through the best use of available resources, to maximize their potential.

REFERENCES

California Department of Education. (1991). *Handbook on the Legal Rights and Responsibilities of School Personnel and Students in the Areas of Moral and Civic Education, and the Teaching about Religion.* Sacramento.

Freire, P. (1980). *Pedagogy of the Oppressed.* New York: Continuum.

———. (1990). *Education for Critical Consciousness.* New York: Continuum.

Gilligan, C. (1982). *In a Different Voice.* Cambridge, MA: Harvard University Press.

Glasser, W. (1984). *Control Theory.* New York: Harper Row.

———. (1990). *The Quality School.* New York: Harper Row.

Hooks, B. (1990). *Yearning: Race, Gender and Cultural Politics.* Boston: South End Press.

Kohn, A. (1990). *The Brighter Side of Human Nature: Altruism and Empathy in Everyday Life.* New York: Basic Books.

Lappe, F. (1989). *Rediscovering America's Values.* New York: Ballantine.

Lickona, T. (1991). *Educating for Character: How Our Schools Can Teach Respect and Responsibility.* New York: Bantam Books.

McLaren, P. (1990). *Life in Schools.* New York: Longman.

Miller, A. (1984). *Thou Shalt Not Be Aware.* New York: Farrar, Straus and Giroux.

Morrison, R. (1991). *We Build the Road as We Travel.* Philadelphia, PA: New Society Publishers.

Noddings, N. (1984). *Caring: A Feminist Approach to Ethics and Moral Education.* Berkeley: University of California Press.

Noddings, N., and P. Shore. (1984). *Awakening the Inner Eye: Intuition in Education.* New York: Teachers College Press.

Peck, M. S. (1987). *The Different Drum: Community Making and Peace.* New York: Simon and Schuster.

Samples, B. (1987). *Openmind, Wholemind.* California: Jalmar Press.

Starhawk. (1987). *Truth or Dare.* San Francisco: HarperCollins.

SECTION II

Processes

INTRODUCTION

Democratic processes in teacher education focus on voicing experiences and sustaining inquiry in down-to-earth ways. This down-to-earth focus is important because the talk of democracy is easier and often not related to the task of getting democracy to work in specific situations. The walk involves a commitment to dialogue with oneself, others, and the world in authentic ways that seek understanding and growth. There is no algorithm for doing this, no simple formula with guaranteed democratic results. The six chapters in this section, however, provide solid instances of the commitment to dialogue, inquiry, and reflection that are integral to democratic functioning. It is not coincidental that half of the chapters in this section are co-authored.

Heidi Watts echoes this theme of walking the democratic talk in her chapter "Only By Living Them." Describing her work at Antioch New England, she speaks to the importance of using circles of discourse, circles of evaluation, and circles of reflection and observation as examples of living and teaching democratically. The processes used within the education department of her institution also reflect this living commitment to shared decision making.

This commitment to dialogue in teacher education is portrayed in the co-authored chapter by Suzanne SooHoo and Thomas Wilson. SooHoo describes her first experience in university teaching in which she sought to limit her directedness so students would be more authentically involved in a democratic classroom process. She honestly discusses difficulties that developed with this process. Wilson then describes his work to develop a curriculum for functioning democratically. The systematic teaching used in his course aims at having students attain higher level democratic skills. They then come together for a dialogue on the possibilities and contradictions involved in their roles as experts and assessors.

The issue of experts and assessors comes through in three chapters. Janet Fortune (Berea College) takes the reader through a short course on the Foxfire Experience, pointing out what is involved in using a student "pledge of participation" and developing the slow process of democratic decision-making skills. The evaluation issue, she mentions, comes up again and again. Lisa Bloom and Mary Jean Ronan Herzog (Western Carolina University) provide two case studies highlighting democratic processes they have used in their courses. Emphasizing how teacher education should provide a model for democratic pedagogy, they discuss how students become involved in course design and objectives. Carol Lieber, Ed Mikel, and Sunny Pervil pursue the evaluation issue head-on in their chapter on radical changes in assessment. After detailing the differences between traditional and democratic assessment, they provide the reader with a myriad of daily strategies to use in inviting teachers in their graduate course to become democratic collaborators in the evaluative process.

Democratic collaboration, of necessity, involves dialogue. William Ayers (University of Illinois at Chicago) presents the approach he uses in dealing with the "unspeakable" issue of race and racism in teacher education. Showing how difficult it is to even talk about race in teacher education, he then gives a moving portrayal of the type of dialogue that is necessary for democratic teacher-educators to participate in the revitalization of teaching. As he points out, this will involve rethinking, reorganizing, and restructuring the entire educational system. And so, the relationship among processes, programs, and problems becomes even more important.

Eight

Only by Living Them

Heidi Watts

"Only by living them can students develop the democratic ideals of liberty, equality and community." This line appears in the statement of purpose for the Institute for Democracy in Education.[1] At Antioch New England we maintain that only by living the democratic ideals can teacher education programs prepare democratic teachers for democratic classrooms, and only by living them can schools create an environment for teachers to teach and students to learn in a way which is appropriate for citizens in a democracy.

In this chapter I will briefly describe the pre-service and in-service programs offered at Antioch New England and the characteristics of a democratic approach which are common to all of them. I will describe the Critical Skills Institute, as a specific in-service program for living and teaching the "basic skills" of democracy. Some of the difficulties and frustrations we encounter in preparing teachers for democratic classrooms are also described, as well as our desire to contribute to the evolution of more democratic schools for both children and teachers in the future.

To understand the "living of them," we need to know what the democratic ideals of liberty, equality, and community would look like in a classroom. Liberty means respecting and nurturing the individuality of each of the actors on this stage: the children, the teachers, the paraprofessionals. It means that every aspect of the curriculum—implicit or explicit, including the schedule, the physical environment, the work required, the books read, and the ways in which people speak and listen to each other—must be attentive to the developmental needs and personal differences of each participant.

But liberty is not license. Equality and community join hands to provide an essential counterbalance to liberty. Equality in the classroom means that if we all are to have the same opportunities to grow to our full capability, accommodations and compromises must be negotiated when one person's freedom impinges upon another's. This is the essence of the social contract and the source of a continuous creative tension in all of our social experience, not the

145

least of which are classrooms, those microcosms of society where teachers and children work together under crowd conditions.[2]

The concept of community gives expression and nobility to the terms of the social contract. With rights come responsibilities. Fairness is an important criteria, and the Golden Rule a guide: To act toward others as you would have them act toward you. But beyond regulation and tit for tat, the concept of community suggests care—that we can be most fully human, we can show our full growth by the ways in which we acknowledge, act toward, and care for each other.

Liberty, equality, and community are high ideals for a society or a classroom, but they are not impossible. Each of us at one time or another has known a time or place where all three were fully operative and dancing in concert with each other. Though a full and complete realization of the ideal democracy for all and forever is impossible, it is surely worth aiming for. In the words of Leonard Woolf, "The Journey not the arrival matters."[3]

Let me offer an example of democracy in action in the school of one of our graduates. At a daily all-school community meeting, teachers and students, third through eighth grade, contribute to an agenda organized into Problems, Plans and Sharing, or PPS as it is affectionately called. Problems range from controlling snowball fights on the playground to messy hallways or a lost lunch. Plans might include what to do if the soccer game gets rained out and where to take an all-school trip. Sharing is reserved for events of interest from home or from the news, for displaying a special piece of work or airing questions and concerns. Sometimes shared items reappear on the agenda as problems or plans.

On one occasion the biggest item in the news was an earthquake in Guatemala. Ten-year-old Gabriela, who was born in Mexico, is very concerned about the earthquake victims. She has brought a picture of a child who was caught in the rubble of his house. She wants to do something for him, and other earthquake victims. There is a flood of questions from the children: Where is Guatemala? How many people live there? What do they do? Do they talk like us? Why didn't they leave before the earthquake? What makes an earthquake, anyway? Could we have one here? Who is helping them? What can we do? The teachers, recognizing the gift of authentic curriculum[4] when it is given to them, pull out a map and begin to list the children's questions. By the end of the meeting, which has run on far longer than anticipated, the children have decided to find out more about Guatemala and about earthquakes. One child has a neighbor who may have been there and could talk with them. A few children volunteer to talk with the librarian and to make a classroom collection on books about earthquakes and Guatemala. They decide to collect bottles and send the refund money to an earthquake relief organization. Two months later they have read and written extensively about Guatemala; they have drawn maps and graphed earthquake intensities, and located quake centers. They have adopted a Guatemalan boy and are exchanging letters with him through the international relief organization Save the Children, and they are eager to continue the journey through other countries in Central and South America.

Authentic curriculum is a term we have coined for thematic curriculum which has an intrinsic, perhaps archetypal, appeal; topics which seem to fit both the appropriate developmental concerns of the child but which also draw on deep universal interests. Dinosaurs, in so far as they allow the child to manage and explore feelings about monsters, hugeness, and mysterious creatures, are one such example; castles and the evocation of "a safe place"[5] are another. In this example of authentic curriculum the children were able to identify with other children caught in a natural disaster, and to study earthquakes—another mysterious and powerful phenomenon in nature. The original impetus came from the concern of one child but rapidly grew into a topic of importance for most of the children, and drew the whole school into a community project. The teachers were able to seize the teachable moment and convert it into curricular content which included skills, concepts, and collaborative work while honoring the individual interests of the children.

The actors on-stage in this example are the children and the teachers, but there are many actors off-stage, a powerful presence in the wings who have an equal stake in the liberty, equality, and community of the classroom. These actors are the parents, school directors, and policy makers, the taxpayers and all those ultimately affected by the quality of the interaction in the triangular relationship between teacher, student, and content in the classroom.[6] These off-stage players have rights and responsibilities as well: the right to have schools graduate knowledgeable, literate, humane individuals; the responsibility to plan for, support, and fund schools to meet these goals. Seen from this vantage, schools become very complicated places, often beset with apparently unresolvable dilemmas in a constant shift of checks and balances. The tension and energy produced by these dilemmas is not necessarily bad: Unsettlement leads to further thinking.[7] Unfortunately, however, when we react quickly under the press of immediate and conflicting needs, we often lose sight of the primary goal—to create and maintain schools consistent with a society based on liberty and justice for all.

If schools are a microcosm of society then here, by practice, by "living them," children come to know naturally and correctly what it means to be members of a democratic society. School is not a preparation for life, school *is* life. School is also life for teachers in training. How can teachers learn to manage democratic classrooms unless they have had experiences within such classrooms for themselves?

Only One Subject Matter

At Antioch New England we offer two pre-service and one in-service M.Ed program. The first, an M.Ed and/or certification program, prepares approximately 20 teachers a year to work in Waldorf schools. Approximately the same number of teachers in training complete an M.Ed program which grants certification in New Hampshire for early childhood or elementary teachers and is built around an "integrated day" philosophy. We also offer an in-service program in professional development for experienced teachers. In many of their courses the Waldorf and integrated day students overlap, as do faculty. The differences between these two programs create useful opportunities for clarifying the aims and practices of each through identification of differences and celebration of similarities. We are striving not for homogenization but for integration in our programs.

The inservice M.Ed program in Professional Development for Experienced Educators enrolls approximately 60 practicing teachers each year, in regional clusters of roughly 15, throughout New Hampshire and Vermont. A cluster consists of teachers coming from a range of disciplines and grade levels who meet regularly during the program. Unlike many programs where teachers can put together the bulk of a degree program from a loosely related collection of courses taken over a number of years, with a shifting student population and a mix of philosophical orientations, the Professional Development Program is a concentrated and intensely collegial experience.

In addition to these three degree programs we sponsor a series of summer institutes under the rubric of "Critical Skills." The Critical Skills Institutes enroll more than 300 teachers each summer, also in clusters of about 15, and are usually organized through a contract with a school district. Critical Skills Institutes are taught by master teachers and deliberately model an inquiry approach to instruction. The principles for Critical Skills are described later in this chapter.

Philosophically, we place ourselves firmly in the progressive tradition. As a way of illustrating what this means to us, I will reproduce here the principles of the Progressive Education Network to which we subscribe:

- Students learn best through direct experience, primary sources, personal relationships, and cooperative exploration.

- Schools pay equal attention to all facets of students' development.

- Assessment is accomplished through multiple perspectives.

- Parents, students, and staff cooperate in school decision making.

- Schools build on the home cultures of their students and families.

- Schools encourage young people to fulfill their responsibilities as world citizens by teaching critical inquiry and the complexity of global issues.

- Schools help students develop their social conscience and help them learn to recognize and confront issues of race, class, and gender.[8]

In our own words, the Antioch New England catalog for 1991-1992 offers this description of an integrated day approach:

a style of classroom teaching that attempts to draw connections between the life of the child and the life of the classroom and attempts to weave together the reading, writing, math, science, social studies, and art components of the elementary classroom. A day in the life of a child in school should not be a sequence of unrelated lessons, but a tapestry of integrated pursuits. Alfred North Whitehead in *The Aims of Education* suggested, "The solution which I am urging is to eradicate the fatal disconnection of subjects which kills the vitality of our modern curriculum. There is only one subject matter for education, and that is Life in all its manifestations."[9] Our aim is to teach all the discrete subjects and skills of classroom teaching and to teach the interdependence of all the components—the ecology of the classroom.

Although the design of the pre-service and in-service programs vary in response to the different needs of novice and experienced teachers, or elementary and secondary teachers, common to all is the commitment to integration of subject matter and to the study of life in all its manifestations.

The unique feature of education programs at Antioch New England lies in the relationship between philosophy and pedagogy. . . . In our programs, major emphasis is placed on clarifying a teacher's vision of the possible person and society and translating this into a plan of action for the classroom. . . .[10]

Antioch New England has a long tradition of working with adult learners in the professions. The average age of our students is 36 and all have had some previous experience with children. We believe that learning is on-going through life, and that learning occurs in the space between experience and the interpretation of that experience. In all our programs we strive for a balance between: work and study; community and individuality; innovation and tradition; flexibility and structure; action and reflection. We emphasize cooperation over competition; we encourage risk-taking and reflection; we value empowerment.

We believe that teachers learn best from other teachers, and often know what it is best for them to learn.[11] Programs are organized so that students meet together in small groups on a regular basis over time. They develop strong ties of personal and professional collegiality. The bonds which form in these cohort groups enable teachers to take risks, to learn from mistakes, to support and challenge each other.

Circles of Discourse

It is no accident that our classes are small and almost always conducted in a circle: Sometimes a simple circle of chairs, sometimes a circle of tables if hands-on activities or writing is involved. A circle is anti-hierarchical. It both symbolizes and facilitates our conviction that in any true teaching/learning situation there is an element of mutuality. Although the learning will be different between teachers and students than between students and students, we are all learners. We all have a right to speak and a responsibility to listen "in the social conversations of mankind" out of which knowledge is shaped and communicated.[12] These circles constitute what Bena Kallick calls an interpretative community:

> one where an active process of interpretation is used to give meaning to learning that is taking place. Meaning, in this place, isn't reducible to a single perspective but is open, ready to yield to multiple intelligences the way shadows yield to light.[13]

In a circle it is harder to hide; we are also less likely to feel singled out and exposed when held in the arms of the circle. When a class is not engaged in some form of discourse in the circle, the discourse continues in smaller groups or in the interior conversations we conduct with ourselves.

The visitor who drops in on an Antioch class is likely to see one of four modes of interaction: whole group discussions in a circle; small group discussions with the instructor circulating among them; student presentations either individually or in a group; or students actively engaged in an activity such as creating a timeline for the history of education, floating clay boats for a science methods class, chip trading for math, or making masks in integrated arts. Faculty are specialists in their fields but generalists as pedagogues. If, as Goodlad says, the ordinary ratio of teacher to student talk in classrooms is three to one, that ratio is deliberately reversed in these classrooms.[14] We believe that what students find out and can articulate for themselves is more powerful and more accessible for further transformations, and will stay with them longer than knowledge which is fed to the student by the teacher. There are times, of course, when a good lecture is just what is needed; faculty expertise is an important resource for students, but it is important to fit the medium to the message and to the moment. Our goal is always transformation, though it may involve transmission and transaction on the way.

Circles of Evaluation

Antioch courses begin with introductions: We introduce students to students, and we introduce students to the content and objectives of the course. Courses end with evaluations. Students evaluate the course, faculty evaluate the students, each trying to reflect upon and communicate what they have learned from and about the other, in processes which are themselves instructional.

The forms of assessment include course/workshops, a two-page evaluation checklist and short answer questions which students fill out for each course workshop, and a verification sheet for each student to be filled out by the instructor at a later date. The v-sheet, as it is called, provides the student with a narrative evaluation from the instructor with attention to four areas in particular: mastery of the course content, evidence of the integration of theory into practice, quality of documentation, and quality of group participation. The v-sheet is the only "grade" which the student receives but it can be translated into pass/fail terms for transcription purposes.

V-sheets and course evaluations are two examples of reciprocal feedback but they are only part of the total evaluation process, which includes both explicit and implicit opportunities for self-evaluation and frequent conversations in a group or between individuals to share perceptions on achievement and growth.

The most extensive self-evaluation process occurs in relation to the internship (the student teaching experience) or the Practicum (the work situation of the experienced teacher). Pre-service students make a contract with their cooperating (master) teacher in which they state their goals for the internship. At the end of the internship the students write an extensive self-evaluation relative to those goals, which is shared with the cooperating teacher and the Antioch supervisor. Experienced teachers also set goals for their Practicum experience and summarize what they have "learned by doing" at the end of each term. Exit interviews, plus group discussions of process and of summative learning, are common. Faculty frequently invite student comments on a course and make changes in response to student suggestions. Evaluation is built on evaluation in a rising circle of give and take, reflection, shared perception, and transformation.

Circles of Reflection and Observation

The circular pattern repeats itself in the helix of reflection upon practice, and reflection-in-action.[15] To put it another way, we try to encourage the integration of theory into practice and the evolution of new theory from that practice.

One important mirror is the journal which each student keeps, whether teaching in an internship for the first time or teaching as a veteran of 30 years. The act of writing about what one has done and seen often produces new insights. For some, writing becomes an avenue for thinking; for others, it provides a means of documenting; and for yet others it gives a legitimate place for the expression of emotion—a catharsis.[16] In addition, the journal provides content for dialogue between the student and the advisor. In a continuous process of encoding and decoding the student acts, writes/thinks, shares, thinks/writes, acts: another circle of interactions to deepen awareness and extend learning.

"Experience is not what happens to you, it is what you do with what happens to you."[17] Huxley's statement has become a maxim for us. The journal writing, like the discussions, challenge teachers to draw out of themselves the meaning in their experiences. Thinking about learning is a learning endeavor. Reflection, and reflection upon reflection, becomes additional course content. In Human Growth and Development students draw on their own biographies as a significant aspect of the work of the course, writing and sharing their own memories of childhood to make sense of the developmental theorists they study. In Conceptual Development the students learn a new skill—like juggling or playing the piano—and observe themselves as learners. In Philosophy of Education students write their own philosophy of education statement and then assess that against their experience in the classroom as students or teachers.

We encourage a "watch bird" mentality, a kind of mindfulness, so that students may be able to see themselves from the outside, to become participant observers of their own behavior. We hope that students can become aware of being aware. The processes of self-evaluation contribute to their ability to stand at a distance and observe themselves in their roles as students and as teachers. Another means to this end is to require students to undertake a close observation of a particular event or a particular child. When students look closely and over time at one child, when they record what they see and hear in different settings, when they try to understand the world from the point of view of that child, they gain insights not only into one child but into many and sometimes into themselves as well. On those insights are built their own evolving theories of child development and out of those insights come better ways to work with children in the classroom.

The action research projects undertaken by Professional Development students are a third form of close observation, an opportunity for each teacher to undertake a significant examination of some aspect of his or her daily activity. Using the skills of research, teachers focus on some aspect of their own practice for the purpose of greater understanding or for change. The stress in these research projects is not on proving something, but on learning something. We have found that "if you want to change something, watch it."[18] These projects may make a valuable contribution to the school as a whole, or to an individual classroom.

Some projects take a creative turn, like the novel for preadolescents written by one teacher and illustrated by another. In preparation for writing the novel the author read the recent research studies on women's voices and on preadolescent girls, and then asked two 11-year-old girls to keep journals for her. She shared the chapters, as she wrote them, with her classes for their suggestions. The illustrator also read portions to her students and asked them to pose for sketches from which, with their continuing suggestions, she created large black and white drawings. The novel, *A Waterslide From My Window*,[19] describes realistically the dynamics in a group of four, two boys and two girls, at home and in a collaborative science study group at school, and how they changed over the year. The students had an opportunity to watch their teachers struggle to express themselves as scholars and as artists. What better modeling can there be?

Other action research projects have taken a social change orientation, such as the BLTs or Balloon Launch Terminators, a project undertaken by two elementary teachers whose students, rather like Gabriela, picked up on a concern about the hazard to animals constituted by balloon fragments. The project is the documentation of the year in which their classes researched the effects of balloon launches on the environment, met with conservationists and balloon manufacturers, and organized a campaign to stop balloon launches. Their efforts were so successful they aroused the ire of the balloon manufacturers and received nation-wide attention with a column in the *Wall Street Journal*.

Some projects result in school-wide changes such as a move toward multi-age grouping, an all-school series of inquiry-oriented student research projects, or greater parent involvement brought on by a community newsletter. Other equally valuable projects which turn inward have looked closely at the interaction of a few readiness children inadvertently placed in a first grade classroom; at the effect on students of learning sign language when a profoundly deaf child joined their class; or the careful examination of her own questioning techniques documented by a first grade teacher. Whether large scale or small, these action research projects are one way of advancing professional knowledge and reflective practice.

Only by Doing

The Invisible Lab School

Absolutely essential to the quality of the learning about teaching is the quality of what occurs in the internship or student teaching experience for the beginning teacher. The conservatism of teachers, the tendency to teach as we have been taught, the almost irresistible move toward the norm in the socialization which occurs between teachers in schools has been amply documented.[20] Not only should good teaching practice be modeled in the courses students take, it is even more essential that it be modeled in the classroom where the student-teaching occurs. We are fortunate in having a few good schools and many good classrooms within commuting distance—most of them public and relatively small. We refer to these schools and classrooms as our "invisible lab school," and place our students in these settings over and over again. Whenever possible we draw on these teachers as adjuncts to teach specific courses, to supervise students, or as guest speakers. There are visits back and forth within the network of schools and over the years more and more of our graduates move from student-teaching status to hired staff in these invisible lab schools. Instead of creating our own special school we are able to give our students experiences in schools governed and constrained in ways similar to those in which they will teach.

Within our invisible lab school network we have examples of team teaching, thematic curriculum, cooperative learning groups, inquiry learning, multi-age grouping, assessment by portfolio and exhibition, inclusion and integration of special students, and a wide variety of holistic learning strategies such as whole language, writing across the curriculum, and Math Their Way. Students visit at least three classrooms and decide, in consultation with the teacher and the Antioch internship coordinator, where they will do their internships. (Each student does two full semesters of student teaching, three and a half to four days a week while taking course work the remaining day. This combination of course work with teaching is another means of making the application of theory to practice explicit. What happens in a classroom at Antioch New England frequently becomes the content of a classroom somewhere else.) The visits give them an opportunity to see that there is no one right way to teach well.

The Education Department

In our own decision-making processes in the Department of Education, we attempt to practice the ideals of democracy just as we attempt to model them in the classroom. We are fortunate in having a large measure of autonomy at Antioch New England. Each department plans and manages their own budget, and each is free, within broad guidelines, to develop and make changes in the programs. We have no tenure, and rank occurs only at the doctoral level. We are developing a niche for ourselves clearly defined as an institution devoted to teaching in the best possible way. We are not primarily researchers. "Publish or perish" is never an issue, though we do support each other in financial and professional ways as writers.

The Education Department is a small department within a small institution. Little bureaucracy, much autonomy, and small units enable us to be unusually responsive to changing times and to our own changing perceptions. The programs I am describing are always in a state of evolution: as we discover ways in which we can do things better, as we become dissatisfied with a persistent problem, we work together to modify the designs, to improve our own practices. Within the department co-chairpersons are ultimately responsible for all facets of the programs, but most decisions are made collaboratively. We try, as a department, to be a democratic community.

The Critical Skills Institute

We have one in-service program which most clearly exemplifies the translation of democratic ideals into pedagogy. We work on the assumption that these critical skills are the "basic skills" in a democracy. The Critical Skills program originated in New Hampshire in 1982 as a collaborative effort between a group of inspired teachers and members of the business community concerned about education. In 1986 the program came under the aegis of Antioch New England. It has grown in numbers every year until now over 300 teachers participate in Institutes each summer.

The Institutes have identified 12 critical skills from which comes the title: problem solving, decision making, critical thinking, creative thinking, community, organization, cooperation, collaboration, management, leadership, independent learning, and documentation. These skills can be introduced, honed, deepened and strengthened at any level from kindergarten through graduate school. As these are critical skills we all need, so the goals of a critical skills classroom are also applicable at any age and in any kind of classroom: to develop critical skills; to attain essential knowledge; to own, invest, and become empowered in one's own learning; to progress toward a concept of self-direction; to hold a collaborative work ethic that is balanced with individual inquiry and accountability; to assume responsible membership in the community to which one belongs.[21]

A Critical Skills Institute consists of a six-day, forty-eight hour week of intensive, experiential instruction; two days of follow-up coaching and support during the school year; and an on-site classroom observation from one of the Institute's master teachers. This follow-up is an essential piece of the design for teachers returning to familiar classrooms who wish to initiate change, often against the norms of the school. To have the assistance of a consultant in one's actual situation is invaluable. Institute staff are master teachers: working teachers with classrooms of their own who have been identified for their excellence in working with adults as well as with children.

The centerpiece of the Critical Skills classroom and of the summer Institutes is the LBRP (Learning By Real Problems). Students are given a "real" problem in need of a "real" solution but designed to integrate the skills, content, and objectives of a given curriculum with reference to what is relevant and significant for students. It is both powerful and empowering. Students are given opportunities in the classroom to use their knowledge and skills to explore issues that touch their lives. This makes it possible for them to move outside the classroom, to take action on issues and to have a tangible impact, often immediately. For example, as part of an exploration of solid waste, young children in Maine moved a local fast food restaurant to take specific steps toward addressing the issues of appropriate packaging and waste management long before the company began national recycling efforts. In another situation, high school students made a conscious choice to change the focus of their study of housing into advocacy for the homeless—culminating in a fundraising march in support of local shelters.

Frequently an LBRP will be evaluated in a presentation to a jury panel composed of policy-makers and persons knowledgeable in the field—as good an example of demonstration of mastery by exhibition as Ted Sizer could wish. One last quotation will serve to illustrate how closely the Critical Skills approach is linked to the ideal of a democratic classroom. "Underscoring every-thing that happens in a Critical Skills classroom is the concept of community. Students experience membership in a classroom community that is initiated through a process of community-building activities, and that is maintained through attitudes of mutual respect and support and individual responsibility. It is reinforced through the egalitarian social relationships and positive interde-pendence that are inherent in cooperative learning.

"In a very powerful way students begin to feel that I/we are important, I/we care, I/we have something of value to contribute, I/we are responsible, I/we can make a difference."[22]

Only by Sharing

"How are we to bring children to the spirit of citizenship and humanity which is postulated by democratic societies? By the actual practice of democracy at school. It is unbelievable that at a time when democratic ideas enter into every phase of life, they should have been so little utilized as instruments of educa-tion."[23] The greatest problem we face is that of anyone concerned about the health of our democracy and the need for democratic classrooms. Where do we find them? As a nation we are strong on rhetoric, low on performance. The number of schools is small and the number of classrooms which are truly devoted to the ideals of democracy and willing to live by them even smaller. Schools profess to be democratic: Terms like equal opportunity, meeting indi-vidual needs, and developing good citizens are bandied about but in actuality children have increasingly less choice, and less personal responsibility for their learning as they progress through the grades. "Only by sharing in some respon-sible task does there come a fitness to share in it. The argument that we must wait until men and women are fully ready to assume intellectual and social responsibilities would have defeated every step in the democratic direction that has ever been taken."[24]

Consider, for example, the travesty of participatory democratic activity in schools such as student government or voting experiences. How many student councils are limited to decisions like where to put the Coke machine and what band to hire for the prom? In how many classrooms in an election year is the requirement to teach about democracy satisfied by having children vote, like their parents, for president—and indeed, what more do we learn from that election than that they do vote like their parents? This is playing at, not living by, the ideals of a democracy. It is not so much that everything we needed to know we learned in kindergarten, Robert Fulgrum to the contrary, but that everything we needed for growing may have been there in the structure of the kindergarten—and has been gradually eroded away by the time we get to high school.[25] Students in our schools, after kindergarten, seldom have an opportunity to make their interests known, to work on real problems, to be heard as individuals, or to take responsibility for helping others. Deprived of both rights and responsibilities, it is not surprising that our adolescents are disenchanted and disengaged from schooling. Nor is it surprising that as graduates they are unaware of where and how it is appropriate to exercise their rights and unaware of their responsibilities toward their neighbors and their planet.

The work of the teacher, like the concept of student government, has been devalued and trivialized. Teachers are treated like technicians, given teacher-proof curriculum, hedged in by standardized test scores on one side, mandated curriculum on the other, and limited to the homogenized knowledge deemed financially safe for textbook publishers. In most classrooms, when Gabriela worries about the earthquake victims in Guatemala, the teacher is touched and sympathetic but must hurry back to the "real" curriculum. He/she knows the children will be tested on Europe this year, South America comes next year, and if the kids fail the test his/her job is in jeopardy. And anyway, he/she also has to get through the math book this week so how can he/she take time for bottle collections, and money-raising discussions? When did a textbook publisher, or a curricula mandate, or even a group of school board directors list direct action on waste disposal or advocacy for the homeless as a legitimate subject for schoolchildren?

To our shame, schools are not set up for teachers with critical skills, for teachers who cherish the spontaneous teachable moment, who know how to create authentic curriculum out of what the children bring in. How many teachers are interviewed with an eye to their aesthetic understanding as well as their credit hours? And yet, how a classroom looks, how the arts are woven into the classroom activities, is a part of the hidden curriculum, the messages about what is and is not important which are communicated to children. How many teachers are hired on the evidence of their ability to learn on the job? And yet, in a society which is changing at an alarming rate, what could be a more important criteria? Here and there a good school, and now and then a good teacher, does exceptional work. But it is an uneasy balance in an unfriendly environment for democratic teaching. Teachers are often burned up rather than burned out.[26]

Where then do our graduates go? Into the cracks. In the best scenarios they find a place for themselves in philosophically compatible schools, private and public, or in schools where benign neglect allows them to practice in the privacy of their own classrooms. Occasionally there is a critical mass of

teachers in one school who are able to make changes by working together.
But teachers have less power than any other actors, on or off stage in the school
play. There are many historical reasons for this, not the least of which is that
teaching is seen as a woman's profession.[27]

Recent reports and reform efforts have documented a discouraging picture of our schools, and have proposed drastic changes. These efforts are
heroic but the forces which act against school change are formidable. Funding
formulas discriminate against the poor in favor of the rich, or force unten-
able choices. The policy-makers are in a highly stratified pyramid of decision making, with miles between the practitioners and the decision-makers.
Our society mistakenly assumes that since we have all been in classrooms
we know what happens there and anyone can do it. (We have the same attitude
toward parenting but are finding out to our dismay, as the fabric of the family
unravels into absent or distracted parents, single parents and teen-age parents
that parenting is, in fact, a very complex and important task.) At the national
level there is covert support for the privatization of education, and a great
deal of fancy talk about improving schools but neither the will nor the
resources to do anything about it. Perhaps most serious of all, we have no
national consensus on what schools should really do with kids and why. How
can we unite to improve schools if we each have a different definition of
"improvement"?

High on our wishlist would be progress toward more democratic schools
for everyone. In our own area we are looking for opportunities to work with one
or more school districts, slowly, over time, to create more democratic environments for teachers and children alike. There are many ways in which interpretive communities formed of school personnel, from administrators to paraprofessionals, working with representatives of teacher education and teacher
regulation institutions, could create new forms and democratically consistent
schools.

We have not, however, yet learned how to contribute effectively towards
this kind of change in schools. Two attempts to form such partnerships failed.
We seem to have evolved effective practices for the democratic education of
whole teachers but have been unable, as yet, to find the keys for working effectively with whole schools. The call for more democratic schools is growing
louder, and our desire to contribute (not just to the education of teachers but
also to the environment in which they can work effectively) is also great. However, we have learned that there is no easy transfer of approaches, that schools
are exceedingly complex systems, and that we have much to learn about how to
work with schools and how to effect change in an existing school culture.

To these two dilemmas—the problem our graduates have in finding
democratic schools in which to teach, and the problems we have encountered
in trying to help schools think through their own needs and address them
effectively—I will add two more, one related to program concerns, another

related to personal concerns. A dilemma within our own practice surfaced when I circulated a draft for this chapter among my colleagues. In reading it, they realized that as our enrollment has grown and our circles enlarged we have lost some of the closeness we once had with students as a sharing and decision-making community. Perhaps within the Education Department we need to articulate and model some versions of PPS for ourselves and our students, or create another form of class meeting which can be responsive to the needs of a larger and more diverse community. Size and scale are always a factor in the functioning of a community or a democracy. It would be a sad irony if growth caused a diminishment in the very values which promoted growth. We learn again that keeping the integrity of a democratic community requires eternal vigilance.

The last dilemma we face is that of feeling continuously overwhelmed with work, the victim of our own good ideas. Largely because we are not burned-up, we are in danger of being burned out. When people have the autonomy to invent their own jobs, and have ownership over their own ideas, there is never enough time to do everything that needs to be done. This is a dilemma common to all good teachers, perhaps to all who work in human services. Involvement and intensity seem to come with the territory. But understanding the reasons for the problem is not sufficient. How do we learn to create priorities, to say no so that we can say yes, to support each other in our own renewal and growth so that we have the energy and stamina to maintain the fire?

These four dilemmas illustrate the range of problems which arise for us across personal, programmatic, and policy levels. It is a representative list, not a complete one. As some issues are resolved, others bubble to the surface. The unsettlements, the challenges are what keeps us alive as learners.

At Antioch New England we are less interested in expanding the scope and size of our present programs than in acting as midwife to other institutions who wish to give birth to their own teacher-education programs living the ideals of a democratic education. We believe we are evolving good workable models for democratic teacher education. We would like to share our experience with other people with the same philosophy who might adapt our ideas to the special circumstances of their own situations.

As I suggested earlier, in any teaching/learning situation worthy of the name, there is a kind of reciprocity. In good classrooms teachers learn from their work with children just as children learn from their work with the teacher. "The gift is to the giver."[28] The learning is likely to be different, but in each case it is real. If we have the opportunity to share our experiences in the evolution of democratic teacher-education programs with other like-minded institutions, I am confident we will gain from the exchange. Teachers and children will also benefit, and the circle of sharing, learning, growing will continue.

NOTES

1. Statement of Purpose, *Democracy and Education* (Vol. 6, No. 3, Spring 1992, Athens, Ohio: Ohio University Press).

2. Philip Jackson, *Life in Classrooms* (New York: Holt, Rinehart and Winston, 1968).

3. Leonard Woolf, *The Journey, Not the Arrival Matters* (Gloucester, Massachusetts: Peter Smith, 1992).

4. David Sobel, personal communication (1991).

5. Anne Fines, personal communication (1990).

6. David Hawkins, "I, Thou, It, The Triangular Relationship," in *The Open Education Reader*, ed. Charles Silberman (New York: Random House, 1973).

7. John Dewey, *Democracy and Education* (New York: Macmillan, 1944).

8. Network of Progressive Educators, *News From the Network* (Fall 1991, Evanston, Illinois).

9. Alfred Whitehead, *The Aims of Education* (New York: Macmillan, 1959).

10. *Antioch New England Catalog* (1992).

11. Kathleen Watts, *How Teachers Learn: Teachers' Views on Professional Development*, unpublished dissertation (New York: Cornell University, 1986).

12. Kenneth Brufee, "Social Construction, Language, and the Authority of Knowledge," in *College English Journal* (Vol. 48, 1986).

13. Bena Kallick, *Changing the Schools into Communities for Learning* (North Dakota: North Dakota Study Group, 1991).

14. John Goodlad, *A Place Called Schools* (New York: McGraw Hill, 1984).

15. Donald Schön, *Educating the Reflective Practitioner* (California: Jossey-Bass, 1987).

16. Tristan Rainer, *The New Diary: How to Use a Journal for Self-guidance and Expanded Creativity* (Los Angeles: J. P. Archer, 1975).

17. A. Huxley, "Visionary Experience," in *The Highest State of Consciousness* (New York: Anchor Books, 1972).

18. Molly Watt, personal communication (1990).

19. Suprenant and Marois, *A Waterslide from My Window*, unpublished master's project (1990).

20. Willard Waller, *The Sociology of Teaching* (New York: John Wiley, 1967), and Dan Lortie, *School Teacher: A Sociological Study* (Chicago: University of Chicago Presss, 1975).

21. Critical Thinking Institute, brochure (1991).

22. Ibid.

23. *A Place Called Schools.*

24. *Democracy and Education.*

25. Robert Fulghum, *All I Really Need to Know I Learned in Kindergarten* (New York: Fawcett Columbine, 1993).

26. Sara Freedman, Jane Jackson, and Kathleen Boles, "The Other End of the Corridor: The Effect of Teaching on Teachers," in *Radical Teacher*, 23 (Boston: Boston Women's Teachers Group, 1982).

27. Nancy Hoffman, *Women's 'True' Profession: Voices from the History of Teaching* (Old Westbury, New York: The Feminist Press, 1981).

28. Walt Whitman, *Leaves of Grass* (New York: Modern Library, 1984).

Nine

Control and Contradiction in Democratic Teacher Education:
Classroom and Curriculum Approaches

Suzanne SooHoo and Thomas C. Wilson

Introduction

The development of democratic education is fundamentally a moral enterprise. The education of potential and existing educators as morals agents "whose actions are subjected to being judged"[1] should be of major importance for any professional teacher-education program. While there is a plethora of writing advocating the necessity of moral and democratic teacher educators, little concerted work which directly describes pedagogical practice and concrete and systematic curricula which might be brought to bear on the democratic education of teacher candidates has been done. This is our challenge.

In this chapter, we offer our current work in reflective pedagogical practice and curriculum development. We proceeded as follows: Each of us wrote an independent response to the challenge. As it turned out, SooHoo concentrated on a classroom experience within a single semester's course (direct pedagogical practice), while Wilson focused on a proposed curriculum designed for a number of various activities over an extended period of time: 12 to 18 months (concrete, systematic curriculum). After reading each other's work, we met to share our impressions. The meeting was audio-taped so that our dialogue could then be transcribed and jointly edited (with the editing kept to a minimum in order not to lose conversational qualities). Our rationale for the dialogue section of our chapter came from Paulo Freire. For five years, Freire has been producing a number of "spoken" books for, as he states it, such a process is "an interesting, intellectual experience, a rich and truly creative experience . . . (and) . . . in fact 'speaking' a book with one or two others instead of writing it alone represents, to some extent, at least a break with a certain individualistic tradition in the production of books, and—why not admit it? By taking us out of the pleasant coziness of our study, it opens us up to each other in the adventure of thinking critically."[2]

For us the key exists in this opening up, in allowing our respective writing to stimulate us to think further about what we have written, where our writing is taking us and "to expose ourselves to the meaningful experience of sharing in a common task."[3]

Who's in Charge Here?

A Narrative about Promoting Student Participation in the College Classroom

by Suzanne SooHoo

"You lost control of the class this evening," commented a student as she was leaving the first evening of my teaching strategies for the elementary classroom class. "What do you mean?" I asked. "Would you let a student take over the class in a REAL classroom?" she asked referring to an earlier incident in which I handed over the chalk to a student who announced he had a better proposal than mine for the development of our cooperative groups.

Initially, her question struck me as incredulous. We had spent the whole first hour of class on a team-building exercise, "Spider Web,"[4] to symbolize the commencement of a community of learners. We discussed how each person was considered a significant member in this classroom relationship and that I, as the professor, was one among many knowledgeable participants in the class. Even if she had missed the point of the activity, had she misunderstood the statement printed at the top of the syllabus?

> This course begins with the assumption that each member of the class is a valuable resource of knowledge. The instructor and students are all teachers and learners, whose jobs are to make this course meaningful. We are equally responsible to contribute to the pool of knowledge. Do you agree?

This article is a synthesis of my personal journal entries. Writing this piece has helped me become clear about this semester's accomplishments. It has delineated my beginning efforts in building a democratic classroom. I will provide three examples of how I attempted to promote greater student participation and responsibility in my classroom by re-thinking traditional teaching practices and creating a pedagogy that removes the teacher from the center of classroom activity. The first part deals with deliberately removing practices where teachers have traditionally directed student activity. The second part focuses on replacing the teacher-directed curriculum with a student-centered curriculum. The last part describes valuing students' experiences as major themes of study.

Rethinking Teaching Behavior—Planned Ambiguity

Was it because this was my first semester teaching in higher education that I found it so easy to see needed reform, or was it my seven and a half years teaching as an elementary school teacher? Perhaps it was my 10 years as a principal that prepared me to challenge the university classroom. Admittedly, I set out to systematically challenge the notion of the teacher being unilaterally in charge of the classroom. I wanted to create a classroom which cultivated diversity, critical reasoning, and democratic participation. In truth, I wasn't comfortable at changing everything at once because I was unfamiliar with students' and administration's expectations. Consequently, it was within a traditional paradigm that I inserted "instances" of alternative practices in my attempt to restructure the classroom.

The first night of class I found students were accustomed to receiving two documents: a syllabus, which listed texts, grading practices, and major study units, and a course assignment sheet detailing weekly topics. I chose not to distribute either documents for two reasons. First, it was my hope that as a community of learners class, *we* would jointly construct a course during the semester, developing the outline as we went along. Second, I, quite frankly, didn't know how to break up and parcel out major themes into neat three-hour blocks. Students responded with anxiety. "Can you tell us what we will be doing each week?" they asked. "No, I can't, can you?" I responded and then asked, "Would you be willing to join me in collectively charting the direction of this course? Let's talk about topics of mutual interest." They agreed, tentatively, and my insides started to knot as I questioned my plans of planned ambiguity.

The second week of class presented another challenge. We discussed what we'd like to put into the end-of-year portfolios which would demonstrate intellectual growth and function as a useful tool for upcoming student-teaching assignments. Students concluded that multidisciplinary, thematic units of instruction developed in cooperative groups would be worthwhile. They did not anticipate that I would balk when they requested to see models previously developed by former students. Perturbed by my resistance, they listened suspiciously as I explained that those units reflected the values and perspectives of *those* authors. I would be interested in seeing curriculum inspired by *them*. Could we agree? With blind faith, most students consented to constructing their own models. The others who could not tolerate the ambiguity scrambled to find commercial units to act as their security blankets.

These college students were accustomed to delineated course outlines and concrete models. They were inexperienced at controlling or creating their own classroom experiences. The challenge for me was to withhold models and definition in order to cultivate a classroom environment which could be negotiated by students and teacher.

Re-thinking Instruction—Curriculum that Equalizes Power

Our text, Lucy Calkin's book, *The Art Of Teaching Writing*,[5] stirred up school memories for everyone about the omnipotent English teacher armed with the critical, red pencil. Each of us could recall a humiliating school incident revolving around substandard writing. Our scarred egos had never healed and we vowed as teachers never to censor children's writing. But how, then, do we teach writing?

Calkin's model honors student voice and casts the teacher in the role of the facilitator, who guides a process that starts with finding an internal voice, to editing conferences which share that voice with an audience. Calkins maintains that students have something very important to say and we, as teachers, need to listen to these ideas to help amplify these voices through their stories. In this process, students are the inventors and the experts of their stories. Teachers guide and help students reflect upon their own narratives. Adults do not impose their stories or language upon students; rather, they help stories to emerge, to be shared with the community of learners and others.

Who's in charge here? Clearly, there is a mutuality of power. The student generates ideas and discovers way to express them. The teacher, acting as a resource, responds to their leads and prompts the development of ideas, expression, and style. The students engage in an interactive dialogue between the teacher and themselves, and also participate in peer conferences.

This writing process, called writers' workshop, makes a radical departure from the traditional teacher-directed instruction epitomized by teacher lecturing in front of the room. Rather, this writing process positions the teacher sitting side-by-side with the student. A horizontal rather than a hierarchical relationship develops and slowly erodes the teacher-in-charge paradigm. "Instead of the teacher thinking . . . privately and talking about it publicly so that the students may store it, both teacher and students engage in the process of thinking and they talk out what they are thinking in public dialogue. As they think and talk, their roles merge."[6]

I felt students preparing for public school teaching needed to be equipped with curricular alternatives which empowered the students and teachers respectively. They could not go out to classrooms outfitted with only philosophy and theory. They required tangible, student-centered strategies and curricula.

Re-thinking Sources of Knowledge—
Valuing Human Experiences

In traditional classrooms, the texts and the teacher are reified as principal sources of knowledge. Human experiences are seldom considered as part of the legitimate bank of knowledge. Most recently, in whole language classrooms, there is a dramatic trend of bringing students' lived experiences into the classroom as the catalyst to teach reading and writing. The teacher listens to these experiences and helps students connect them to class curriculum. The key for the teacher is to mediate between experiences and study themes.

An opportunity occurred this semester to capture a teachable moment. It involved a confrontation between a learning-disabled adult student and three students in the class. This incident allowed us to examine how the notion of homogeneity pervaded our understandings about classrooms and order.

The adult with the learning disability was prone to make socially inappropriate comments in class. One evening he was more zealous in his comments than ever. Consequently, he verbally monopolized both large and small group discussions. At the end of the evening, three students confronted him and informed him that he was rude, boisterous, and tactless. After class the three students complained to me.

"It's your job to get him out of the program."
"You know he doesn't belong here. He doesn't fit."
"You shouldn't mislead him by taking his money when you know he couldn't ever possibly teach."
"He's a poor role model."

They believed he had no right to be in our classroom or program. Protesting, "He doesn't fit," they assumed he didn't fit their concept of teacher. Their lack of tolerance for his difference blinded them from seeing other successful alternatives for this teacher. Sensing they were ready to send him to Never-Never-Land, I decided it was time to conduct a session on teaching in the pluralistic classroom.

The following week I gave students a case study[7] written by an elementary principal, a regular education, and a special education teacher describing a dilemma regarding the mainstreaming efforts of a special education student. The case focused on a young boy's difficulty in assuming regular education expectations and the regular education teacher's difficulty in adjusting her standards. Students volunteered to role-play the case study. Classmates watched their peers seek strategies requiring integration of instructional appropriateness, social acceptance, empathy, and compassion.

Following the simulation, public self-disclosures of discomfort at addressing student differences were made. "Why is it our first instinct is to exile any student that deviates from the social norms?" we asked ourselves. "Why do we not gravitate to those who are different in an attempt to understand them better?"

The class immediately linked the case study exercise with the situation that had occurred. Feeling responsible to the learning-disabled adult because they had failed to support him earlier, two students conspicuously offered him a place in their cooperative learning groups. The students who had confronted him began to tolerate him, trying hard to appreciate him. The case study activity held a mirror up to the students, revealing their discrimination of people with learning disabilities and their inability to respect difference.

We subsequently studied the social and cultural forces that have influenced our thinking and our preference for "sameness" over "difference." Patriarchy, bureaucracy, and behaviorism were examined as the historical legacy schools have inherited. The "seen and not heard" patriarchal influences struck a familiar cord for the students. The concept of students hanging onto the lowest rung of the bureaucratic hierarchical ladder with no invested power raised eyebrows. Peaking their interest was behaviorism's transmission model of pouring knowledge into the empty minds of students. We began to understand that these three pervasive social influences promote student passivity, compliance, and conformity. Therefore, we were not surprised when we saw the teacher as the authority-in-charge of the classroom's curriculum, instruction, and students' educational destinies. We expected to find classroom practices impregnated with values of compliance, uniformity, standardization, and homogeneity. We were prepared to find schools not only uncomfortable with variations but also to find schools that systematically attack the concept of difference due to the hegemonized valuing of sameness.

The confrontation between the learning-disabled student and the other students provided an ideal example of prevailing school practices influenced by the "sameness" paradigm. Because it helped us examine the values behind our practices, this teachable moment was worth re-mapping the course activities. This strategy of connecting human experiences to major study themes values human experiences as an important classroom resource.

Embryonic Stages

This semester's tinkering was a modest beginning at attempting to undermine the conventional notions of the teacher-in-charge. I am still a long way to shared governance, discussing ethics, and critical dialogues.

Going into the semester with a vague idea of cultivating a democratic classroom, I tried to solicit the participation of all students and celebrate the multiple resources in the classroom. I also knew I wanted to create an environment which would encourage the joint construction of meaning. But I didn't know how to do this. I merely promised myself that I would continually seek ways as I became increasingly familiar with the university classroom. The methods and curriculum that were subsequently developed may be considered primitive by some but was an authentic exploration in preparing a classroom for critical pedagogy by me.

How Do We Know We Are Ethical and Democratic?

A Rumination on Ethical, Democratic Reasoning, and Action Curriculum

by Tom Wilson

Based on works in professional ethics,[8] I would like to offer a three component, 45-hour moral, democratic teacher-education curriculum which, in modification, could be adjusted to meet the time requirements of most pre-service teacher-education programs.[9] The fundamental purpose of this curriculum is to increase the democratic and moral consciousness as well as the potential for action of students in teacher-education programs through the integration of philosophy, moral psychology, and critical analysis.

As for the philosophical, I agree with Soltis[10] that it is important for educators to know something about philosophical ethical systems. While to know if one is an instrumentalist, a deontologist, or some combination thereof may be intriguing and lead to self-reflection, such knowledge is hardly sufficient. An ethical, moral,[11] and democratic pedagogy needs to go beyond philosophy to incorporate insights from both psychology and critical analysis. With respect to psychology, James Rest[12] states the issue quite well.

> Until recently psychologists and ethics instructors have tended to go their separate ways, in my opinion, to the detriment of both their disciplines. Though psychologists have done a great deal of work on moral development, they have not thought much about the specific ethical problems that students will face after graduation in their lives and their careers, the kind of information that ethics instructors know well. For their part, many ethics instructors have not taken advantage of the findings of psychological research, nor have they evaluated their courses using the methods and tools of psychological research. Therefore, I propose that ethics instructors and psychological researchers collaborate for the sake of improving ethics courses, evaluating programs, and advancing research.

Concerning critical analysis, its inclusion incorporates within a democratic curriculum the notions of critical consciousness,[13] dialogue, reflection and action,[14] and theories of action.[15] The inclusion of the critical in moral reflection brings an often ignored perspective framed in such themes as domination, oppression, class, race, ethnicity, gender, and culture to bear upon educational issues. The assumption here is that traditional philosophical-based educational ethics curriculum often is apt to miss, if not actually ignore, these themes. Such a position is not to argue that the critical offers *the* answers to ethical problems, but rather, since it in and of itself rejects any notion of value neutrality, it should be integral to any discourse on democratic teacher education.

The three component curriculum also brings into consideration authentic assessment practices, and the involvement of practicing, school-based educators in the curriculum process. Historically, assessment of students has relied upon examinations, observations of students in discussion sessions, papers of various lengths and formats, and perhaps other impressions garnered from informal contracts with students.

While there is support for traditional assessment and evaluation approaches as being more than adequate at least in business ethics,[16] my position is that while they may be necessary they are hardly sufficient. A more complete and authentic curriculum and assessment[17] would include the results of speculations and research based on a cognitive developmental perspective of moral reasoning,[18] as well as critical educational praxis.[19]

The involvement of practicing educators makes problematic the reliance on postsecondary faculty as the sole agents of both instruction and evaluation. This problem centers upon another cherished notion that academic faculty are the most qualified to "teach" democratic ethics whether they are from schools of education or from philosophy departments. The issue thus becomes a democratic concern for the larger educational community's interest or, at the minimum, potential interest in moral and democratic professionalism of teachers.

This curriculum assumes that it is possible that the members of the public education sector communities are basically qualified and can be directly involved in the curriculum as "critical friends." If this is true, then reciprocally, both education faculty and external educators are apt to increasingly value moral and democratic instruction, encourage its development, and see its salubrious relationships to their own endeavors.

With the rationale of incorporation philosophy, moral psychology, and critical analysis in conjunction with the issues of assessment and practitioner involvement hopefully clear, the specific three components of the curriculum now can be offered. These are:

1. Interpreting a situation; recognizing a democratic, moral issue as a dilemma when it arises.

2. Deciding what to do ideally; deciding the reasoning to guide action.

3. Deciding and implementing the decision.

Component I: *Recognizing Democratic Dilemmas* **(15 hours).** In this component, students are presented either audio or video mini-drama dilemmas apt to be found in teaching. The dilemmas, as cases, are drawn from experiences reported by teacher-practitioners.[20] As the dilemmas unfold, the student is asked to take the role of the teacher as if he/she were in the situation. The student's dialogue is audiotaped, transcribed, and evaluated by both faculty and practitioner to ascertain if the student was able to recognize a democratic ethical issue and to respond in a coherent, well-reasoned manner. The student then meets with a faculty member (ideally one versed in philosophical ethics, moral psychology, and critical theory) and a practitioner to discuss the dialogue: What *was* the dilemma; how did parties involved see the issues; what were the conflicts; what might be the consequences of the action chosen? This procedure takes place at the beginning and the end of the teacher-education program. By comparing the two testing administrations, inferences can then be made as to changes in the student's thinking.

Again, faculty and practitioner assessors would have to be as ethically democratic and critical as they hope the students might become. This is a crucial issue, for if Gardner is correct, many well-intentioned individuals may still carry in their heads the understandings of a five-year-old child, five-year-old theories, of how the world works physically, culturally, and morally.[21] Assuming—and it is a huge assumption—that, through dialogue, some sense of assessor moral competence could be captured, the process of using faculty and non-academic professional educators would seem to have a meritorious impact on students.[22] To paraphrase Bebeau,[23] such benefits include:

1. Helping them to see themselves as linked with a group of professionals in a relationship which sanctions the discussion of ethical and democratic issues.

2. Establishing a more congenial relationship with professionals that might carry over into students' future professional life.

3. Helping them to recognize that both faculty and non-academic professionals struggle with ethical and democratic issues, and that a fair number of them have been successful without compromising their own self-interest nor the rights of others.

Component II: *Examining Democratic Reasoning to Guide Action* **(15 hours).** In this phase, students examine their own thoughts and struggle with moral and critical ideals which might guide and influence actual behavior. Students would have great latitude in determining the manner in which this moral and democratic reflection might occur with one caveat: The reflection must take place. From a cognitive developmental perspective, ideal democratic reasoning approximates stages five and six (if six actually exists) of Lawrence

Kohlberg's framework. Theoretically, students might take one or more of these instruments, which are designed to capture moral reasoning: The Moral Judgment Interview (MJI),[24] The Sociomoral Reflection Measure (SRM)[25] or The Defining The Issues Test (DIT).[26] The best candidates, it seems, are either the SRM or the DIT, since the MJI scoring requires a high level of training, up to two hours per protocol interview, and interview recording and transcription.

Of particular importance in Component II is providing students with the critiques of moral development theory including the issues of context,[27] and male bias.[28] Such criticism is vital because it provides for context and gender as illustrative frames to examine the democratic nature of moral development theory itself.

Democratic reasoning can also be approached through the use of the Conscientizacao or C-code,[29] which attempts to make operational the critical perspectives of Paulo Freire.[30] The C-code uses verbal samples of individuals responding to self-identified protocols which are either visual or written. A legitimate protocol is one that (1) represents an honest response, (2) reflects in some way the answers to several questions: What problems do you have? Should things be as they are? Why are things as they are? and What can be done to change things? and (3) represents individuals' responses to their own and/or their peer group's life problems and not those of another sociocultural group.[31] While the samples can be gathered either from written responses or through interview, the interview is preferred as it allows for more extensive and in-depth dialogue. The disadvantage of the interview is the time required and its labor-intensive quality. For the purpose of this teacher-education curriculum, rather than having students' responses scored by a second party, they might either score each other's or score their own. Since the intent primarily is to engage in dialogue about the nature of critical consciousness, democracy, and their moral nature rather than any one individual "level," disinterested scoring is probably not required.

A third possibility for examining democratic and moral ideals would have students read various works on school practice and reform, including their own constructed versions and responses to the dilemmas from Component I. These readings then would be subjected to analysis much as that suggested by Foucault,[32] in which discourses are not only about what can be said and thought, but also who can speak, when, and with what authority. Words and concepts change their meaning and their effects as they are deployed within different discourses. Meanings are derived, then, not so much from language but from contexts with their institutional practices and power relationships. Additionally, discourses constrain the possibilities of thought and, beyond what can be said, they are about what cannot be or is not said; they are constituted by exclusion as well as inclusion. Students, therefore, would be encouraged to examine education writings, their own and others, to undercover power relationships, who speaks to whom about what, and what is allowed to be said and what is not.[33]

It should be recognized that the effectiveness of assessing moral and democratic ideals as I have defined them presents a dilemma in and of itself. If democratic and critical thought includes the ideas of free choice, nondominating structures, and non-hierarchical arrangements, then how can an "external to-the-actor" procedure be developed to use with the actor? Yet, if all externally derived instruments are rejected, how can it be known if interventions make a difference in democratic consciousness development? It seems that the best resolution might be in "teaching the instruments," making them philosophically transparent to those who are its recipients. That is, the theory is taught in conjunction with the practice of that theory. This becomes the norm that drives Component II.

Component III: *Deciding and Implementing the Decision.* In Component III, students are confronted with issues of fortitude, ego-strength, and interpersonal skills in order to carry through with a decision to resolve a democratic dilemma with which they are faced. Otherwise, the paean to principle is apt to catch in the throat of exigency, or as the homily states, "the road to hell is paved with good intentions." This component seems to be the most illusive, and at the same time, most important.

Components I and II may assist the student in profound ways, yet the impact remains minimal until that student is able to carry out ethical and democratic acts. The will to act in and of itself is value-free. Jesus, Ghandi, Hitler, and Stalin, in all probability, had high ego strength. It is the ego strength in the service of principled and democratic consciousness behavior, the recognition of one's own potential as a moral agent, the awareness of one's being indeed responsible to act ethically, and be judged accordingly, to which Component III is addressed. Rest[34] is correct, I believe, in hypothesizing that "resoluteness, deliberateness, and task orientation may be deep-seated aspects of personality organization." While as such they may not be much affected directly by instructional techniques, the theory and practice of improving professional competence as developed by Argyris[35] seems to have potential for assisting students in actualizing and acting on their moral convictions and commitments. Argyris's work centers upon means to uncover discrepancies between beliefs and action. He posits a "theory-in-use": an implicit model that can be inferred from behavior but may differ sharply from the actor's "espoused theory." An observer can employ the inferred theory-in-use to predict the actor's behavior, but if the actor's espoused theory says something else, those with whom the actor deals may be misled. Moreover, any attempt to discuss the situation may simply elicit the espoused theory, thus further confusing all concerned. If an individual also has defensive motives for resisting such discussion, there will be still more barriers to open discussion.

On the basis of extensive management studies, Argyris has also suggested that certain variables are especially likely to create such barriers. This attitude involves several key assumptions about how working relationships should be conducted, in which the parties involved must: (1) achieve a purpose, as defined unilaterally by the person in charge, (2) "win," (3) suppress negative feelings, and (4) emphasize rationality. This cluster of assumptions has been labeled Model I by Argyris. It is an extremely common model for relationships in most sorts of organizations, including teacher education programs.

The alternative to such construction is an open communication system in which the participants continually re-examine the governing variables of their system. Argyris calls this a Model II environment whereby one seeks to discuss the undiscussable, make explicit the implicit, and question premises. The belief here is that the problem of control, domination, and authority in teacher-education programs, as well as in most of current life can be dealt with only when they become subjects of Model II-type dialogues rather than remaining out of bounds as in Model I (and in Foucoult's discourse analysis). Such dialogue is developed through the concrete use of brief protocols and "script writing," which enables students to uncover the contradictions in their thinking and thereby learn the mismatch between their espoused theories and theories in use.

Other pedagogical processes to assist students' propensity for democratic action might include structured experiences, laboratory learning (including, yes indeed, classical personal growth experiences), role plays, direct interpersonal skill training, and simulations, all of which should be tried and learned from.

Component III thus moves to help students to act in accord with understandings and beliefs derived from Components I and II. Component III's focus is to determine ways by which the nature of moral, critical, and democratic behavior can be captured or, in Freire's words, "concretized." As such, Component III is straight-forward politically. It is a critical and moral educational theory which holds that an emancipatory, democratic teacher education can only occur, or be constructed in situations characterized by "*mutual trust . . .* of ideals, facts, and values and *between* the people that share and act upon them."[36] The knowledge so generated through trust is emancipatory for it forms the basis for the transformation of culture through self-reflective process directed against domination and guided by dialogical and open relationships.

Assessment of Component III's success is difficult. Expert assessment and observations might be one approach, as explored by Sheehan, et al.,[37] in relating moral judgment to physical performance. In conjunction with Sheehan's findings, Kohlberg's[38] work with naturalistic and clinically based moral action interviews could perhaps be used. Action interviews would probe jointly to determine precisely how the student decided what to do and how to do it when carrying out a democratic plan of action. As well, the action interviews might be employed in a retrospective manner wherein respondents would reflect upon a moral and democratic strategy which they attempt to implement in the "real world." To tap what Kohlberg calls the practical, as opposed to the hypothetical, reasoning requires the uncovering of personal meaning which drives behavior. Careful study of experimental phenomenology[39] and application of appropriate qualitative evaluation procedures[40] might provide further procedures by which the experience of implementing democratic decisions could be better understood by students, faculty, and practitioners.

Conclusion

It needs to be made clear that the entire 45-hour program needs to reflect its own intent; it, in and of itself, must be ethically and critically sound. The entire curriculum should be assessed not only by using its internal notions of moral development, critical consciousness, and theories of action, but also its overall democratic and procedural properties. Amy Gutmann[41] writes that any democratic education must meet the criteria of non-repressive and non-discriminatory practice. Michael Kealey[42] has applied John Rawls'[43] extensive theoretical notions of justice and the difference principle to organizational functioning in terms of a preferred social arrangement that minimizes regret over the actual consequences of interaction. While full explication of the applicability of Gutmann and Kealey must await another time, it suffices to state that both offer rich possibilities for securing some sense of the curriculum and its assessment properties take place in a just, democratic participatory ethic of non-discrimination, non-repression, and non-regret in which students do not become the objects of someone else's research agenda, but are ideological actors in the total process.

Dialogue

Tom: Suzi, my understanding is that we were not to plan in advance what we are going to do in this dialogue. So perhaps we can just respond to what we discovered in each other's portions of the chapter.

What I looked for were themes and contradictions. The themes I was looking for were arguments that were structurally the same in both of our pieces and I saw several. You write about examples of how you attempt to promote greater student responsibility in the university classroom by rethinking traditional teaching practices. I think this is a structural manifestation common to both of our writing because in mine, although a more technical kind of thing, there is this tension between teacher as "expert" and student as novice. And in one sense this is true, for the teacher should know more about creating or helping students become empowered in the classroom than the students do, thus the teacher becomes an expert, to use expertise to provide for students' active engagement in the creation of the classroom.

I have the same expert-novice problem in my three-component ethical literary model. It seems to me that the research and instrumentation that I use which other people have developed has to be used in a manner which does not treat students as subjects of someone else's expertise. But at the same time, there are things, ideas, and purposes that I, as an "expert," believe must be done. Absolutely, I want to create a classroom which incorporates diverse critical beliefs and democratic participation. I do want potential teachers to respond to moral dilemmas as part of professional education; it should not be optional for them. Now I admit this is a control issue and a contradiction; the research effort does control, yet if one does not want to talk about moral issues, then one should not consider teaching as a profession.

Suzi: Once again you seem to hit right at the core of the contradictions. In the process of writing this piece, I found I was working through a teacher control problem by experimenting with alternative practices. By the end of the semester I became more clear about a pedagogy that increases student participation. Now I'm wondering, how do you engage in this deliberateness without being controlling and manipulating the classroom participants? I could honestly say this first semester I was constructing, playing, hardly deliberate. The entire teaching experience was in a somewhat amorphous state. I didn't consider myself an expert. So at the end of the semester, this question of deliberateness is more significant to me. Because now I know what I know, and I have to respond morally to the fact that I'm now the expert and therefore could fall prey to using this new knowledge as a form of control. I wonder which is more effective in our work with the schools. Is it better to define an agenda upfront like union leaders and supervisors and risk anti-authority sentiment or would it be better if our agendas come out of the milieux of problem-solving?

Tom: It seems to me that a negotiated agreement needs to be established, yet how does one establish this contract, this constitution of the classroom wherein everyone agrees that this is the way it is going to be, where issues of control and contradiction are discussed openly and where the agenda is upfront. I think this is Chris Argyris's essential intent.

Suzi: I've seen you do this quite successfully when you say, "Here's an agenda. These are some thoughts and feelings. What do you all think? Could we work this way?" I've seen people embrace this modis operandi. But, I've also seen the other and I don't know if you would agree, but it has to do with developing trust. Something instinctively says to me that there is

a readiness, a number of shared experiences that happens prior to a negotiated agenda. People get to know each other and then allow themselves to
be engaged in negotiations. What instincts do you have about readiness?

Tom: Readiness would be something discussable. I wouldn't decide
when people were ready, because that would be a unilateral decision
that I should not make. I might say, "I think we're ready for this for the
following reasons . . . the data leads me to this conclusion." Often I
might state, "This is just a hypothesis . . . do we want to do this?" Yet at
some point as a teacher-educator I will say, "We are going to do this."
For example, we are not going to debate whether we're going to talk
about democracy, that's a given. If someone wants to be in a teacher-education program to be an educator, then he or she ought to respect the
moral dimensions of teaching. Morality, ethics, and democracy are the
givens of the discourse. I am opposed to getting into an argument or discussion such as, "Well, the pros for the holocaust and the antis for the
holocaust will have a debate." There are some things we don't debate, it's
beyond debate and I think democracy is one of them. To talk about
democracy in process is critical. This isn't to say that there is an ideal
state of democracy—this does not exist. There is only a democratic process and to be a teacher, with a moral public trust, means engaging in
democratic and moral discourse. We might question readiness to do certain kinds of activities or processes within them, but we must keep in
mind the base mission of the creation of democracy.

Suzi: Who determines this agenda of democracy? One can't predict
what shared experiences agendas will evolve as a result of shared experiences.

Tom: When you and I call people together to have a shared experience,
it seems to me that we already have an agenda in mind and we want
them to have a shared experience. We do want them to think differently,
that's what education is all about. We want people to think better, or
more adequately; that's the agenda, that's what we are doing. The reason
we do that is to share experiences so we can talk deeper. Yet, we must
make it explicit that this is what we are doing and why we are doing it.

Suzi: You built the Coalition (Wilson has been a regional coordinator
of Ted Sizer's Coalition of Essential Schools) not as a result of announc-
ing to the world, "This is what it's about," but rather through informal
networking. I'm not so sure you built your reputation as a moral educator
by going around saying, "I'm a moral educator" on a T-shirt, and therefore this announced agenda is what brings those people to you. In fact,
I've seen a lot of informal things happening. People collect around you
because you wear a number of different T-shirts.

Tom: But Suzi, so do you agree on this? Yet isn't the moral and ethical always there?

Suzi: I would agree.

Tom: What do you think of the three-component ethical literacy curriculum?

Suzi: I like it. I want to try it. The part that is most attractive to me is how you made a balance between scholarly research and informed practices with authentic (personal) experiences. You invited the community to be a part of the project; you empowered them by calling them "critical friends." I hope you meant anyone in the broad context of community.

Tom: The total curriculum is open to critical friends, people of interest, and so on. When we get down to the assessors (I don't know what other word to use), this notion of "sitting down beside someone" to see what values exist is critical because one wants someone as assessor who understands ethics and democracy. I wouldn't randomly select from a population for just anyone to be an assessor. I want someone who knows something about ethics and philosophy.

   I don't want to be self-righteous, but we are moral educators and we struggle with this notion of expertise all the time. I hope to get moral reasons why we struggle. And some of us do recognize dilemmas when we see them and if there's any truth in Larry Kohlberg's work, there is some sense that moral argumentation is different because of stages within thinking processes. And not to be too smug about any one theory that we have to apply, it's hard to expose people to Kohlberg's theory or Paulo Freire's notions of critical consciousness if one doesn't know anything about these two; it won't make sense. An assessor would have to be conversant with the theory, the praxis, the research within the components of the curriculum.

Suzi: How does one become moral? Is it through families, experiences, or training? That would color what this model would look like. Can a person be moral and not ever been trained?

Tom: Ghandi? Christ?

Suzi: If that is the case, what appears to have alienated me is that same thing that happens with the critical theorists and that it gets way into something, it becomes a piece that is scholarly, and has a language, and is assessed, it's instrumented. How did Ghandi measure his morality?

Tom: Read Bob Howard's dissertation[44] tracking Ghandi's moral development, trying to assess the stages of his reasoning and his experiences which contributed to his reasoning.

Suzi: This idea of an expert body of knowledge defining morality can be distancing to people from the broader community. I would want the group of participants to construct the assessment, whatever way that looks.

Tom: I agree to a point, but to be an assessor means one knows something about that which is to be assessed. I heard you say it, education is this moral, public trust so if we don't directly deal with assessment, then we don't know if what we are doing is effective. Otherwise it just becomes an experience. What you're doing in your classroom is a fine way to start, but I guess I want a more formal curriculum. How would you know your students are getting better in their sense of thinking?

Suzi: I don't know exactly, but I know how I want to proceed. Yesterday I opened up the class syllabus and said, "Here is a proposal, and it's negotiable, any piece of this is negotiable." And I'm willing to pull anything off and insert anything else. I use the metaphor of syncopated rhythm in my head hoping we will achieve a sense of rhythm of learning with each other and jointly constructing the syllabus.

Tom: I love the metaphor, but I want to push that students cannot be allowed to escape the moral. Remember Gutmann argues that one doesn't debate whether education is going to be democratic or not. One must have choices in school, yet you can't start a Nazi school because, by definition, it would be discriminatory and repressive and that's not democratic.

Suzi: Can you start a discussion about Nazi schools to probe the issues?

Tom: Yes, but not argue if it's OK to have Nazi schools; a voucher school that is repressive would not be appreciated. Suzi, one final comment from me. I found your part of the chapter most reflective and thoughtful. It seems to flow much better than mine. It represents an authentic, concrete democratic struggle to truly liberate both teacher and student from standard, taken-for-granted practices.

Suzi: Tom, this was a phenomenal experience—writing individually, then engaging in a dialectal conversation to flush out contradictions. Thank you for contributing to and building upon my existing knowledge.

We (Suzi and Tom) agreed, at the end of this dialogue and upon reading and editing its text, to examine our own ethical and democratic natures. That is, to what extent did we, for example, in our discussions, use the kinds of practices we proposed? Are we internally consistent? This is something the reader may also want to contemplate.

NOTES

1. W. Frankena, *Thinking About Morality* (Ann Arbor: University of Michigan Press, 1980), p. 44.

2. P. Freire, and A. Faundez, *Learning to Question* (New York: Continuim, 1989), p. 2.

3. Ibid.

4. J. Gibbs, and A. Allen, *Tribes* (Santa Rosa, CA: Center Source Publication, 1978).

5. L. Calkins, *The Art of Teaching Writing* (Portsmouth, NH: Heinemann, 1986).

6. M. Grumet, *Bittermilk* (Amherst, MA: University of Massachusetts Press, 1988), p. 219.

7. R. Silverman, W. Welty, and S. Lyon, *Case Studies for Teaching Problem Solving* (New York: McGraw Hill, 1992).

8. M. Bebeau, "Teaching Professional Ethics," *The Science Museum of Minnesota Encounters* (Sept./Oct., 1983) and J. Rest, *Moral Development: Advance in Research and Theory* (New York: Prager, 1987).

9. For a more detailed description of the curriculum than space allows here, see T. Wilson, "A Curriculum for Educational Ethical Literacy: Philosophical, Psychological and Critical Perspectives" (Irvine, CA: University of California, 1991a).

10. J. Soltis. "Teaching Professional Ethics," *Journal of Teacher Education* 32(3) (May/June, 1986), p. 11.

11. While distinctions between the word "ethics" and "morality" have been made by Camenisch, I use the words interchangeably, as is the case, I believe, with most educators in daily conversations. See P. Camenisch, "Goals of Applied Ethics Courses," *Journal of Higher Education* 57(5) (1986), pp. 493-509.

12. J. Rest, "A Psychologist Looks at the Teaching of Ethics," *The Hastings Center Report* (Hastings-on-Hudson: The Hastings Center, 1983).

13. P. Freire, *Education for Critical Consciousness* (New York: Continuim, 1981).

14. P. Freire, *Pedagogy of the Oppressed* (New York: Herder and Herder, 1970).

15. C. Argyris, *Overcoming Organizational Defenses: Facilitating Organizational Change* (Boston: Allyn and Bacon, 1990) and C. Argyris, R. Putnam, and D. Smith, *Action Science* (San Francisco: Jossey Bass, 1985).

16. A. Caplan, "Evaluations and the Teaching of Ethics," *Ethics Teaching in Higher Education*. Edited by A. Callahan and S. Bok (New York: Plenum, 1980).

17. The sense of assessment as used herein is captured by its etymology, that of an assessor as one who "sits down beside someone." See C. Onions, *The Oxford Universal Dictionary of Historical Principles*, 3rd rev. ed. (London: Oxford University Press, 1955), p. 13.

18. L. Kohlberg, "Moral Stages and Moralization: The Cognitive Developmental Approach," *Moral Development and Behavior*. Edited by T. Lickona (New York: Holt, Rineholt, and Winston, 1976) and C. Gilligan, *In a Different Voice* (Cambridge, MA: Harvard University Press, 1982).

19. W. Smith and A. Alschuler, *How to Measure Conscientizacao: The C-Code* (Amherst, MA: University of Massachusetts, Center for International Education, 1976).

20. While full expectation of democratic/moral dilemmas remains to be developed, such factors as race, class, ethnicity, gender, testing, tracking, resource distribution, grading, "common" curricula, voucher, and choice plans are saturated with moral and democratic issues.

21. H. Gardner, *The Unschooled Mind: How Children Think and How Schools Should Teach* (New York: Basic Books, 1991).

22. One strong possibility for potential assessors would have them partake of the three-component model as students themselves, wherein *their* assessors would be those individuals identified as knowledgeable about ethics, democratic forms, and critical approaches.

23. *Teaching Professional Ethics*, p. 2.

24. L. Kohlberg, A. Colby, B. Speicher-Dubin, and M. Lieberman, *Standard Form Scoring Manual* (Cambridge, MA: Moral Education Foundation, 1975).

25. J. Gibbs, and K. Widaman, *Social Intelligence: Measuring Developments of Sociomoral Reflection* (Englewood Cliffs, NJ: Prentice-Hall, 1982).

26. J. Rest, *Moral Development: Advance in Research and Theory* (New York: Prager, 1987).

27. E. Mishler, "Meaning in Context: Is There Any Other Kind?" *Harvard Educational Review* 49(1), 1979, p. 1-19.

28. There are other significant empirical research limitations to each of these assessment measures. The reflection called for in Component II would incorporate understanding of these additional reservations, see *In a Different Voice*.

29. *How to Measure Conscientizacao*.

30. *Pedagogy of the Oppressed*.

31. *How to Measure Conscientizacao*, p. 57.

32. S. Ball, ed., *Foucault and Education: Disciplines and Knowledge* (London: Routledge, 1990).

33. For an example of discourse analysis of two texts on school reform, see Wilson, T., "Comparing Discourses: Democracy, The Coalition of Essential Schools and The Eight Year Study" (Orange, CA: Chapman University, 1991b).

34. *A Psychologist Looks at the Teaching of Ethics*, p. 34.

35. *Overcoming Organizational Defenses.*

36. K. Sirotnik, and J. Oakes, "Critical Inquiry and School Renewal: A Liberation of Method Within a Critical Theoretical Perspective." Occasional Paper No. 4. University of California, Los Angeles: Graduate School of Education, Laboratory in School and Community Education, 1983.

37. D. Sheehan, S. Husted, D. Candee, C. Cook, and M. Bargen, "Moral Judgment as a Predictor of Physician Performance," *Moral Education Forum* 5(1), 1980, p. 2-7.

38. L. Kohlberg, "Essays on Moral Development," *The Philosophy of Moral Development*, Vol. 1 (San Francisco: Harper and Row, 1981).

39. D. Hide, *Experimental Phenomenology* (New York: G. P. Putnam and Sons, 1977).

40. G. Willis, ed., *Qualitative Evaluation* (Berkeley: McCutchan, 1978).

41. A. Gutmann, *Democratic Education* (Princeton, NJ: Princeton University Press, 1987).

42. M. Kealey, "Ethical Aspects of Organizational Governance," *Review of Social Economy*, XL(3), Dec. 1978.

43. J. Rawls, *A Theory of Justice* (Cambridge, MA: Belknap Press of Harvard University Press, 1978).

44. R. Howard, "Mohandas K. Ghandi: A Biography of Moral Development." Ph.D. dissertation, Harvard University, 1986.

Ten

Democracy in Education:
A Foxfire Experience

Janet C. Fortune

Introduction

There is a slowly growing call in United States education for wider participation in classroom decisions and in the creation of institutional regulations. As teacher-educators, we hear difficult questions from our students concerning the alleged demise of the public schools, the inadequate preparation of classroom teachers, the high student and teacher dropout rates, and the place of public education in a capitalist economy. These questions require us to consider the discrepancy between democracy as espoused in theory and democracy as embodied in the current lives of our citizens. Our purpose here is to begin to examine the less than democratic conditions of higher education as a social institution, which exists within a country priding itself on the promulgation of democratic ideals.

We hold firmly at least two convictions that would not allow us to ignore a voice calling for movement toward a more democratic condition in education. First is our belief that democracy is a goal worth working toward on both a broad political level and on that closer, personal level through which we are each impacted in our day to day lives. We, as teachers, students, citizens, must renew our efforts toward democracy and allow other people the ability to do so as well. Secondly, we believe learning best takes place when students are actively involved in, take ownership of, both the process and product of their education. Therefore, we believe democracy is best taught as a process and best learned through active participation in decision making, as well as active participation in classroom work. As teachers of teachers, we are called to enable our students' efforts to become active change agents and decision-makers in their lives as teachers.

EKTN-Berea College Collaboration

These philosophical strands found their way into a January 1991 short-term course at Berea College, a 1,500 student liberal arts college in south-central Kentucky. The short term lasts 20 academic days each January and is designed to provide students the opportunity to explore outside their majors and to provide instructors the opportunity to expand the curriculum.

The three instructors for this course, "Democracy in Education: A Foxfire Experience," chose to use $1,000 in funding from a Ford Foundation grant and the association between Berea College's Education Department and the Eastern Kentucky Teachers Network (EKTN) as the groundwork for a course on democracy and the classroom. This association began following Eliot Wigginton's 25-year success with the Foxfire teaching approach in Rabun Gap, Georgia. Foxfire teaching incorporates 11 Core Practices: student decision making, real world connections, academic integrity, group work, reflection, evaluation, community involvement, teacher as facilitator, active student participation, and the need for an audience.

In 1985, Wigginton was awarded a 1.5 million dollar grant from the Bingham Trust for Charity of New York to sponsor his desire to share the success of Foxfire's Core Practices with other classroom teachers. That same summer, Wigginton came to Berea College to teach in one of the college's two-week Mellon High School-College Cooperative Learning Seminars, which bring high school teachers to Berea College for courses on issues in the liberal arts taught by college professors. The Mellon program aims to build a network for mutual assistance and intellectual conversation, including the invitation of Berea College professors to public school classrooms and vice versa.

At that time the high school teachers who participated in Foxfire teaching were scattered throughout eastern Kentucky. As they began to implement this non-traditional Foxfire approach in their classrooms, they felt a need to connect with each other for support, resources, and follow-up. In the spring of 1987, a coordinator was hired and the Eastern Kentucky Teachers Network became the first of the Foxfire teachers networks nationwide. EKTN now has teachers writing their own mini-grants, attending conferences and workshops for professional development, and communicating through a computer network linking some 30 teachers who share classroom and professional ideas over modems. To provide support and follow-up on classroom instruction, in-service training, and teaching resources, a teaching associate was hired who later became one of the three instructors in the Berea Short-Term course.

Since its inception in 1855, Berea College has been committed to serving the people of the Appalachian region. Reflecting and building on this commitment, Berea's Education Department has for years taken students to visit the schools, teachers, and towns of eastern Kentucky. In 1989, EKTN began helping with the funding of these trips and sponsoring students' investigation of

Foxfire teaching, settlement schools, and the educational and economic needs of Appalachia. Part of this funding included the Ford Foundation grant for the short-term course on Foxfire pedagogy as a more democratic approach to teaching at all levels of education.

Privilege and Power: Structuring the Course

Planning for the actual nature of the course began in the spring of 1990, when two members of the Education Department and EKTN's teaching associate sat down to determine our understandings of democracy and Foxfire, the confluence of the two, and how best to put these definitions into action in our classroom in a time span of 20 academic days. Time was a critical factor, and this was born out in every aspect of planning and conducting the course and, upon reflection, all aspects of student experiences. Unfortunately, time always was in short supply. Even though we were and are committed to team teaching as an important and viable pedagogical concept, three teachers multiplied the inherent difficulties of scheduling threefold. This became even more critical during January when we had difficulty finding time to reflect on the events of each class session.

During the planning, basic questions and assumptions emerged. Nothing was easy about this course; which is not to say it was not enjoyable or inspirational, because it was. However, uncovering these basic questions and assumptions concerning the nature of education and the construction of the classroom were, most assuredly, not easy nor comfortable. Building a conversation of democratic change in education makes us newly responsible to the inequities we see and the privileges we enjoy.

Before we could move to consideration of ways in which our teaching could potentially alleviate inequities and respond more fully to students' needs, we had to consider the ways in which a classroom environment benefits the instructors as it does not the students. That is, in addition to considerations of a stronger, emerging student voice representing increased decision-making power and self-authority, we had to consider those taken-for-granted privileges awarded to us on the basis of what we will call "academic privilege." By this we mean those benefits enjoyed because of one's relationship within the institution and the concomitant relationship with one's students. These are not the benefits derived from expertise, whether it be pedagogical or discipline-related; hopefully, expertise would be a combination of both. Academic privilege includes the systemic, daily benefits which bind us together as instructors and not-students within the context of the classroom.

Academic privilege ensures that, as instructors, we have the powers of evaluating; of deciding issues of importance, interest, and relevance; of determining the course curriculum; and of choosing the adopted text. As instructors we are more assured of a voice within the institution. We are able to make decisions as to who enters the institution, who enters the major, who leaves the institution, and under what circumstances. Our position has given us the ability to decide what pedagogical techniques intercede between the discipline and the student. Our position has given us the ability to listen to some voices in the classroom, to ignore others, to praise some, and to be critical of others. We are pretty well guaranteed of being treated professionally and of having our opinions and judgments treated with respect. We are also assured of a particular physical placement in the classroom. We are able to criticize the institution with greater freedom and less fear of repercussions; of course, the farther up the tenure track, the fear lessens and the freedom increases. Our academic privilege precedes us and does not rely on us as knowledgeable individuals for its sustenance. It does not rely on the vital differences between unique participants for its continued existence or for the creation of its idiosyncrasies.

To define expertise as separate from academic privilege is to describe a classroom environment of creative individuals engaged in the mutual task of deciphering and answering the questions of the discipline rather than centering on the questions of the instructor. The instructor participates in the class through knowledge of the discipline, respect for that which she/he does not know, and the ability to enable meaningful pedagogical experiences. We set ourselves the task of conjuring up an educational world in which students have power and use it without fear. In this educational world, teachers would recognize and respect this legitimate use in sharing of power and be changed by it.

Identifying our areas of privilege as instructors could help us in the critique of the structure of the classroom and higher education as an institution, but it was obviously not the entire process. Our subsequent task was to identify those areas in which students would actually want to participate, and those structural inequities which are inappropriate to a classroom based on the needs of all its members. The following questions seemed essential to us: What privileges do instructors hold which would benefit students? What processes of the classroom would students want to hold and control? What dispersion of power allows for full and active participation by all members? While maintaining a viable learning situation, what do instructors have that students should want?

This discussion was grounded in our study of John Dewey's educational philosophy, of Foxfire's premise of student-centered pedagogy, of our own concept of democracy as a process, and of our own classrooms and students. In retrospect, a longer term would have allowed us to pursue these questions with more deliberation with the course participants. As it was, this discussion did come to pass, but the students felt as if it had taken place previously without them—as, indeed, it had—and that perception added a whole new dynamic to the conversation since the instructors felt ready to move on and the students felt their participation to be integral to the process.

As instructors, discussing this level of student responsibility and participation was frustrating. We felt pulled by our position in the institution and the need to meet its requirements; by the vast, slow process of democracy and our desire to teach the basic premises of Foxfire; and by our different intellectual agendas. Most difficult, during planning and throughout the course, was facing the challenge of giving up our own position and privilege in the classroom. This was just the first of many moments of personal reflection and reckoning and of attempts toward melding vastly different theoretical differences and teaching styles.

From this planning emerged the "givens" of the course—its basic framework. These givens were the choice of texts, the centering of the course on an understanding of the Foxfire process within a democratic setting, the sharing of responsibility and instruction time equally among the three instructors, the inclusion of student projects designed to establish a sense of community and comraderie, and the need for grades as an institutional necessity. The course catalog description advertised a class trip to visit Wigginton in Rabun Gap (which was quite a draw for enrollment but was still open for student vote). Because of expenses exceeding the Ford Foundation grant, the course carried a 25 dollar student fee. Early in the course, these parameters were presented to the students and discussed nearly every day thereafter. In the planning sessions we also decided on an approximate course outline, consisting of one week of in-depth study of texts, one week concentrating on the Foxfire approach, and one week working on projects using the Foxfire process.

Democracy as Process and Product: Content of the Course

We decided to open registration to all interested students. Of the 21 students who enrolled, 17 were education majors with various levels of preparation for a teaching career. Three students were beginning majors in child development in a department other than education, one student was an exchange student from Middlebury College. Of the 21, 7 were men and 14 were women.

The first day of class was spent in introductions and interviews reflecting on the belief that the work of a democratic classroom requires security, understanding, and community. On the second day of class, the agenda included discussion of personal and group goals and our "givens," an introduction to the Foxfire Core Practices, and the possibility of a class project. Our intent on these opening days was to proceed with the discussion of the privileges students want and expect in the classroom, to access the students with educational philosophy and Foxfire in particular, and to familiarize students' needs and desires in the planning of course activities.

The class shared characteristics of their most memorable learning experiences with the intent toward constructing a learning situation exemplifying these characteristics. They shared concerns about learning and putting into practice Foxfire's theories. Students wanted to know whether they would be capable of implementing the Foxfire approach in their own future classrooms, and voted to visit classes in Rabun Gap to see the Foxfire pedagogy in action by Wigginton himself. It became clear that our students' visions of democracy in this course necessitated, or would find its interpretation in, direct experiential learning, decision making, and our responsiveness to suggested course activities. The consensus of the group was to learn about (but in the process to "experience") Foxfire. The overall goal set for the class was to understand and to be able to implement the Foxfire process.

As students began to look at ways to do this, ideas began to flow. At this point the instructors introduced what had been decided among the three of us as our expectations (derived from the givens decided upon during the planning sessions) of the class. We presented these expectations as follows for consideration by the students: completing assigned reading materials which we felt essential to the understanding of the course; maintaining a daily journal kept by students and instructors to demonstrate growth and insight as the class progressed, and to meet the recordkeeping needs of EKTN; and demonstrating a working knowledge of Foxfire.

The problem of product had been presented; that is, what is it we want to learn in the time we have? What experiences and pedagogical methods, that is, what process, could/would make this possible? The creation of a product is inseparable from an understanding of the process of production. In this instance, understanding Foxfire as not synonymous with democracy, but as a more democratic approach to teaching, required changing the process of production.

It would seem most beneficial to discuss the solutions presented by the class participants, how well they worked, and, finally, how well they and the situation responded to experimentation with democracy in the classroom, for experience with Foxfire, and for students' gaining greater responsibility and balance in the college classroom. Planning for these learning activities took place in a weaving of prior knowledge created by both the instructors and students. The instructors who formed the warp held class views ranging from determination that democracy means full participation in all decisions over to adherence to implementing Foxfire even though some decisions would have to be established for the class by us. The students, who brought with them hesitancies created by years of nonparticipation in classrooms and lack of student authority in education, variations in concepts of democracy and knowledge of Foxfire, and differences in commitment to change in the field of education formed the weft.

One of the key principles or ideas which quickly emerged centered around the need for self-evaluation, with each student responsible for and determining what was important to that individual and the grades which would necessarily have to be submitted to the college. Some students felt wholly prepared to make decisions about course goals and to evaluate completion of course work. Others felt a strong need for more direction and guidance, and were uncomfortable assigning a grade to their work. This quickly became one of the two most contentious and difficult problems of the class. We may have indulged in dreams about not giving grades, but, for students to receive course credit, grades were required. No one maintained that we not give grades or that all students receive the same grade, exemplifying the conundrum of wanting evaluation but not wanting the judgmental side of valuing. The students were no exception to the notion that we want judicious encouragement.

The issue of evaluation took a great deal of class time to resolve, if, indeed, it was ever resolved; it's also difficult to talk about here because it webs together with so many of the other areas of decision and learning activities. The discussion took so long in class, our students began to think we'd never do anything to evaluate. On the positive side, the class provided a forum for students to explore personal attitudes of evaluation. As instructors we became more aware of student concerns about the uses of evaluation. The necessity for grades as at least one form of evaluation kept the instructors in the position of evaluator, and determined that the class must perform some tasks which could and would be judged in the form of grades.

The class eventually decided to work in groups on projects reflecting an awareness and understanding of Foxfire principles. These projects were to be evaluated by criteria established by the group. Each group, in conjunction with the three instructors, was to decide on a grade at the end of the term. These projects were the joy and pleasure of the class. Each group was required to demonstrate use of as many of the Foxfire Core Practices as possible, to have a finished product suitable for an audience, and to have each member of the group learn to do something she/he had not done before.

The products were remarkable. Each one demonstrated hard work and determination, and the students only had two and a half weeks (interrupted by the trip to Rabun Gap) to learn and accomplish something they'd never done before. One group wrote the script for, videotaped, and edited a news report on progressive education; none had ever done any aspect of this project previously. Another group (of only two) obtained funding from local merchants for a magazine they wrote, compiled, and managed to have printed by deadline. A third group assembled a scrapbook history of the class including numerous photographs and interviews with class members. The fourth group arranged to observe, teach, and make materials for the College's preschool. The final group designed and displayed an informational bulletin board on the Persian Gulf with the intention of trying to transmit information without bias.

Each group of students chose its own project, kept extensive records of the work process, conferred with the course instructors as guides, researched outside sources extraneous to the class, provided evidence of the Core Practices, and maintained standards for evaluation. We, the instructors, held our collective breath throughout this whole process. We are in complete agreement in believing teachers often get in the way, and that responsibility given breeds responsibility taken. Every class has some level of success, but we are convinced that in this course the decision making, setting of personal standards, and benign leadership led to an abundance of pride and achievement. Working in small groups was advantageous to the less assertive class members. One group did admit that they quickly chose each other because they knew personalities and work habits. These students admitted that another step in breaking ground in learning, beyond learning a new skill, would be to step toward accommodating other people and helping other individuals develop new skills and cohere into a viable, strong group.

The issue of evaluation directly relates to difficulties in defining the nature of participation within democracy. True evaluation requires instructors to build their own competence and stand on it with confidence as they watch closely for and recognize signs of burgeoning expertise in their students. This is complicated when student participation is limited. One hopes that people constructing a democratic environment will accept the need for participation, but diversity means that we cannot all participate in the same way or to the same degree. How does a democratic classroom respond to its most reluctant member? Rather than using established methods and timetables for class participation, we wanted the class to struggle with this dilemma—not only for the present circumstances but also because of the democratic commitments embedded in their chosen careers and adult lives. But even the discussion of reasons for and methods of participating was agonizing since the discussion itself requires some level of participation (even agreement with others' opinions necessitates a modicum of participation).

It is our concerted opinion that the educational history of some of our students played against us and them in this regard. Active participation, in the classroom and in broader democracy, is difficult and can be threatening. One can, in growing up in educational institutions, develop habits of acquiescence or outspokenness or the gamut between. In much the same way, asking 18-year-olds to make wise civic decisions without a background of responsible actions and consequences is foolhardy. But, in our limited time situation, exploring avenues of participation became frustrating, so much so that one group of five students began to feel as if they were dominating the class, which allowed others to remain silent. At one point they informed us of their intentions to quit talking during class so that someone else would have to. In discussions between this group and the instructors, we concluded that strong arm tactics such as these had no place in democracy, that group and personal growth could not occur through manipulation, and the difficulty of restrictive time was a problem of the course, not a problem to be used to force student movement of desired outcomes. The lesson was and has been valuable in many facets. The class as a whole wrestled with making a democracy work when the participation of some was more visible that others and some felt they were being coerced into participating in uncomfortable ways. One student designed a pledge of participation to share with the group:

- I pledge to recognize the worth of my ideas, when they arise, and assume the responsibility of sharing them with the class.

- I must also abide by the dictates of my conscience. That is, for example, if I see the class experience moving in a detrimental or unproductive direction, then I will alert my classmates and work to get the group back on track.

- I must make an effort to become acquainted with my peers, becoming familiar with their strengths and needs for growth.

- Consequently, I will be attentive to their needs by not interrupting or dominating the experience and, when appropriate, encouraging and nurturing their participation. (submitted by Donovan Fornwalt)

The principles or ideas which formed the activities of the class emerged from the discussions of the first few days. Students wanted to build community through an atmosphere of collegiality and trust where members would feel comfortable inquiring, disagreeing, and sharing responsibilities.

One suggestion for a community builder was a communal activity. We (along with the rest of the world) had been watching the advent of the war in the Persian Gulf, knowing with more than usual acuity that we were watching history unfold. Opinions concerning the war varied as widely as opinions on democracy and class participation. The class elected to go see "dances with Wolves" as a communal activity and as text for discussions of perceptions and interpretations of historical data. In a horrible coincidence, on the night of the movie, the invasion by U.S. troops was announced. One class member was shortly called to active duty.

The class also issued invitations to guest speakers. Eliot Wigginton spent a morning talking informally with us, clarifying understandings of Foxfire, and emphasizing the need for structure and rigorous pursuit in the students' Foxfire projects. On two separate occasions, teachers from EKTN spoke with the class about their Foxfire successes and failures and provided inspiration for visions of teaching alternatives.

Members of this class were obviously concerned about creating democratic structures within their own teaching situations. They were also concerned about the nature of decision making in their current educational institution, Berea College. An invitation was extended to the college president, John Stephenson, who addressed student questions and concerns about administrative decision making and responsibility, the college's political stance, and the relationship between students and administration.

Going to Rabun Gap was the capstone experience in community building. Although the instructors had made arrangements before January, the decision to go was still left up to the class and the remainder of the planning was in the students' hands. In the course of the trip, community was developed through traveling, eating, being housed together on the mountain, and the inevitable "bull sessions." One student, in reflecting on the trip, shared, "We talked about community all month—it took being snowed in on a mountain to build trust." True to form for January, the snow did indeed come. The first night in Rabun Gap, everyone shared in preparing and eating a spaghetti dinner and shared experiences with the Foxfire staff music teacher at Rabun County High School.

Students spent the next morning in conference with the Director of Teacher Outreach and in snowball fights. Rather than risking being iced in the second night, everyone packed and headed perilously down the mountain and back to Berea. No one was able to spend time touring through classes or watching Wigginton teach, but a closeness developed which sometimes requires the mutual dependence of being away from home and campus and school stresses.

We, the instructors, did adopt texts for use by the class, but they received more attention than use. The relationship between Foxfire, the democratic process, and the texts seemed clear and identifiable to the instructors but less so to the students. The use of books as texts wasn't so much seen as superfluous as just less close to the target than the other course activities. The texts were not what students' needs and interests required, but represented the connections the instructors had already made based on prior experiences. In this instance, the experiences themselves were what the students wanted rather than hearing about the instructors' experiences and connections. The class chose to use as texts: *Sometimes A Shining Moment* by Eliot Wigginton for information on the Foxfire approach; the speakers and guests; "Dances with Wolves"; the trip; themselves, their work and experiences.

A Hell-raisin', Butt-kicking Class:
Evaluation and Reconsideration

Experimentation is a tenuous, slow, compromising, delicate process. Any change asks for close examination. What has been considered trivial may now be important; work previously considered significant may need to be let go. Letting new light into your vision of what class is supposed to be is hard.

We've mentioned before the constraints of time on this course. Two students mentioned the stress of working under such a tight schedule. One student, currently a student teacher, remarked on the very slow process of developing decision-making skills in his students and of convincing them that they could learn to participate in this process. With 20 days always in the back of his mind, allowing the short-term course this same slow process was stressful. The second student said he had used the break between short-term and spring semester to recover from his exhaustion. For the instructors, any afternoon which did not include time for reflection, planning, and reconnoitering meant that we were one day behind and less well prepared for the following class. With other professional responsibilities, there were too many days when we couldn't confer. One of the characteristics of the memorable learning experiences described by students at the beginning of the course was patience, the time to repeat attempts toward success. Were we to do this course again, we would make accommodation for time necessary for process work.

The issue of democracy was a very present and constant stress. We all struggled with problems of lack of participation from some class members, too much from others, and the time-consuming task of decision making. Some students felt frustrated with the time spent defining and developing a democratic environment because they had expected to spend short term studying strictly Foxfire. Other students felt democratic decision making was absolutely essential and everyone should be required to participate in the process. As instructors, we felt caught by these frustrations and our own frustration of wanting complete student participation but knowing that forcing participation was antithetical to our class goals. Periods of anger, fear, pressure, and tears were evident throughout the course. One student wrote at the time, "We went through a day-to-day process that was so strenuous at times I just wanted to quit going to class. But I learned so much about myself by struggling to get along in a community of diverse people. It was just hard for me to listen to someone who stands for something that I'm totally against." Another student wrote, "This class has been very stressful. This past month I feel as though I have eaten, breathed, and dreamed this class. It has gone against any kind of class structure that I have ever known. We have struggled with ideas nonceasingly. My mind has screamed, 'Give me a syllabus, tell me what is required of me!' I can't ever remember taking a class that has caused me to think so much."

We, as instructors, can attribute some of the stress and dissension surrounding the issue of democracy to our differing definitions of democracy and notions of how Foxfire and democracy would fit together in the classroom. Although these differences were apparent during our planning sessions, they became clearer during the course of the class. Our disagreements were a source of consternation to the students. As we have reflected on these disagreements, though, we believe it's important for students to see instructors disagree, compromise, argue, compromise again, and take responsibility for outcomes. After all, this is the process of democracy.

Over the short-term period and in subsequent reflection, certain characteristics of democratic processes have emerged as of primary importance to our students. The creation of community may be foremost among these. The feelings of security, belongingness, and acceptance which exemplify community laid the groundwork for the democratic process to take place. With the essence of community, the democratic classroom can evolve as both process and product. The democratic classroom is a goal or product toward which we work involving egalitarian participation, responsibility, and rewards. It is also a process since, in reality, members come and go and are able to participate more or less depending on abilities, awareness, and desires. Community and the democratic classroom both involve the slow process of decision making and the accompanying tests of patience. As this short term progressed, it became clear that our students also felt that in a democratic community or classroom they must have the freedom to participate in restrictions. That is, when creating the most beneficial learning environment, groups are free to create structures and boundaries and operate within those boundaries through disagreement, compromise, and respect.

One difficult lesson for the instructors of this course was learning to let go of privilege and hidden agendas while maintaining the substance of expertise. Our students taught us, through their unflagging persistence and patience, to be responsible for our own full participation as members rather than excusing ourselves as instructors. Maybe we should give ourselves a "B." As one student said in evaluating the class, "This course was a hell-raisin', butt-kicking class. So I justified my grade as a 'B'. Of course I learned too much to be graded—growth is not gradable. A 'B' represents my effort and quality of my work. Thus that is what I put down. Self-evaluation is another form of grading—if I earned it I'm sure I'll get it."

Beyond Short Term

This January course was a microcosm of the work which is necessary and possible in the regular semester-length courses of the college curriculum. A belief in the active involvement of students in the process of their own education requires movement toward a more democratic environment in every class.

However, this belief and its enactment are mediated by certain institutional restraints and methods of operation. We would like to share our experiences and thoughts of these restraints as organized in three categories: the bureaucracy of the institution, pedagogical considerations, and expertise in the disciplines. This discussion arises from our experiences trying to slowly implement more democratic classroom procedures and with acknowledgement of our own difficulty with relinquishing power as teacher-authority in our courses.

First, we fully recognize the need for preparing undergraduates for teaching. But we have found teacher education to be so bound by state and college requirements that much maneuvering is necessary just to fulfill them, not to mention exceeding or meeting individual differences. Education majors can find themselves caught between long lists of courses without time for the intellectual, experiential exploration and reflection of the learning process—the very process teachers should share with and model for children. Certainly all undergraduate majors are in a crunch, but we are concerned here specifically with teachers of children and their preparation as both thinkers and practitioners.

Another consideration of the institution is the same contradiction of grades and evaluation that K-12 institutions grapple with. Rather than asking "What is of value?", we seem to continue to ask only "What is measurable or attainable?" We feel higher education must begin asking what is of value and whether grading the products of students in our courses is getting us any closer to a just education for our students. Perhaps, rather than letting numerical grading scales rule the content and evaluation of courses, we must come to realize that evaluation can take a multiplicity of forms without losing its effectiveness in gauging progress. A growing number of K-12 programs are choosing alternate methods or combinations of methods of evaluation (e.g., portfolios in Kentucky's Education Reform Act); maybe the time has come for higher education to stop pointing its proverbial blaming finger at schools and start more cooperative ventures.

We would like to see schools and departments of education taking the lead in alternative courses and evaluation, which brings us to the consideration of academic rigor. We do not advocate courses of study with no standards or evaluation. The notion here is for rigor to include the experiential as well as the theoretical, the intuitive as well as the analytical, and the creative as well as the reiteration of established routine. Academic rigor must recognize the creative, the imaginative, and the same evidences of cooperation, patience, and reflection we should be watching for in children as learners. In teacher education, it is hypocritical of us to uphold these characteristics of children as learners and deny them in adults as learners. We hear education majors talk of being accused of a lack of rigor. It's imperative that teachers of teachers support their students, guide them to excel, and excel themselves.

Consideration of academic rigor helps to move us to our second category of experiences and thoughts: considerations of institutional constraints on pedagogy. We have come to see the tenure process as a mixed blessing in this context since one may be evaluated by peers with vastly different notions of value for the educational process, value within a discipline, and/or value within pedagogy. The increase in student control, among other changes, of the more democratic classroom may have dire consequences for a faculty member seeking tenure. Returning to the issue of evaluation once again, it's important to judge by the correct criteria. Movement toward a more democratic classroom is no excuse for an abdication of responsibility but neither should it be a burden on the educator's professional progress.

Of course, this issue is larger than just tenure. It concerns what subjects and methodologies have come to be known as acceptable for higher education. We don't want to advocate losing a sense of history or knowledge of the classics, but we'd like to add the concept of truthfulness to the concept of a search for truth. A search for truth implies a search for the right answer, the one true ending to a quest. Truthfulness is the integrity of the search and research and the necessity of the student in this quest, itself. We must pass on the process, not just the product, of the search since none of us will eventually be able to engage in the search ourselves. Hence the importance of appropriate, democratic pedagogy. Learners learn through engagement with the process; if teachers want students to learn division, poetry, conflict resolution, the Electoral College, then students must learn to divide, read and write poetry, resolve conflicts, and elect. Anyone who has ever divided, written poetry, resolved conflicts, or participated in an election knows these are rigorous activities with their own inherent dignity.

Our third category in considering institutional constraints is that of expertise in the disciplines. We do not use the term 'expertise' in reference to that advanced level of knowledge and ability to manipulate the images and methodologies of a field toward which all students work. We use 'expertise' to refer to the expert who sets her/himself apart both from the students of the field and from practitioners of other fields. This expert holds the content of her/his field as separate from other fields and the student as one who must be guided piece by piece through the field as the expert knows it. This person is wary of alternate methods of research, of new developments within the field, and of intrusions from other disciplines. Wary, not skeptical or wakeful about new developments, is absolutely appropriate. Democracy is an interdisciplinary term. It seems to necessitate viewing problems holistically, from a number of different perspectives and through a number of different lenses. Teacher education, existing as it does at the crossroads of the disciplines, must rely on the answers and quests of these disciplines. Movement toward democracy in the education of teachers requires the cooperation of "experts" within the different disciplines, each able and willing to share knowledge and searches with the teachers of children.

How do we deal with these constraints in the regular semester-length courses? For us, there are two questions to keep constantly in mind, questions we often share with student teachers. First, what's important or what is of value, and how can this course be structured so that students learn what is of value? Second, how can the field be opened so that students become active practitioners and learners? A key question is, who's doing all the work here? Or, put differently, who is the most active person here? If we, as instructors, are the most active then we may be the only ones learning; we may have set the situation up to show off our own expertise or as an optimal learning situation for ourselves rather than our students.

In our regular courses, we begin with a tentative syllabus. That is, the course has goals or things which must be accomplished but the route toward those goals is not routine, it can bend with the prior experiences and thoughts of these particular students.

We also begin the semester with much discussion of grading. We acknowledge the necessity of grades for the institution in which we exist and clearly state our responsibility for giving those grades. However, once again, the route toward those grades is not routine. Students have the opportunity to state criteria by which they wish to be judged, to choose those activities which they feel will best show what they have learned, and to write evaluations of their own work. For example, a written essay or research paper is not always the best medium through which to show one's thought process. A presentation, interview, journal, an aesthetic rendering, or whatever, may more clearly show research in progress. The point is to give expression to the process in which one is engaged. Our students do study educational theory and are able to repeat the words of the theorists. What we want them to learn to do, however, is to digest those words, process them, and express their understanding. If that requires a different medium from the research paper or in addition to the paper, so be it. Sooner or later, as teachers, these same students will be asked to express their understandings in the form of classroom structures, lesson plans, and disciplinary procedures.

Our classes generally take the form of seminars and the format of questioning. The students are often asked to take parts of reading assignments, dig for the central concepts, and teach those concepts to the rest of the class. We also ask students to interpret particular readings aesthetically, for example, to construct a paper sculpture to interpret John Dewey's concept of experience or Dewey's notion of the relationship between teacher and student. Students critique each other and themselves while maintaining, with the instructor, a watchful eye for intellectual integrity. We have also asked students to construct learning situations for themselves which require them to learn a skill never tried before through some method beyond using the library. The point is to re-experience the ego involvement, the "failure," the patience, the attempts and more attempts of learning so that when we have discussions in the classroom, they have that recent experience to which they can refer.

Through this alternative research, we hope our students come to know the multitude of ways of experiencing, questioning, responding, learning, and interacting with their world. The children they teach will experience their worlds in ways other than going to a library, even though this is extremely important. But, literacy includes having the experiences and using all the senses so that reading and writing can come alive within one's thinking.

Since orders for texts must be submitted months before the beginning of each semester, adapting them to the particular needs of specific groups of students is problematic. Certain books are important enough to be required course reading; John Dewey's *Experience and Education* is one example. But the usefulness of survey texts can vary widely from one class to another. We have tried to get copies of texts for projected use and have them critiqued by students already acquainted with the subject area discussed. We have also begun to compile articles and chapters for extended reading to give students when they leave a course. It's also helpful for students to read more widely among periodicals on an issue of particular interest. For us, the importance of a text is that it provide that "hook" which joins the student's prior knowledge with the information being presented and sometimes that hook has to come from a broader definition of text which includes people, observations, and the students' writing.

In keeping with the question "Who's doing the work here?", when circumstances call for decisions to be made or arrangements to be done, students are either included or form the leadership. Decisions relating to only one person are made in conference with the instructor; group decisions are made by the group. Arrangements for field trips, etc., are made by the students; students videotape each other; students must arrange for and use some form of technology in presentations. We are responsible for creating a learning environment in which students feel free to succeed and to make mistakes, and to help students learn to connect with people in all walks of life who are willing to help them learn. In other words, to help students see their learning and their education as their own.

These are our fledgling steps toward creating a democratic environment in our classrooms. It's difficult, but important work often is. We feel our students are stronger for their abilities to control and understand their own learning. We feel their students will reap the benefits of having thoughtful, dedicated, challenging teachers.

I wish to thank J. Wilder, M. Rivage-Seul, and our students for joining me in experiencing this class.

REFERENCES

Dewey, John. (1963). *Experience and Education*. New York: Collier Books.

Wigginton, Eliot. (1985). *Sometimes A Shining Moment: The Foxfire Experience*. New York: Anchor Press/Doubleday.

Eleven

The Democratic Process in Teacher Education:
Two Case Studies

Lisa A. Bloom and Mary Jean Ronan Herzog

Western Carolina University is a small state university nestled in a rural, mountainous area of North Carolina. Although Western's teacher education program has included innovative faculty over the years, the core approach is built on a traditional structure that must be changed to meet the needs of preparing teachers for a democratic society. Faculty have been driven by the standards of the North Carolina Department of Public Instruction and National Council for Accreditation of Teacher Education. Colleges of education, like public schools, are "failing because they, too, are products of the factory model of education—authoritarian, dogmatic, and boring, boring, boring."[1] We realize that in spite of the efforts of dedicated, innovative faculty, this criticism can be leveled at our own university. In this chapter, we describe some initiatives recently taken to institute changes in our education programs. We are experimenting with democratic principles in our courses, and the bulk of this chapter is a description of two such efforts. First, however, we offer some reflections on the need for democratic teacher education.

The Need for Democratic Teacher Education

In 1916 Dewey asked, "Why is it, in spite of the fact that teaching by pouring in and learning by passive absorption are universally condemned, that they are still entrenched in practice?"[2] Decades of reform have come and gone, with very little change. Most recently, the 1980s, a decade of celebrated educational reform, ended on a flat note with one overriding consensus. Conservatives and radicals alike agree that public education is in dire need of dramatic change. Finally, in the 1990s, attention is being paid to the systemic, structural problems in public education. For example, Tom Skrtic argues that traditional school organization works against the possibility of true reform, an argument that has persisted throughout the century.[3]

The bureaucratic structure of schools restricts the freedom of teachers and students. Curricula and methods are handed down from above, uniformity is rewarded, and innovation is discouraged. The "effective schools movement" of the 1980s, for example, institutionalized one "effective" way to teach, and prescriptions for following this formula were abundant. This reform movement virtually ignored "the very heart of schooling: the relationship of a teacher to students over subject matter."[4] Schools that buy these narrow prescriptions leave little room for innovation, individuality, experience, or relationships.

The same issues plague institutions of higher education. Curriculum is dictated as authoritarian dogma by state and national accreditation associations. It is assumed that there is a set of "best practices" and the mission of teacher education is to "train" future teachers to act according to formulas and prescriptions. Both undergraduate and graduate students, like their public school counterparts, are encouraged to be passive in their student roles and authoritarian as teachers rather than democratic and reflective.

Teachers teach the way they were taught.[5] Most teachers are products of public schools, colleges, and universities where didactic methods prevail and curriculum is prescribed by some higher authority. Students preparing to become teachers are rarely exposed to democratic participatory models, or they may experience schizophrenic patterns in their programs. While some faculty approach teacher education through democratic practices, students ultimately toe the authoritarian line. They might learn about the value of democratic, progressive approaches in several courses and then take the courses in "assertive discipline" and "effective teacher training" required by the state. These required courses are in direct opposition to democratic participation, and contribute to a cycle of disempowerment of teacher educators, teachers, and students. If lasting reform is to succeed, this cycle needs to be broken. Colleges of teacher education lead in the movement to restructure the traditional bureaucracy, not just by telling teachers what to do but by providing models of democratic pedagogy.

Initiatives for Change

Recently, several faculty at Western Carolina University have recognized that providing these models requires a restructuring of traditional teacher education. Faculty are planning an optional teacher education program that integrates general education, professional education, and teaching experiences. Participants will be involved in public school experiences which are closely tied to seminars conducted by students as well as university and public school faculty. A set of core beliefs that reflect a democratic pedagogy have been developed to form the framework for the optional track.

Western Carolina University has an Office of the Institute for Democracy in Education (IDE) that serves as a network for developing productive relationships among public school teachers and teacher education faculty. A small group of teachers who use democratic practices have been able to use the IDE as a vehicle for sharing their ideas and supporting each other. These initiatives are developing within the traditional structure. In the following section we describe some specific courses as examples of attempts to transform this structure.

Special Education as A Laboratory for Democratic Practices (Lisa Bloom)

Incorporating democratic principles in graduate-level courses in special education has become a priority for me. Students in these courses are typically on-the-job teachers working toward graduate-level certification in special education. The diversity of experiences and teaching roles that these students bring to class makes meeting their needs and covering course content a challenge. Engaging students in course development helps me meet that challenge. In the following section, I will use a course titled "Educational Programs for Students with Mental Retardation" to illustrate this process. My focus will be on the approach of this course rather than its content.

At the beginning of the course, I told the students that though we had some dictated competencies to cover, the course was their course and would be run democratically. I gave students the required state competencies in the form of a traditional syllabus and asked them to prioritize the competencies according to their needs and interests, add issues they would like to address, and indicate how those goals could best be achieved through the semester. I used their suggestions to develop a new syllabus and course schedule. Activities they chose included guest speakers, class discussions of readings, simulations, films, and lecture. Students collaborated in locating guest speakers, films, and readings for the course. Their participation in designing the course objectives and activities helped them develop ownership of the course content.

Students also developed course requirements. They agreed to do outside reading in professional journals on topics that were most relevant to their teaching area, to complete an individual project that addressed a critical need in their area, and to present their projects to the class. In lieu of a final exam, the students decided to undertake a group project that would make a difference in the lives of children with mental retardation.

Examining issues in this course was as much the students' mission as it was mine. Students were responsible for leading class discussions and summarizing the discourse at the end of class. To facilitate this process, I asked students to jot down their ideas for discussion questions as they completed outside readings. I began most classes with a discussion question related to a theme of the course. The students discussed the issues among themselves first and then reported their findings to the group. I then asked them to continue the discussion by posing their own questions and sharing their own stories related to the topic. While I did not keep my own opinions quiet, my opinions were only one voice in the class, and I let students know when their discourse caused me to rethink my own position. Lecture was a very small part of the course and only occurred when students thought they were lacking information that I or another student could provide.

Individual projects also gave students the opportunity to be actively involved with course content. Three examples are included. Sarah, who works with autistic children, explored using computer technology as an alternative mode of communication for her students. Her project included library research and observations of classrooms that were using alternative communication. She produced a videotape and an in-service program for her two classroom assistants so the technology could be implemented in her own classroom. She also received a grant to purchase necessary equipment. Mary Sue's job included assessing young children with developmental delays. She researched play-based assessment, a new trend in preschool assessment. Mary Sue reviewed current research and produced a videotape which demonstrated a play-based assessment and illustrated its value over more traditional assessment. She used this videotape within her organization to teach other workers to use this new form of assessment. Elizabeth, a high school teacher for students with moderate mental retardation, interviewed various agencies, reviewed current literature, and developed a program to assist her students to make a successful transition from high school to adult life. This type of program was practically nonexistent in the local high school, and special education teachers worked in isolation from community agencies and resources prior to Elizabeth's work.

Each project was based on the individual experiences and needs of the students and represented a current issue in special education. A couple of students initially thought that it would be much easier for them if I would assign a project. Choosing a project required an examination of the current literature and an analysis of each student's professional situation to determine a need. Choosing their own projects forced students to examine and identify the critical issues in their own area.

The group project was probably the most satisfying aspect of the class. As a result of a discussion, the students chose a project that would make a difference in the community instead of a final exam. In an attempt to contribute to the prevention of mild mental retardation in the area, we decided to produce a booklet for parents and their newborns. The booklet was designed to encourage parents to stimulate the language and cognitive development of their children.

The students first called several hospitals, health departments, and other agencies to determine if there was a need for the booklet. Students researched the content, wrote the the booklet in clear language, and field-tested it with two mothers. They made presentations to the local Rotary, Optimist, Lions, and Kiwanis clubs. Each organization made a contribution to the printing of the booklet. They also presented the booklet to the local hospital and county health department and received an overwhelmingly positive response. The hospital is currently giving a copy to each new mother in the community and the health department adopted the booklet to use with their "at risk" program for low income mothers. Even though the course is over, students are still working to have the booklet distributed to hospitals and health departments throughout the state.

What did the students gain from this project? Aside from knowledge of prevention of mental retardation, they also learned how to do a professional presentation and to interact with the community to identify problems and solutions. But most importantly, as one student commented, "This was the first time I really felt like a professional." The consensus of the group was that the best part of completing the project was that it had a purpose beyond fulfilling course requirements. This idea is not new. One of the core principles of the Foxfire approach developed by Elliot Wigginton is that there must be an audience beyond the teacher for student work.[6] An audience affirms that the work is important and worth doing. Additionally, the need for teachers to be recognized as professionals and have the respect of the community is emphasized in much of the current literature.[7]

The group and individual projects gave students the chance to apply current research to their own situations to benefit themselves and their students. In an examination of the *Handbook of Research on Teaching*, Smith and Lytle found that out of 35 research reviews none were written by school teachers.[8] The questions of teachers and the interpretive frames they use to understand and improve their own class practice are missing. These authors suggest that one approach to bridging the theory-practice gap is to encourage teachers to research questions that are important to them, that is, to become teacher-researchers. By giving students choices on projects that related to their interests and needs, research becomes meaningful.

At the end of this course, students agreed they had learned more from the course than they had anticipated. Most importantly, students realized that using a participatory approach in their own teaching situations would help foster independence in their special-needs students regardless of age or severity of disability. They appreciated their involvement in designing the course and the opportunity to concentrate on relevant projects and readings. One student commented that it was the first time she was actually interested in completing outside reading. They were very pleased with the results of the group project and hoped that efforts to have the booklet distributed beyond the immediate county would continue even though the course was over. Students also developed professional relationships with each other that would continue well beyond the end of the semester. Several students were concerned about their grade (before grade reports) because of the lack of tests and required assignments. In that sense, they felt I should provide a little more structure for future classes. They suggested that I impose deadlines and grading criteria. I still struggle with this notion.

Curriculum Course as A Laboratory for Democratic Practices (Mary Jean Ronan Herzog)

The majority of the students who take my curriculum course are teachers who are enrolled in Masters degree programs. As a professional studies requirement, it serves students in all certification areas in education. It also draws some students from counseling, nursing, speech pathology, and higher education.

I approach this course from a critical perspective and use the concepts of democracy, experience, and community as central themes. The students undertake an in-depth project based on their interests, needs, and expertise. Some students have developed qualitative research projects that closely connect graduate study with teaching practice. In a couple of cases, students and I expanded original class projects into larger research projects that I have been able to include in my other classes to illustrate concepts and principles. The following discussion of one such class project will illustrate this process.

A graduate student, Peter Freer, was teaching fifth grade at the time he enrolled in the class. For his project, he studied democratic theory and applied it in his classroom. He had been experimenting with experiential practices and set his class up as a microsociety. One of the central features of his classroom became democratic participation. His students became involved in developing the class structure, including revised disciplinary policies. After Peter finished the course, we expanded his class project into an ethnographic study examining student and teacher perceptions and attitudes about their classroom experiences. The data collection procedures that I used included individual interviews with Peter, focus group interviews with his students, and classroom observations. Later, another graduate student conducted classroom observations in Peter's class as part of a qualitative study on democratic classrooms. That student is now a first-year teacher of high school English and is attempting to apply these principles in his own classroom. So the networks develop.

In my courses, I now use the ethnography of Peter's class to illustrate the application of democratic theory. I present the case study of Peter's class to my students, show a videotape of the focus group interview of the fifth graders, and have Peter as a guest speaker. He invites my students to visit his class, and they often do. Several of them have implemented democratic practices in their own classes. The case study that I present to my classes is a description of four aspects of Peter's class: the teacher, the classroom and curriculum, discipline, and the students' feelings about their experiences.

Case Study of A Democratic Fifth-Grade Class

The Teacher. Peter Freer started teaching with a traditional perspective but, over the six years of his career, has evolved to a non-traditional, democratic, experiential approach. His day-to-day teaching experiences influenced his change as did his graduate program, particularly through readings of John Dewey. Peter also said that George Wood's chapter in a curriculum text[9] that we use for the class was also very influential.

Peter is not a typical teacher. He teaches martial arts classes after school. He drives a motorcycle, wears a pony tail, and has been known to break bricks with his hands. He works on the weekends as a "security advisor" (i.e., a bouncer), in a nightclub. He is completing a Masters' degree in intermediate education and says he enjoys reading the works of Krishnamurti, the mystic Indian poet. He characterizes himself as an anarchist. He spent his early childhood in Millbrook, New York, in a community characterized by the cultural and social revolution of the 1960s. Both of his parents are teachers. He moved to the Appalachian mountains of North Carolina when he was an adolescent and has been teaching middle school for six years.

The Classroom and the Curriculum. Peter's self-contained fifth-grade classroom is in one section of a pod in an open-structure school. Each classroom is separated from the others around it by bookshelves and other partitions. In Mr. Freer's class the desks are sometimes in rows, grouped for projects, or pushed back to make more room to sit on the floor. "Creativity, insight, intelligence" are the reminders on the bulletin board at the front of the room. There is a plethora of home-made objects around the room: a lifesized mummy, flags of different countries and states, a bracelet factory, a bank, and a space-ship.

Peter uses the *North Carolina Standard Course of Study* as a tool of freedom and guidance. It prescribes content areas, skills, and processes but does not dictate methods, materials, timing, or style. He described the state curriculum requirements to the students at the beginning of the year, and they discussed ways in which they might be able to meet those requirements. Ultimately, they did so through an integrated curriculum which was developed as a collaborative effort between the teacher and students. The curriculum was not driven by textbooks, schedules, or standardized tests.

The classroom was organized as a "micro-society" in which students developed a classroom government including a constitution and elected officers. They constructed states with fictional histories patterned after the United States. The development of the states covered many content and skill areas in addition to politics and history. For example, the students learned about the history of energy as the society progressed from wood burning to coal burning to electricity. They learned mathematics by measuring and constructing buildings out of corrugated cardboard. Businesses were included in the microsociety; groups of students in the class created a comic book company, a bank, two bakeries, a newspaper and a television station. They printed their own currency. It became so realistic that some students surreptitiously created a scam business that the class had to stop.

During the year, the class decided on a project that reached out to the community outside of the classroom. They built a shelter on the school's nature trail. They had to plan carefully and through the process they learned about measuring area and perimeter and how to square the sides of the building. They worked as a cooperative group and organized landscaping, water, building, and clean-up crews. The end product, the shelter, was a source of pride and accomplishment for all of the students.

Classroom Discipline. Since Peter wanted the classroom to be a total learning experience, discipline policies had to be integrated with curriculum, rather than separate and isolated. This required student participation in developing and administering classroom discipline policies and procedures. During the school year, the students tried four different disciplinary systems.

1. Assertive Discipline—The students initially selected a familiar system, Assertive Discipline.[10] It is commonly used in schools in the region; in fact, it is quite popular throughout the nation. Assertive Discipline is a behavioral approach that uses increasingly severe consequences as punishments for misbehavior. Although there are variations, consequences typically progress as follows: The student's name is written on the board; check marks are placed next to the student's name for additional infractions; the student is sent to another teacher's room after maximum check marks are reached; next, the student is sent to the principal's office; and finally a phone call is made to the parents. Classes receive rewards such as a party, a movie, or candy for following class rules and behaving in the prescribed ways.

2. Modified Assertive Discipline—The class used Assertive Discipline for a month before becoming dissatisfied with it. They felt that it did not help them accomplish their main goal of behaving responsibly. They did not like putting names on the board and noticed that the same names were always there. They voted to modify the system by placing color strips on the culprit's desk. Soon, however, they came to realize that they preferred a system not tied to external rewards.

3. Military Discipline—Halfway through the year, a guest speaker from the Coast Guard visited the class and talked about military discipline. The children thought this sounded great and decided to institute a military style discipline program. In describing this approach, Mr. Freer said that the children would:

> stand at attention when I came into the room and would not sit until I told them they could be seated. They would not approach my desk unless they had permission to approach. We ate square meals. We did not sit down in the cafeteria until I told them they could sit. The other teachers said that they were the most well-behaved class in the school.

About two weeks into the military approach, the children got tired of acting like robots. They decided that it did not allow them the freedom to think for themselves.

4. Peer Review—During experimentation with the three approaches described above, Peter submerged his own preferences to those of the children. He did not particularly like any of their choices, but felt that the students would learn more by developing their own system. The final approach, he said, seemed to evolve as a higher ethical and intellectual choice. Peter and the students discussed the reward and punishment basis of the systems that they had tried and moved toward one in which the teacher was not the central authority figure in the classroom. A peer review approach was their choice. It is based on real-life experiences and discussion of the positive actions and negative behaviors of individual children. To be fair and effective, it must be carefully guided by the teacher.

During class meeting time, usually on Fridays, each child stands in front of the class and receives feedback about their behavior, attitude, and contribution to the class. Both students and teacher give suggestions to the child under review. The goal is to help bring students to their own conclusions. The following example will illustrate the process:

Bobby was excessively aggressive on the ballfield during recess, and the other students did not like the way he yelled at them. The peer review session started with students complimenting him for showing improvement but saying that he should stop yelling. Some of them talked about how it made them feel when he yelled at them. Others suggested that he be more careful, pointing out how he might feel if he were in their shoes. One student recommended that he chew gum to relieve his stress. Peter told a story about his own brother who was aggressive and intolerant. His point was that it was with positive support that players will improve. The students agreed that criticism only makes you play worse. As I observed the peer review sessions, I was struck by the openness and concern displayed by the students.

Young people are often assumed to lack empathy and the ability to take the perspectives of others. Schools are often based on a belief that they have to have external punishment and reward systems to motivate students. The students in Peter's class told me about the peer review approach and their feelings toward it. Their reasoning was quite sophisticated, and negates the common view that children are incapable of making decisions based on critical thinking and the higher good. We collected the following comments from Peter's students during a focus group interview. These comments are their responses to the question, "Have you learned anything about yourself from the peer review approach?"

> **Sam:** We learn to discipline ourselves. It really means something. It teaches us how it is in the real society.
>
> **George:** At first when you have to get in front of the class, you're kind of nervous. Like going to the doctor. You don't really want to go, but you know you have to, and it's good for you.
>
> **Kirrin:** In our class we get to make decisions not only for ourselves but for the others around us.
>
> **Nathan:** Our peer review approach taught me that choices are hard to make and you have to think about them before you blurt out your ideas.
>
> **Betsy:** We tried punishments and rewards and neither worked. After awhile no one cares about either.
>
> **Adam:** When you're good so you can get candy or something, you're being good for the wrong motivation.
>
> **Katie:** Most classes are dictatorships more than they are democracies.

The students also gave us advice for prospective teachers:

> **Dennis:** Teachers should let the students have a voice in planning what's going to happen in the classroom.
>
> **Theresa:** If teachers explained the math lesson instead of just telling you to go to your desk and do it, kids wouldn't get in so much trouble.
>
> **Nancy:** I like it when teachers listen.

Reflections on Teaching and Learning

Peter considers his classroom an environment of possibility. He says that if he were not allowed to teach the way he does, he probably would not continue teaching in public school. He said, "It would not make sense to me to sit in a classroom and read to children and have them answer questions out of the book. It is utter stupidity to carry that kind of teaching on. It's backward. I remember doing it and getting very little out of it." Peter says that he is motivated by having fun and making learning fun for the students. If they are learning, his work is kept to a minimum. He said that the students just keep on learning and all he has to do is provoke or provide an atmosphere, an environment conducive to learning. He said,

> I think it's turned out to be progressive and creative. Creativity is like happiness. It comes uninvited. We just let it happen by providing an environment in which the kids could make it happen. My job is not to try and create creativity. It is just to provide an environment in which it is possible for it to happen.

Peter takes an unusual approach within a traditional school environment. His story is not meant to be a prescription or formula. It is not about technique. He rejects the standardization that has been imposed on teaching in small, rural schools as if they are the fastfood restaurants littering the countryside.

This case study started as a graduate class project and moved beyond the confines of the semester. In my courses, I try to make the principles of experience, democracy, and community a part of the life of my classes as well as issues for students to study. Teachers who are interested in applying these principles in their own classes have started to forge networks. They initially become acquainted through graduate classes, then they visit each others' classrooms, and develop relationships and collaborations. For example, several graduate students from several semesters, including Peter, recently participated on a design team that developed a proposal for a restructured system of schools in the region. As in Lisa's courses, helping students develop relevant projects, informed by theory and designed to grapple with authentic problems, makes their projects inherently meaningful.

Democratic Pedagogy in the Undergraduate Curriculum

Using a democratic pedagogy is more challenging at the undergraduate level than at the graduate level. Short class periods and large classes contribute to the difficulty. Because undergraduate students have had little experience with educational decision making, we find that they are initially uncomfortable making choices in their education, and actively participating in class. Typically, their college and public school experiences so far have involved few choices, little if no involvement in planning the curriculum, dependency on faculty approval and grades, and irrelevance of what they hear in lectures to what they have experienced in public school classrooms. Additionally, they often perceive faculty-student relationships as "we" versus "they" relationships. Although each undergraduate class has a handful of students who are determined to be actively involved, many seem to be oriented toward grades and course requirements rather than course content. Because of their experiences they seem to prefer passively listening to lectures rather than actively being involved in class issues. If given a choice, they prefer multiple choice exams over essays.

It is easy for us to take a "blame the victim" attitude, but we have to realize that it takes time and constructive experience with participatory education for students to develop trust in the process. Some of the ways we are trying to incorporate democratic practices within the traditional structures are similar to the approaches we take with our graduate classes. These include class procedures structured to promote active discussion and participation,[11] choices on group or individual projects,[12] choices about ways to meet class requirements, and alternative approaches to evaluation (including self-evaluation). To illustrate, we will include examples of democratic practices from each of our undergraduate classes.

In their foundations of education course, I gave a simulation assignment that required students to develop a "New American School." In doing so, they had to deal with the contrast between authoritarian and democratic governance. They read about and debated the issues in small groups and as a whole class. They incorporated their reflections from their field experiences into the discussions. The majority of the students eventually decided that a democratic approach is more humane and would probably be more effective but they also realized that they were facing a long, uphill battle to achieve democratic ·schools.

In my undergraduate courses in special education, like graduate courses, I give students the opportunity to develop proposals for group or individual projects that relate to course objectives. One of the requirements for the project is that they identify someone who will benefit from it beside themselves. Compared to graduate students, undergraduate students are at a disadvantage in finding an audience for their work because they are not closely tied to a school system. But by asking students to identify a purpose for a project, undergraduate students have developed links with community agencies, parent groups, regular and special education teachers, etc. For example, one small group of students researched recreation and leisure activities for adults with mental retardation. Their resources included the library and several community agencies. As part of the project, they organized several recreational activities throughout the semester for adults with mental retardation in the community and students at the university. This project benefited the community and gave students the opportunity to gain experience with adults with disabilities.

We also encourage active involvement by asking students to determine the number of tests (if any), the alternatives to tests, to assist in locating guest speakers, etc. We ask students to engage in problem-solving when the need arises. For example, if class attendance starts to dwindle, the problem is presented, and students generate the solution. Once students learn that their voices are heard, they use them more often, especially during class discussions.

To encourage self-evaluation, we ask students to develop criteria for grading their projects and to evaluate their projects based on their own criteria. We find their criteria are for the most part more stringent than our own, and the number of "tell me what you want" comments have diminished. Honest self-evaluation, although difficult, leads to reflection and growth.

We also link undergraduate students with schoolteachers who are using democratic practices so that they can see that we are not merely eccentric or ideological. We think that having undergraduate students actually experience the beauty of a democratic classroom will help them to change their notions of teaching. This is difficult because the field assignment process involves placement of over 400 students each semester. We have no control over the quality of the placements. A few students are placed with superb democratic teachers; others are placed with ineffective and authoritarian teachers. To capitalize on the learning that can result from the former, we use videotapes of classrooms and bring those teachers into the class to talk about the issues. Our students then have the opportunity to use these teachers as resources in doing their class projects.

By giving undergraduate students a voice, they become more comfortable with active participation in discussions and decision making. By involving students in course development they become more invested in the learning process. By giving students choices on projects and helping them make connect with democratic teachers, they begin to develop experiences from which to construct meaning.

Conclusion

These struggles with democratic pedagogy strengthen our understanding of the need for an alternative to the traditional teacher education program. As we experiment with these practices, we are building a body of knowledge and, at the same time, a case for restructuring teacher education. We try to structure our classes to foster a sense of community that involves developing relationships within the class and dealing with class problems (e.g., class attendance) democratically. As students begin to realize they have a voice and they develop a sense of trust, they become more intrinsically motivated. As Beyer

and Wood suggest, to be comfortable with participation you must have experience with it.[13]

At the heart of it, we are trying to create a new story for teachers and
prospective teachers. We are trying to get our students to erase the blackboards
of their minds that prescribe teaching as "standing in front of students in rows
of desks, giving instructions, using textbooks and worksheets, and being in
control." The new story portrays teaching and learning as an active, participatory process that depends on building relationships, developing classrooms as
communities, and encouraging individuality, expression, and ultimately liberation.

NOTES

1. Edward B. Fiske. *Smart Schools, Smart Kids* (New York: Simon and Shuster,
1991), p. 256.

2. John Dewey. *Democracy and Education* (New York: Macmillan, 1916), p. 89.

3. Tom Skrtic. *Behind Special Education: A Critical Analysis of Professional
Culture and School Organization* (Colorado: Love Publishing Co., 1991).

4. Larry Cuban, "Please, No More Facts: Just Better Teaching," *Education Week*
(March 11, 1992), p. 30.

5. Mary M. Kennedy, "Some Surprising Findings on How Teachers Learn to
Teach," *Educational Leadership*, 49:3 (November, 1991), p. 16.

6. Elliot Wigginton, "Foxfire Grows Up," *Harvard Educational Review*, 59:1.

7. See, for example, John L. Goodlad, "Why We Need a Complete Redesign of
Teacher Education," *Educational Leadership*, 49:3 (November, 1991) and Gene I.
Maeroff, *The Empowerment of Teachers: Overcoming the Crisis in Confidence*, (New
York: Teachers College Press, 1988).

8. Marilyn Cochran-Smith and Susan Lytle, Research on "Teaching and Teacher
Research: The Issues that Divide," *Educational Researcher*, 19:2 (March, 1990).

9. George Wood, "Democracy and the Curriculum," in Landon E. Beyer and
Michael W. Apple, Eds., *The Curriculum: Problems, Politics, and Possibilities* (New
York: SUNY, 1988), pp. 166-190.

10. Lee Canter, "Let the Educator Beware: A Response to Curwin and Mendler,"
Educational Leadership, 46, (1988).

11. See, for example, Ira Shor and Paulo Freire, *A Pedagogy for Liberation:
Dialogues on Transforming Education* (Massachusetts: Bergin and Garvey, 1987), pp.
39-44.

12. See, for example, Elliot Wigginton, "Foxfire Grows Up," *Harvard Educational Review*, 59:1.

13. Landon E. Beyer and George H. Wood, "Critical Inquiry and Moral Action in Education," *Educational Theory*, 36:1, (Winter, 1986).

Twelve

Skin-Game:
Race and Racism in Teaching and Teacher Education

William Ayers

NOTE: A skin-game is a swindling game or a trick—an act of exploitation based on fraud. Skin—our covering, our surface—separates as well as connects inner from outer. More specifically, it is the limiting layer of our beings—limiting in a precise physical sense, and constraining in a much more transcendent sense. Indeed, when W.E.B. DuBois proclaimed in 1903 that "the problem of the Twentieth Century is the problem of the color line," he was speaking of skin. Color, race—yes, skin—has proved to be a complex social invention, the most enduring focus of human pain and suffering in our time. And it shows no sign of letting up.

Will America educate African-American youngsters?

"Boyz 'N The Hood," John Singleton's stark portrait of growing up black in urban America, opens in death and school. Four youngsters detour from their regular morning route to visit the site of last night's slaying—up a street marked "one way," down an alley proclaiming "wrong way," under the yellow police tape signalling the scene of the crime.
"What happened?" asks one of the kids, wide-eyed.
"Somebody got smoked, stupid."
"At least I know my times tables."
A precocious discussion follows concerning the separation of plasma from blood cells as the scene fades to the classroom. Black history and motivational posters share the walls with children's paintings: a casket, a police

helicopter, an L.A. squad car. The teacher—white, well-meaning, a bit har-ried—is relating the Thanksgiving myth and the "unity of the Indians, excuse me, Native Americans, and the European settlers." She's modern, "progres-sive," struggling to find the more respectful phrase, trying to include the chil-dren's history and their own ideas in her lessons. When Tre Stiles interrupts the class, she asks him if he'd like to come up and lead the class. She's "student-centered."

"Yea, I can do that." Tre is confident.

"Come on up," she urges. "Instruct us. What will be the basis of your lec-ture?" She sees Tre as somewhat out of line, arrogant, and her voice drips sar-casm.

"Huh?"

"What will you tell us about?"

Tre teaches that Africa is the birthplace of humanity, and that African-Americans have a proud history. Within minutes he is involved in a fistfight with a classmate, and Tre is suspended from school—like thousands of other African-American males in America every day. As he makes his way slowly home, we hear the teacher lecturing his mother over the phone. Again the voice, patronizing, pseudo-scientific, slightly harassed. "He's highly intelli-gent; he has an enormous vocabulary. But he has a very bad temper that makes it very hard for him to interact with his peers." And then the inevitable ques-tions: "Are there any problems at home?" "Are you employed?" "Then you are educated?"

Tre's mother is furious, of course, though she's heard it all before, and she is determined not to let Tre become a victim. The teacher is annoyed. They are speaking past each other over a yawning chasm, and at the base of that chasm is the question of whether America values all of its children.

Will America educate African-American youngsters?

The answer depends in part on the relationship between school and soci-ety, and on the nature of society itself. Schools are creations of societies, and they are shaped in powerful ways by the forces that spawn them.

One can understand South Africa, for example, by looking closely at its schools—stratified along racial lines, strictly segregated, a few challenging and highly successful places for the children of the white rulers, a mass of failing sites for those who work the mines and mills and live in the shanty-towns. Or one can understand the intricacies of apartheid in the larger society, and deduce from that how the schools must look and function.

Societies, of course, are dynamic and so are schools. There is no fixed, absolute relationship between them. In fact, precisely because schools are insti-tutions that reflect social norms and practices, and because they are places where large numbers of people gather, they are often sites of conflict and call for reform or revolution in the larger society. Schools are a part of any given social order, and schools are natural venues for resistance and popular struggles against the status quo.

American schools serve a society stratified by race, a society with identifiable structures of privilege and oppression based on race, and the schools both reflect and serve that stratification. Chicago schools, for example (which are 12 percent white, 15 percent Latino, and 73 percent African-American), serve 80 percent of the bilingual youngsters and over half of the poorest children in Illinois. Chicago schools need more resources but receive less: Chicago can raise only $1,447 per student on its tax base, less than half the $3,208 raised by an average suburban district and considerably less than all-white districts like Lake Forest ($10,000) or Rosemont ($12,000). Sixty-eight per cent of Chicago students are poor enough to qualify for federal reduced or free lunch programs, and yet state aid is based on the erroneous notion that 22.5 percent of Chicago kids are poor. When former governor James Thompson called Chicago's schools "a black hole," his excited rhetoric stirred the full range of racial justifications and social tensions.

Chicago schools, of course, are in terrible shape. The failure is bought and paid for. About 35,000 students out of a population of 440,000 are absent on any given day, while 1,000 teachers (4 percent) are absent every day. Thousands of students are serving suspensions on an average day. Over several years between 40 percent and 50 percent of the total students who entered high schools in Chicago dropped out.

The average child is functionally illiterate by the age of 16 in Chicago, one of the richest cities in the world. And that average child is African-American and poor. For each year spent in our schools, that child's achievement scores fall relative to his or her white and affluent counterparts. In other words, in Illinois we have created what amounts to two parallel school systems—one privileged, stable, effective, and largely white; the other ineffective, disabled, chaotic, starved for resources and disadvantaged in countless ways, and largely African-American. The system accomplishes massive failure for African-American youngsters alongside an equal and opposite success for students who are white and middle-class. What can justify this structure? To think in some covert or subtle or indirect way that African-Americans are somehow not fully worthy is to be able to live with this outrage in our midst.

Will America educate African-American youngsters?

Andrew Hacker (1992a) offers his white college students a weird and provocative challenge: Say it turns out that a terrible mistake was made, and that you were to have been born exactly as you are, but with one difference—you are black. How much monetary compensation would you deserve? Answers range from hundreds of millions of dollars a year to hundreds of thousands, but no one says they deserve nothing. In other words, whites know that they benefit from being white; they also know that black people have suffered and continue to suffer due to inequities imposed upon them by a white-dominated society.

What is seldom talked about, but is as real and as serious, is that white people increasingly regard the presence of African-Americans in society as completely lacking in value. Africans were kidnapped, brought to America, and sold as chattel because whites were willing to do anything to acquire the cheap labor they desperately wanted and needed. Following emancipation and for over a century, African-Americans held a solid if inferior place in the American workforce. Poorly paid, last hired and first fired, continuing to "predominate in those occupations that in a slave society would be reserved for slaves" (Hacker, 1992b, p.30), African-American labor power still had real value. Today there is a new reality and a new message: The economy has changed, new waves of immigrants have moved into the economic margins, and black people have no value whatsoever in the eyes of the ruling group. "It is bad enough," says Hacker, "to suffer slavery, segregation, and discrimination. It is even worse to know that most of your fellow citizens would feel a lot happier if you simply disappeared" (Hacker, 1992b, p. 30).

Nowhere is this lack of valuing and this forced invisibility more apparent than in the schools. In many schools nothing about the presence of African-American youngsters is considered valuable or important. Rather, that presence is always a problem, a deficit, an obstacle. Lillian Weber (1992) claims that the presence of black youth "is looked at fearfully, as something that is an encumbrance, a problem, one that one would wish to discard, to get rid of . . ." (p. 1). Weber is discussing the question of black or multicultural curriculum but she finds that curriculum questions must be considered in the context of valuing. She points out that not only are African-American youngsters found to be lacking in value but that there is a strong message that they will never become valuable or contributing adults either: "Where there is *no* conception at all that they are *going* to be contributing to the society or finding *any* place of membership in the society, I have to ask, what *is* the role of the school, and even, if there *is* any?" (p. 2).

Three large problems interface and feed this crisis of valuing. The first is jobs, productive work, labor that is intimately tied to a sense of positive identity and self. Without some hope for a productive future, the dignity of work, and the ability to contribute, how can young people make sense out of school and the work of school? If the connection for youngsters between school and a better tomorrow has been broken—if, for example, a sizable group of kids, say five or ten in a class of 30, can point to a friend or relative who endured all the demands of school and is still not making it—how can educators in good faith encourage participation? How can motivational posters of Michael Jordan or heroic pictures of Martin Luther King, Jr. make a difference?

Second is the premise of school based on deficiency, which, besides being pedagogically unsound, forces people to redefine themselves in negative terms in the struggle for educational resources. Education is offered after (and on the basis of) degrading and dangerous generalizations. How can families and youngsters resist this degradation? How can they fight for an education that allows them to name both their hopes and aspirations as well as the obstacle to their freedom?

Third is the problem of creating schools and classrooms that nurture and challenge the wide range of youngsters who actually appear at the classroom door. Rigid, unresponsive classrooms hurt all children, and are disastrous for poor, immigrant, and African-American children. How can educators create classrooms where all youngsters are visible, honored, and valued? How can we build environments that embody high expectations and still respond to the real needs of children? How do we break the pervasive cultural myth that success is linked to neighborhood conditions and family situations rather than to classroom response to students' circumstances?

Chicago has held a long tradition of blaming children and families for the collapse of the schools. In an oft-quoted aside, the superintendent of the Chicago Public Schools defended his office from criticism in 1987 by noting that "When you put garbage into a system, you get garbage out." He was referring, of course, to black children.

Will America educate African-American youngsters?

At the center of John Dewey's thought was a particular idea of democracy and moral action. To Dewey the world was a place without certainty, without absolutes. He spoke of the unity of knowledge—he had in mind that knowing is inseparable from doing, that we create values as we live and as we act on our own choices. For Dewey all the old dualisms were not only bad philosophy, they were socially dangerous: mind/body, theory/practice, individual/collective. He saw the individual as a distinctly social being, and society as a dynamic collection of individuals. While there are no guarantees, while there is always uncertainty, contingency, and the possibility of peril just ahead, Dewey urges us to do the best we can *given what we know*.

We know, for example, that racism is a dagger at the heart of our society. Knowing requires action. There is no greater challenge for those who claim to be progressive or democratic than to confront and fight against the structures of privilege and oppression based on race that characterize our society, our schools, and the entire social enterprise of schooling, even as we create classrooms of hope and possibility, critique, and challenge for all youngsters.

The question confronting democratic educators is this: How can education for democracy exist without a direct and persistent challenge to the structures of racism at the center of society? The question for progressive educators is the same: What progress can we hope to achieve unless we confront and overturn the structures that distort and twist whatever might be hopeful in our schools? And for teacher educators those questions echo in a third: How shall we teach teachers in such a way that they are not only aware of ethical issues such as equity and justice, but that they are prepared to act in light of them? How shall we prepare teachers for effective action in urban schools?

Teacher education is in large part a failed enterprise. Teacher education is, of course, part of the apparatus and establishment of schooling, part of the certification mill, and so it is deeply implicated in school failure. Half of the graduates of teacher education programs leave within the first five years of teaching. Somehow the obvious message is dodged and never reverts to colleges of education. Furthermore, the hundred largest school districts in the United States—through a series of temporary certifications and adjunct arrangements—employ teachers trained from somewhere other than colleges of education. In other words, districts that are largely poor, African-American, Latino, and immigrant are facing a catastrophic shortage of teachers while affluent and white district are not. Again, the responsibility of teacher educators and teacher education programs is being shirked.

I teach a seminar that meets at 3:00 P.M. every Wednesday—35 undergraduates, average age 22, average background white ethnic, maybe second generation in America, dominant gender female. These folks work hard all week as student-teachers, several hold down jobs in the evenings and on weekends, and all are pretty stretched out. They come to me tired, crabby, resistant.

This is what I see when I come through the door: chairs with swivel formica desk tops bolted three and four together, an imposing gray metal teacher's desk, paint crumbling from walls, dirty windows, and the gray of the city beyond. And also this: The two men in the group are as far apart as two people can get, Mike 'way in the back squeezed into the far corner, Barry in the front, his seat scooted just a bit in front of all the others. And along the left-hand wall are the five African-American students, close together in what looks like a deliberate formation, perhaps a protective shield.

The class is called "Teaching Children of Various Cultures, Backgrounds, and Conditions," a clumsy name for an indistinct and sloppy idea. Somewhere in some committee a compromise was struck, and this class is the result.

One day I put on the board, "In my classroom we _____ differences," and ask them to fill in the blank. Someone says "respect," another "tolerate," and a third "understand." No one says "learn from," "investigate," certainly not "celebrate." I want to challenge these future teachers to think about culture, to open up to differences, to examine their own lives and beliefs in light of a deep encounter with the complexity of other people's lives. So where do I go from here?

One of the great myths of teaching is the idea that there is one center of the classroom. Teachers often act as if there is only one true story of classroom life, with 30 or so misinterpretations. In reality more than 30 true stories are being played out simultaneously and interactively in any given classroom. Classrooms are yeasty places, with teachers spending much unnecessary energy punching down the rising mass. While it can be uncomfortable acknowledging all the different centers of classroom life, I've been carried out of teaching deadends on many occasions by students pursuing their own important questions:

"But some differences are just too sad, too horrible. Why would we even pretend to celebrate them?" Linda is Italian-American, working-class, refreshingly iconoclastic and blunt, always willing to step out on a limb.

"Like what?" asks Karen, challenging. Karen is African-American, sharp, articulate, engaged. She has a fine (some would say hyper-sensitive) antenna for injustice, and she can detect a racist impulse before it can gather a real head of steam. "Like what?"

"Well, like say a kid's retarded, or has Down's syndrome, or is in a wheelchair. That's different. But it's horrible."

"Why?" ask Karen.

"Would you want to be retarded?"

"A lot of people think I am, " Karen smirks. General laughter. "But seriously, is it horrible to the kid? I mean, it's just the way he is. What may be horrible is how the rest of us react to the way he is. But maybe being him isn't so bad."

So you're in a wheelchair. You can get around, do a lot, make things happen. And then you need to go downtown, and you go to the bus, and no way. Because the definition of "rider" or "citizen" or "public" as far as the bus service is concerned only includes human beings who walk on two legs. No one else counts. Now that's horrible.

No, no, no! Yes, yes! People are talking all at once and I'm watching 10 or 12 disconnected parts of conversation. Suddenly Karen pulls the scattered pieces back together, speaking loud, above the others: "Ok, ok. But what I'm saying is, how people treat me *because I'm black* is horrible—how people treat me, see?—but being black is not the bad part. *Being* black is cool, being treated a certain way is shitty. See?"

An awkward silence. "That's stupid." It's Linda again. "Because being black is not like being in a wheelchair."

"It might be worse," says Yolanda quietly, flanking Karen. "It might be that it's more complete, more total what other people think."

Another day I say, "come close." I try to look a little conspiratorial, and so I peer over the top of my glasses as I gesture with my hand to pull the circle of chairs tighter together. "Come close," I repeat, "because we're going to talk about something that is difficult and often troubling and it will help if we are able to look into one another's eyes and not raise our voices."

"Is racism a problem?" I ask the question and everyone squirms. Even me.

Is racism evident in the schools? In this city? In our families? Where does it come from? How do you deal with it?

"Well, I saw David Duke on TV," says Judy. "And he's unbelievable." Is he an example of racism? Is he a racist?

"Sure," says Terry. "People are prejudiced and that's a problem everywhere. Duke is extreme."

Is prejudice the same thing as racism?

Well. Yes and no. "No." Yolanda is speaking authoritatively. "No, because racism includes prejudice, but it's more. It's like policies and programs that discriminate—that's a big part of it."

"That's in the old days," said Jennifer. "That's not part of today."

No?!?

I pull out a thick packet of articles about hate crimes and racist incidents in a one-month period from newspapers across the United States. The packet has been assembled by the National Coalition of Advocates for Students, and leafing through it is chilling: "Slur Mars Meeting on Racism," "White Supremacist Groups on the Rise," "Third Youth Attacked, Painted by White Teenagers in NY." The cumulative effect leaves some students looking embarrassed, some dulled, others enraged. The expressions—like so much else— split along racial lines.

I pass around an article from the *Chicago Tribune*, "Race Still an Issue." The article notes that 82 percent of African-Americans consider discrimination based on race a problem, while 47 percent of whites think that it is not a problem.

Why is that?

We shift to men and women—and the terrain feels easier. "My husband doesn't think sexism is a problem," says Judy, "because nobody whistles at him or threatens him. I know it's a problem." A tentative bridge is being built.

On this tough urban campus, there is very limited security for students at night. It took me a while to notice, but women wait for one another in order to walk to the parking lots or the train. Women don't go out alone, but the men disperse casually—in their own time—without a thought. Here is a simple case of stratification (in this case based on gender), of structures of privilege and oppression that nobody deserves or earns. They just happen without being sought out, and yet how one responds to these realities is an open choice. And of course, these realities structure a response: Men often think there is no problem; women know better.

We move back to race. Who is in a better place to understand racism, whites or blacks?

"Anyone can understand it," says Norma. Oh? Who raises it? Who usually notices it? And when it is raised in a mixed group, who feels annoyed, who imposed upon? "I'm always aware of it," says Karen. "If people look at me funny, my first thought is race."

"Maybe you're overly sensitive," says Judy tentatively. "Maybe it's only sometimes about race."

True. But that's part of the way race is constructed and structured. If I'm downtown and can't get a cab, I'm just mad. If Chuck can't get a cab, he's mad and he's certain that race is part of it. Or when you watch the reaction of the Red Sox fans to Jim Rice and Carl Yazstremski—like Sonia Sanchez says, "It's America's favorite pastime, and the name of the game ain't baseball."

"What about reverse racism?" It's Janie, an honest question.

Oh, yes, reverse racism, the only kind of racism *acceptable* in America today. Instead I ask: But if racism is more than rotten ideas, and includes policies and programs as Yolanda argued, policies that promote inequality, then how big a deal is reverse racism?

Big!

Not big!

It's almost time to go, but Karen wants to tell a story before we leave. She got a traffic ticket last month and went to traffic court yesterday to take care of it. She's a single mom and a college student, and hasn't any money to spare, so she asked the clerk for a standard form called a "Pauper's Petition" in order to plead guilty but avoid the fine. As she told it, the clerk smirked as she handed her the form and said in a patronizing voice, "Fill this out as best you can, honey."

"Hell," said Karen. "I'm black and I'm poor. I'm not ignorant. I wanted to punch that racist clerk out."

Here are two job descriptions from our College:

1. *Urban Teacher Education* (assistant professor). Research, teaching, and service in urban education; emphasis on elementary education, with content speciality desirable; candidates should be able to collaborate with colleagues to develop an exceptional teacher education program; emphasis on multicultural aspects of curriculum and instruction is sought.

2. *Teacher Education Leadership in Urban Settings* (open rank). Demonstrated commitment to scholarship and to excellence in teacher education in urban settings, with command of theory and practice of teaching and teacher education. Leadership role in developing teacher education programs, addressing issues such as teacher career development, supervision, and teacher involvement in school improvement. Instruction preservice teacher education courses (elementary level preferred), advisement of students and outreach activities are expected.

These descriptions are intentionally general, awaiting specific individuals with particular interests and points of view to breathe meaning and life into them. At the same undeniable priorities and goals embodied in these descriptions, and certain key words are meant to leap out: "urban," "multicultural," and "teacher education," a phrase repeated seven times.

The key words in themselves do not constitute consensus on meaning. Take "teacher education." To some the meaning is broad—someone who teaches teachers, someone involved in the improvement of teaching. From this perspective a philosopher could be as important as a mathematician, a humanities scholar as valuable as a social scientist. To others, however, teacher education denotes specific, definable attributes involving a specialization in subject-matter content and a "research focus" explicitly named "teacher education." The same divergent views express themselves in relation to the other key words, notably urban and multicultural.

Since criteria for hiring faculty are largely not formalized (there is no test score to refer to, although a doctorate is a kind of test—note that, in 1990, 904, or 3.5 percent, of all doctorates went to black men and women) people tend to rely on personal judgments, issues of collegiality, and "fit," and this becomes a slippery slope indeed. On the one hand, racism can express itself as tokenism, that is, hire this person because she is black; on the other hand, racism can be expressed as the traditional holding-to-the-standard—without regard to any connection between it and later and without questioning whether the standard is artificial or overly rigid.

A tokenist position is reflected in comments like: "Her presentation style was outstanding"; "She seems like someone who could deal with the complex issue of race without being threatening or confrontational"; "We need (many) more people like her to diversify our faculty and to provide alternative role models for our students." The more traditional exclusionary position might hold that "She has no apparent expertise in a content specialty"; "She is potentially a good person but not a close fit"; "I don't think (she) fits . . ."; "She does not strike me as someone who has thought a lot about students, how they learn and change, how teaching can be improved or enriched, how teaching and schooling are or can be related, and so forth."

Or a tokenist position might be that she would "fill one of the major blank spots in the College," or that she "overlapped a great deal with [the other black candidate]", while the more traditional position might argue for exclusion because "she doesn't fit our needs," "she does not appear to have a conception of teaching and learning to guide her . . . [and] no rationale for why she chooses the approaches she does over others," and "I'm not sure what's there." Nothing personal, nothing sensible—just business as usual.

Will America educate African-American youngsters?

In a sense, all education is about power—its goal is for people to become more skilled, more able, more dynamic, more vital. Teaching is about strengthening, invigorating, and empowering others. Few agree on how to get there, but there is general accord that good teaching enables and strengthens learners.

While education is about empowering people, the machinery of schooling is on another mission altogether. Schooling is most often about obedience and conformity; it is about crowd control, competition, hierarchy and your place in it. It is rule-bound and procedure-driven. Schooling is enervating, and it fosters dependence, passivity, and dullness. In fact, many normal discerning students, wondering what kind of intelligence will be rewarded in school, conclude that being quiet, dull, and invisible is the dominant expectation and act accordingly. Or they drop out altogether.

Dependence is more than a psychological condition; it is structured into certain relationships. When resources are distributed inequitably along racial lines, for example, and when access is uneven or unfair, dependence is a predictable outcome. Similarly, when we separate thought and action, theory and practice, we are structuring dependence.

In the first year of the Chicago school reform, the dramatic decentralization of the city schools, the parent-led Local School Councils were free to seek "training" and education from any source they chose. At the end of the year many Council members had two complaints: They felt that they had inadequate knowledge and training to do the job; they also felt that they had been worked to the bone, had burned-out on meetings, and had been trained to death.

This paradox can be understood by looking at the nature of the training experience and the expectations of the participants. A strong sense that some piece of skill or knowledge was out there that should be given to council members, rather than that no adequate training is available prior to the actual doing of the job. That is, being a Council member is itself the only true training for being a Council member—where specific knowledge or skills are needed (making a budget, say, or writing a funding proposal), specific experts can always be brought in. This was not, in the main, what happened. Typically Councils were offered packages—a curriculum on hiring the principal, a curriculum on law, a curriculum on budgeting—and these were built on the top-down, either-or, we-know-you-don't-know, theory-practice paradigm. The hidden curriculum in these instances is invariably powerlessness.

If we want to participate fully in the revitalization of teaching and teacher education, we will need to perceive ourselves and our work in new ways. We will have to move beyond brilliance, beyond living in our heads, beyond an exclusive focus on correct ideas. We will have to address all the destructive dualisms, the either-ors, that obscure our vision. We will have to create a holistic language, a language both clear enough and complex enough to capture the realities and possibilities of teaching. We will have to reinvent our profession if we hope to help reinvent schools, and we will have to be prepared to take action in solidarity with others.

We should stay alive to questions, to contradictions, to ambiguity, to the next utterance in the dialogue. And, yes, to spontaneity. We should be for intellect, for a continual desire to see more, to know more. And we should be for a morality linked to action. We can fight for a stance of interconnection, commitment, struggle, and continuity. We can integrate an understanding that the people with problems are also the people with the solutions, and that experience (our own as well as others') is a powerful teacher if we will only wake up and pay attention.

We need to reorganize and restructure and rethink the entire educational enterprise, top to bottom, if we are to make a real difference. Instead of university faculty and school staff as fragmented parts of a whole, for example, we can think of teachers as working now at the university, now in a public school. Or, perhaps educational resources can begin to be reorganized to provide for teacher-researchers rather than the currently constituted cadre of researchers above the army of teachers. Good teaching is always in pursuit of improvement, after all, always in that sense experimental; teacher-researchers inquiring into the improvement of teaching may be a sensible goal. Academics and researchers can then stop hiding behind their sanctified methods, their exclusive rhetoric. They can give it all away now.

Leon Litwick, in his 1987 presidential address to the Organization of American Historians, notes:

> The significance of race in the American past can scarcely be exaggerated. Those who seek to diminish its critical role invariably dismiss too much history—the depth, the persistence, the pervasiveness, the centrality of race in American society, the countless ways in which racism has embedded itself in the culture, how it adapts to changes in laws and public attitudes, assuming different guises as the occasion demands.

Racism is more than bias and prejudice. In fact the common liberal view that the source of the injustices and inequalities suffered by African-Americans is prejudice has turned things upside down. The structures of privilege and oppression linked to race and backed up by force and power are the root and renewable life-source of bias. In other words, the endurance and strength of prejudiced ideas and values lies in the structures of inequality based on color. We must fight the power, the power of ideas and the power of institutions.

In education labels and titles are often unhelpful, even deceptive. Tre's teacher, for example, may be "liberal" or "progressive" by some definition—she displays the work of her students, she includes their ideas in her lessons—and she may be an agent of oppression by another. She may be both at once. And so the question remains: Will American educate African-American youngsters? In part the answer depends on each of us.

Skin-Game

We are earth-bound,
Body-bound,
Wrapped in little leather sacks,
The color of dirt or dust

We are water-born,
Body-borne,
Defusing mysteriously through blood and slime,
Coated in a shallow rind of scales.

We are shadow-seeking,
Soul-reaching,
Peeling back the bark—skin and all—
Moving with raw nerves
Touching hopes, stirring dreams,
Naming what stands in the way of freedom.

REFERENCES

Hacker, A. (1992a). *Two Nations: Black and White, Separate, Hostile, and Unequal.* (New York: Charles Scribner's Sons).

———. (1992b). The New Civil War. *The New York Review of Books*, 39(8), p. 30-33.

Weber, L. (1991). Black or multicultural curriculum—of course—but what more? Unpublished paper presented at the North Dakota Study Group, Chicago, February, 1991.

Thirteen

Radical Change in Assessment:
A Catalyst for Democratic Education

Carol Lieber, Ed Mikel, and Sunny Pervil

This chapter discusses our approach to graduate coursework in democratic education for experienced teachers. We derived this approach from a vision of the fully democratic society: one in which all people interrelate respectfully within a community founded on caring; in which all collective decisions are mutually determined; in which justice prevails; and in which all individuals and groups are free to pursue the realization of their unfolding human potential.

The three of us recently planned and, to various degrees, had responsibility for teaching a week-long graduate course in democratic education. We brought widely varying experience in teacher education to our participation in the shared course. Among the three of us we have done school administration, teaching at the high school and elementary levels, educational research, educational program evaluation, student assessment, educational consulting and university teaching.

Out of this collaboration, especially the day-by-day working through of the course, we have come to fashion a rationale for democratic teacher education. This rationale posits an image of schooling as embracing a fully democratic culture reflective of the broad social vision noted above. Grounded within this image is a conception of the sort of professional development such schooling would require of teachers. Foremost, teachers would become equipped with radically unconventional assumptions about the processes of assessment and corresponding know-how from direct experience to act on the conviction that democratic assessment can become the organizing principle in transforming school life.

Foundations of an Approach to Democratic Teacher Education

"A democracy is predicated on the idea that ordinary men and women are capable of governing themselves."

Adolf Burke, 1971

"There is no daily democracy without daily citizenship."

Ralph Nader, 1971

How we educate all of America's citizens, including the nation's teachers, remains a question of both pedagogy and politics. American schools have inherited many missions; among the most important is educating for democracy. To ignore the connection between schooling and the politics of public life is to ignore the crucial relationship between living in a democracy founded on the principle of self-government and educating a citizenry that is prepared to participate responsibly in it. As John Dewey (1901) expressed it: "Since a democratic society repudiates the principle of external authority, it must find a substitute in voluntary disposition and interest; these can be created only by education."

In Dewey's view, democracy ought to exist in all social realms. Schools are particularly vital because they are places where we cannot only deliberately create democracy, but devote ourselves as well to continual learning about and practicing the "living arts" of everyday democracy as "a mode of associated living, of conjoint communicated experience" (Dewey, 1966, p. 87). If we as teacher educators wish to inspire our students, the present and future teachers of children, to become citizen-teachers and advocates for democracy, democratic education will need to find a home in our courses and our classrooms. If we arc to take the mission of democratic education seriously in our departments and schools of education, we will have to take a hard look at the "learning culture" in which we live and work. We must become keenly aware of all the patterns of behavior and related meanings held by teachers and students that together constitute all activities of teaching and learning in the classroom.

What are the hallmarks of the "learning culture" of democratic education? It is foremost a culture in which all members are *at once* concerned for their individual interests and well-being *and* the interests and well-being of all others. This essential contradiction, which Jesse Goodman (1992) has characterized as a "dialectical tension between the values of individuality and community," is both a wellspring of the democratic ethos and an eternal dilemma. It is axiomatic in an enduring and thriving democratic culture that "each individual's [or group's] self-actualization can be fully realized only within a just and caring society" (Goodman, 1992, p. 9).

The essential contradiction of democracy and its various tensions are kept in balance only through the responsible and active participation of its members. These "living arts" include sustained interest in civic discourse, a respect for everyone's right to be heard, open-mindedness, a willingness to compromise, and tolerance of diversity. Classrooms certainly offer a daily test of its members' competence and dedication to democracy's "living arts."

Assessment, Accountability, and Standards in Democratic Education

In broad terms, educational assessment is the making of judgments about learning that is occurring in classrooms or schools using standards of one form or another. These judgments are intended to influence persons assumed responsible or accountable for the learning that was assessed, most especially teachers and their students. The entire process turns on the critical and difficult tasks of setting standards and attributing accountability.

Assessment standards may run a gamut from specification of minimal attainments to lofty prescriptions for extraordinary accomplishments and encompass many points between. That there is such a range of possible formulations of standards only hints at the issues lying behind how assessment standards are determined; among these are: by whom standards will be formulated, to whom will which standards be applied and under what conditions, and to what purposes will assessments made on the basis of chosen standards be used.

Although these issues always lie just below the surface of any classroom, they are often faced only implicitly or obliquely by teachers. The full force of the issues is quite evident, however, when they are aired in forums attracting a broad geographical or demographic participation and hearing. Here profound disagreements come into play, animated by diverse orientations to the fundamental values and institutions of democracy, by strongly opposing material and social interests, and by highly varied outlooks on the present and future of our society and our schools. As Harold Berlak (1992) writes, "Given the fundamental differences and multiplicity of perspectives, there is clearly not now, nor is there ever likely to be a national, state, or even district-wide consensus on, or single vision of schooling purposes and policies" (p. 205).

Tied as it is to the setting of educational goals and policies, programs and priorities, assessment is ultimately a most public enterprise. Somehow the body of standards that assessment calls upon must account for the public imperative of democracy: that the community seeks the well-being of each within the welfare of all. Such an ideal community is never fully realized but always in the process of becoming. It can only fulfill the promise of becoming ever more democratic by the full participation of all its members in collective decision making on the current state of the community and the course it should take in the future. If members fail to participate (or be represented), there will be gaps in the community's awareness of all the particular interests and valuations at stake and of all proposals for collective arrangements that may satisfy all particular aspirations represented in the community. Accountability, in the democratic sense, is also short-circuited when participation falls because members can only be considered accountable for public obligations to the extent that they have participated in the mandating of them.

Assessment and accountability are thus critical for teachers who wish to create and sustain democratic cultures in their classrooms. Standards for democratic assessment must be considered emergent and mutually determined. To be sure, elementary and secondary school students are not adults and cannot be accorded equal status in decision making. (Indeed, by its formal nature, the teacher-student relationship is never one of equality, whatever the ages of the persons involved.) Yet, the teacher should act as nearly collaboratively as possible in the spirit of democratic responsibility and full participation. The teacher serves as the community's principal agent and final arbiter of each member's (student's) obligation to the community ("community" has multiple and nested meanings, including the community of the classroom, the school, the locale, region, state, and nation). But in acting to ensure the "welfare" of the community, the teacher must also provide for the "well-being" of each member. In this role the teacher must account for the special interests and values of each individual and group present in the classroom, their distinctive capabilities and the conditions of their lives, and the support they have received from others and given to them. All these bear heavily on the process of assessment, shaping a context by which judgment can invoke standards democratically.

Openings to the Democratic Classroom Through Assessment

Elementary and secondary school classrooms are very busy, complex, and often unpredictable places where events are typically highly interrelated, though perhaps separated by time or location. In such a highly interactive place, balancing the desires and interests of all individuals and primary affiliation groups with commitment to the common welfare of all in the classroom community is paramount to sustaining a democratic culture.

In such a milieu, how can teachers keep their footing secure and their bearings clearly set toward democratic education? The myriad points at which some form of assessment can take place can provide such an anchor. These are "entry points," "pivot points," and "check points" for evolving democratic teaching. Although assessment does constitute a major realm of classroom practice in itself (as the current debate over testing, standards, and alternative methodologies will attest), we can justifiably view assessment as involved with virtually everything teachers do in their classrooms. At these moments—*in situ* or apart from classroom scene—teachers engage in a process of reflection, including reflection on self. There is a rich opportunity to consider what is at hand, to make judgments about its quality, and to decide what course to take. These are key points at which a teacher can gather a clear sense of his/her most deeply held principles and values and the possibilities offered by the situation for enacting them. From these points of assessment and reflection, a teacher can decisively reaffirm, extend, renew, or recast the foundations of teaching practice.

We believe that teachers can fundamentally reorganize the whole of their teaching by adopting a democratic paradigm of assessment. The following pages contain a description from our graduate course with practicing teachers. Such a paradigm stands in stark contrast to the conventional paradigm of educational assessment. A shift to democratic assessment practices would profoundly alter how we teach and interact with our students. To be sure, it is risky if only for the fact that we cannot make it all up ahead of time! It is messy, as is any democratic effort in which we respect a student's exercise of choosing and voicing. It is open-ended and collaborative, which means we must spend classtime exploring and ultimately designing assessment processes that meet the needs and interests of our students and ourselves. Because democratic assessment is participatory, we must engage students in reflection and self-assessment, just as we involve ourselves. We must encourage student leadership and provide opportunities for informed agenda setting and decision making. Above all, democratic assessment assumes that we are engaged in a genuine partnership with our students, in which we respect both the learning community we create together and each individual's contribution to it.

Revitalizing Professional Development for Teachers in Democratic Education

Given the unceasing demands and complexity of classroom life, a program for democratic teacher education must foster a professional learning that reaches "into the bones." Learning must run deep because teachers do not face compliant social conditions in their schools. Rather, they must transform social relationships, curriculum mandates, requirements for standardized testing, and unstimulating and inhospitable physical environments that generally lock out possibilities for democratic education. To be up to these daunting challenges, teachers must possess, we believe, a thoroughly developed practical philosophy of democratic education. We use the term "practical philosophy" to refer to an array of explicitly avowed principles, a body of related craft of teaching knowhow, and a general strategy for reflecting upon any measure of classroom life and, especially, of the teacher's presence in it. Above all, a practical philosophy of democratic education for teachers must be well grounded in what may be called an alternative paradigm of assessment.

Careful reflection is at the heart of any assessment that is well done. Professional learning and development cannot occur in any meaningful sense without systematic self-reflection: the deliberate examination of self and of self in relation to others and to social and physical circumstances. Professional development can easily spring from any assessment activity permitting a teacher to engage in probing self-reflection, especially where s/he has the counsel of others who are directly involved or who are familiar with the subject at hand. Teachers do not, therefore, have to be the principal subject of an assessment to use it as an occasion for professional growth. There need be only a genuine opportunity for self-reflection and re-creation of practice.

Whatever the occasion or format of self-reflection for professional development, the process focuses the teacher on what s/he wishes to attain (especially on that which is most highly valued) and the craft know-how required to make it happen. As purpose and capability are independent, their relationship will shift over time, and can shift dramatically and frequently as a teacher conscientiously attempts new methods and tried to inaugurate new models. If a teacher is conscious not only of purpose and craft but also of their interrelationship, s/he may engage in self-reflective professional learning that constitutes development of a practical philosophy of democratic education for teaching.

Assessment is the motor that drives the curriculum and influences how we teach and treat our students. If we give two exams a semester, we will teach to those exams. If we give no options or choices regarding readings, topics, and projects, we are asking students to fulfill our learning agenda, not their own. The traditional assessment paradigm is instructor-driven and anti-democratic. The instructor selects what will be assessed and chooses the means of assessment. The assessment process most often involves one-way communication, from instructor "down" to the student. Finally, the purpose of traditional assessment is to assign a grade and a comparative rank order to a student's work; it rarely engages a student in reflection and self-assessment and frequently becomes an obstacle to new learning and understanding.

The paradigm shift from traditional to democratic assessment is one of emphasis. We are not suggesting that all traditional assessment be tossed out; neither are we suggesting that qualitative standards be placed with individualized anarchy. Rather, we urge teacher educators to broaden and deepen their commitment to a wider range of assessment experiences which promote democratic values. In short, if we don't incorporate democratic assessment into our teaching, we are not practicing "the living art" of democracy in our classrooms.

In the remainder of this chapter we will discuss in detail how we have attempted to promote the ideas that can develop a practical philosophy of democratic education. We have organized our coursework on the assumption that a practical philosophy of teaching must be unshakably oriented toward the radically different paradigm of democratic assessment. We turn next to describing the features of this paradigm.

TRADITIONAL ASSESSMENT PARADIGM	DEMOCRATIC ASSESSMENT PARADIGM
The assumption of student **inequality** implies that some students will learn; others won't. Some will receive an A; others will receive an F.	The assumption of **equality** implies that everyone can learn and everyone can achieve. Everyone has the potential to receive an A.
Monologue of instructor dominates. Lecture format conveys to students that "teaching is telling."	**Dialogue** in small and large groups as well as facilitated conversations (using newsprint to record and assess ideas) enable instructor and students to seek emergent truths, new insights and questions, and deeper understanding through "give and take" that emphasizes active listening and continual feedback.
Coercive instruction utilizes fear, shame, threats of punishment, and repressive control in order to "make students learn." Students are assessed on their outward compliance to arbitrary rules and standards.	**Invitational learning** emphasizes voluntary cooperation, self-discipline, and mutually determined expectations and consequences which nurture a desire and will to learn. Students and instructor assess whether, how, and to what extent goals are met.
Conflicts, mistakes, and errors are perceived as negative and often lead to harsh judgment of the student, a "bad" grade, or an immediate punishment. Conflict is to be eliminated as quickly as possible or avoided altogether.	**Conflicts, mistakes, and errors present learning opportunities** for students to assess their thinking and actions and improve their skillfulness. Democratic assessment encourages open acknowledgement of academic and interpersonal difficulties and assumes a commitment to resolve conflicts constructively through class meetings, one-to-one dialogues, negotiation, and mediation.
Students experience **dehumanization** when assessment of their work and growth is reduced to a numerical measurement and/or excludes interactive exchange between instructor and student. Depersonalized assessment can build a wall that prevents genuine communication between instructor and student.	Face-to-face conversation, verbal "quick-checks," and personalized written exchanges between student and instructor **affirm the dignity of the individual** and can help break down the adversarial distance between instructor and student.
Traditional assessment places more	Democratic assessment places more

(continued)

emphasis on **external rewards** (grades, incentives honors, pleasing instructor).	emphasis on **internal rewards and satisfaction** in the learning process itself. The internal reward is in the doing and successful completion of a project or task.
Traditional assessment is often **contrived and disconnected** from the real world and from students' own experience and understanding.	Democratic assessment attempts to be **authentic and purposeful**, linking what students learn to how they live. Authentic assessment often engages students in presenting their work to real audiences and tackling real world problems in their schools and communities.
Choice is extremely limited or non-existent.	**Students have the freedom to make choices** about what they learn, how they learn it, who they learn it with, and how they demonstrate what they've learned.
Instructor takes full responsibility for leadership and learning climate, diminishing the sense of student accountability and ownership of learning process.	Responsibility for the learning climate is shared and **both instructor and students continually develop and practice leadership skills**, ensuring that everyone shares accountability and ownership of learning process.
Autocratic, unilateral decision making guarantees that instructors have all the power because they make all the decisions.	**Shared decision making** ensures that people affected by decisions are involved in making decisions. Instructor and students practice a decision-making process which incorporates consensus and compromise and assesses consequences and implications of choices before making responsible, informed judgments.
The voice of authority is the only legitimate voice.	**Student voice** is equally valued and encouraged.
The over-reliance on a **single point of view in a given situation** necessarily simplifies thinking and encourages absolute judgments and intolerance, limiting the ability to take on the perspective of "the other."	The inclusion of **multiple points of view** necessarily complicates thinking and encourages tentative judgments, empathy, "perspective-taking," and greater tolerance of ambiguity.
Presumption of **cultural uniformity** in	Acceptance of **cultural diversity** in

which a dominant, monolithic cultural perspective forms the learning experience of all students. Traditional assessment accepts the premise that all students share the same cultural perspective and make meaning in the same way.

There is one right answer. Quantitative, right/wrong assessment conveys to students that **"learning is remembering."**

There is **one right approach** or method of learning and **one dominant medium** (usually a timed "objective" test) which a student must use to demonstrate what he or she has learned.

Instructor sets **predetermined goals** for course and **predetermined standards of quality and criteria for assessment** before meeting students.

Emphasis is on **competitive learning**, which often pits one student's success against another student's failure. Students receive a clear message that there are a few "winners" and lots of "losers" that for me to be better or best, you have to be worse.

Academic achievement is the dominant or only outcome that is assessed and therefore diminishes importance of social

which a variety of cultural perspectives inform the learning experiences of students. Democratic assessment accepts the premise that students do not share the same cultural experiences and consequently make meaning in different ways.

There are many ways to answer a question, and solutions are often context-dependent. Qualitative assessment conveys to students that **"learning is to be used and applied."**

Democratic assessment encourages instructors and students to become adept at using a **variety of learning strategies and approaches** and encourages students to use a wide range of media and experiences to show what they have learned **(demonstrations, action-research, dialogue, written and oral reflection, presentations, portfolios, exhibits, photodocumentation, the use of visual and recorded media, direct application to real problems).**

Goals and standards are emergent and mutually determined. Students identify personal learning goals and everyone participates in setting standards of quality and criteria for assessment.

Emphasis is on a **personalized approach to independent learning, cooperative learning, and collaborative problem-solving.** Students receive the message that they can all be "winners" and that collaboration can often enhance achievement and learning outcomes.

Academic achievement, social efficacy, and personal growth are all assessed; therefore, all three dimensions of learn-

(continued)

TRADITIONAL ASSESSMENT PARADIGM *(continued)*	DEMOCRATIC ASSESSMENT PARADIGM *(continued)*
efficacy and personal growth.	ing are valued.
The final product or "the big exam" is often the only means of assessing a student's progress. Students and instructors do not systematically question and reflect about what they are thinking, feeling, and learning the rest of the time in a course.	Instructor and students are engaged in ongoing, **experience-based reflection** about what they are teaching and learning and how they are experiencing (cognitively, socially, and affectively) the learning process.
Knowledge is one-dimensional. Legitimate knowledge is the linear-sequential knowledge of evidence and "the expert." Students are most often the passive recipients of other people's knowledge.	**Knowledge is multi-dimensional.** Students actively participate in constructing their own knowledge of the world, other people, and themselves through evidence and research, and exploration of values, feelings, and perceptions, reflection and insight, direct experience, and interactive dialogue.
Traditional assessment focuses on the individual at the expense of the group. Students are often alienated from the instructor and each other, **living and learning among a group of strangers**.	Democratic assessment pays attention to the whole community as well as the individuals in it. The process of **building a pro-social community** is valued and the well-being of the community is constantly being assessed.

One student described the paradigm change she intended for her classroom in her final course project:

> Welcome to Room 1. As you enter you see a brightly decorated classroom. In all, it's a pretty good room. There is one desk for each student and a special time-out desk that is apart from the rest of the desks. There is also one big desk, up in front, near a window and the big blue cabinets that contains all the teacher's manuals and the worksheets. Students are not allowed in this area without permission. There are several tables around the edges of the room. One is large and holds the two computers and the one printer this class gets to use with the teacher's permission, but only two people at a time. The other tables are cluttered with work in progress or things the students bring in for "Show and Tell." The teacher has done a good job of hanging cute bulletin board displays around the room. The students are allowed to look but they do not touch. They know it belongs to the teacher and she wants to keep it nice so she can use it again next year. In all, it's a pretty good room. The

teacher is nice. She gives out stickers and candy if you do your work. If you don't, you have to do it in the office. Every day students start work by writing in their journals. There is an open-ended sentence on the board to copy and finish. The teacher takes lunch count and attendance, then picks someone to deliver them to the office. The class schedule is almost always the same: Word Study, research, spelling, English, composition, math, science, and social studies. Almost all of the lessons come out of the curriculum guides the district has given the teacher. The children take lots of standardized tests. But it's a pretty good district, and a pretty good school where this pretty good room is located. There's just one little problem: Pretty good is not working.

Instead of worrying about teaching all the lessons out of the teacher's guides, maybe I could teach my students how to think for themselves without having to ask permission to do it. They can be taught how to solve problems, not the kind that are in the math book but real issues from their everyday lives. Suppose they were taught how to take an idea they had, ask some questions about it, do some research, and see what they found out. What if they were allowed to use whatever resources they wanted to for their research, including each other, me, the computer, AV equipment, the library, other classrooms, other people, their parents, the community, the world? To do this would require a very special work place. Let's go back to Room 1.

Welcome; As you enter this time you see students engaged in different activities. Each of them is working or discussing work with one another. Students move freely around the classroom to gather materials they need, meet to talk with each other about their projects, and interact with their teacher. The focus of the classroom changes as the students learn from each other. A feeling of cooperation and respect is obvious everywhere you look. The bulletin boards are covered with student-generated work they have proudly displayed. Gathered on one table is a collection of books that the students especially enjoy; some of them they wrote themselves. There are centers all over the room. Students are encouraged to settle their disagreements themselves by discussing the problem together and coming to a consensus about a solution. Class meetings are held once a week to discuss anything that is on students' minds. Everyone is given a chance to speak while the others listen. Classroom procedures are all carried out by the students. The teacher is always there to facilitate their learning. The children are evaluated by multiple assessments based on the work they have been doing.

It is a little noisier than it was last year and a little messier than it was last year, but last year it was just a pretty good room and now it's terrific! (Fell, 1992)

Overview of Course and Initial Preparation

We began talking about teaching this class for a year before it occurred. To finalize our plans we met once a week for a month to make outlines of the day-to-day activities. We created a resource file of journal articles for the students based on their interests expressed in a survey we sent out two weeks before the class began. Each student was sent a letter presenting 20 possible topics that we were considering. Students were asked to reply by indicating which of the listed themes, or any others they wished to suggest, seemed most important or vital to them to be included in the final syllabus. Returns were received from 14 of the 15 students. Their overwhelming favorites determined the final selections of the daily topics. On the morning the class began, we arrived very early to set up the room. We were able to keep resources and video equipment in the room. Each of us brought our own personal collection of books and video resources numbering over 100 items. The students helped us compile these into a "Democratic Classroom Bibliography." We used George Wood's *Schools that Work* for the course text.

The course was then organized into daily nine o'clock to three o'clock meetings using the following succession of the chosen thematic studies: multiple definitions of the democratic classroom, democratic classroom environment, democratic discipline, peaceful conflict resolution, multicultural understanding, thematic curriculum, and student projects designing classroom change toward democratic education. Each of these thematic studies considered a rather broad realm of classroom life encompassing the physical environment, social climate and authority relationships, curriculum resources and materials, the processes of study, and intended learning outcomes. The various studies overlapped and inter-related in many realms; looking beyond our own classroom experience, we can also identify realms of the larger social world patterned in terms of similar themes representing interwoven purpose, relationship, and activity. We used strategies that modeled the theme of that particular day of class. For example, as students studied the theme of conflict resolution, we practiced activities that they might use to solve conflict in their own lives. They could also use the same techniques we taught them with their students.

Our assessment of the students reflected the democratic activities and strategies we had given them, as well as the "new" paradigm ideals. In this chapter we detail a variety of assessments: Some are explicitly for the purpose of evaluation, and others are implicitly within teaching practices. The explicit assessments were guidelines given to students on the first day of class. The implicit practices were ongoing and provided the instructors with information about students' learning during the process of study. This ongoing information assured the learners' continued growth and provided the teachers with the opportunity to reflect on principles, review experience and imagine options.

Explicit Assessment

Standardized Testing as Assessment. Perhaps nothing has constricted American education from becoming more democratic over the last four decades than the predominance of standardized testing and its shaping of assumptions about formal assessment in schooling. (For a thorough discussion of standardized testing, the psychometric paradigm, and their antidemocratic influence on assessment, see Berlak, 1992). Standardized testing enforces a view of assessment primarily as a sorting exercise. At certain predetermined decision points, judgments are made about the quality of student learning (or aptitudes or intelligence or predispositions), comparatively and summarily. While testing surely does not supply the only means or logic of assessment carried on in American schools, it is emblematic of a pervasive antidemocratic mentality that lies behind the typical practices of school assessment.

Testing is meant to produce results expressed in the briefest of terms, most often a single number or set of a few numerical scores. This sort of quantitative distillation allows each individual tested to be considered an "instance" or "case" of some aggregate category. If the test is norm-referenced, students will be ranked along some scale from low to high. If the test is criterion-referenced, students will be determined to have reached or fallen short of the designated criterial level of performance. In either case, the student becomes a candidate for membership in a group of people who share certain defining characteristics. All members of such a group—"high" or "low" achievers, those who are "at risk" or "gifted"—are seen by the testing logic as "types" who merit a level of regard and treatment appropriate to the status of results they have obtained.

From where those who are tested stand, the process is oppressive. Tests set up artificial situations of time limitations and rigid procedures. They often pose unfamiliar tasks that are largely disconnected from one another, and that are frequently introduced by unclear or peculiar directions. No appeal can be made to modify what is to be done to make it sensible, inherently interesting, or related to things previously done. After the testing is completed, the efforts are sent off to distant places to be evaluated by anonymous experts whose decisions are unassailable.

Although standardized testing is seldom used in day-to-day work, the testing mentality pervades school assessment. In the following pages, we discuss how we set about to disavow the conventional practice of assessment and in our course bring the new democratic paradigm to life.

An End to Letter Grades. At the heart of the intended new form of assessment was eliminating the traditional system of letter grades. We wanted particularly to shift students' attention away from the spectre of a final grade to the prospect of completing and sharing a culminating project. This project was to mark a serious venture in remaking their own classrooms more democratic. The only grade available to students was "A." It was not automatically given, but it was expected that all students would end with it eventually. The absence of a scale of letter grades meant that no student would be officially designated more successful than any other; neither would students be forced to compete for the differential reward of a grade. This is not to say that we desired uniform learning or did not anticipate that some projects would be more sophisticated or more ambitious. Rather, by the multiple criteria or "standards" we observed, any student working conscientiously throughout the course should achieve the level of professional learning an "A" was meant to represent.

Standards in Democratic Assessment. Completion of the culminating project depended upon the diligent work—collaborative work as well as individual work—from the first day of class on. But completion of the project, unlike the scheduled administration of a standardized test, was not time-bound to a climactic decision-point. Any student could reasonably delay project completion until s/he and the instructor were satisfied. This stipulation embodied the student's heightened affirmation of democratic principles for teaching, a more reflective understanding of the concrete implications of these principles, and the requisite craft skill to realize designs in successful practice.

Unspoken Permission from the University. The practice of giving an entire class of graduate students an "A" is not viewed as particularly unusual. We have never been questioned about our grading policy. At most universities graduate students hardly ever receive a grade lower than "B." Our practice prevents the ludicrousness of sorting people into "A" and "B" categories. It expresses the value that everyone is capable of doing "A" work. There must be documentation and evidence that the student has met the requirements of the course. If the student has not met the requirements, s/he receives an "incomplete" until the work is found satisfactory. Copies of each student's project and his/her journals are kept on file. The students' projects are shared with other interested students. This policy does not lower the quality of the work in any capacity. If we felt that the competition game would give us quality student work and learning, we would use it. We have found quality work comes from sharing and the knowledge that the work will be used and valued by others. At present the university has expressed no objections to this practice.

Implicit Assessment

Implicit assessment is evaluation that is embedded in the strategies the teacher uses to deliver the curriculum to the students. The use of these strategies provides the instructor with ongoing feedback about the thoughts and feelings of the students. It provides the teacher with moment-to-moment evidence that the focus remains on the objectives, and that both teacher and student are moving in the direction of accomplishing these objectives. The strategies themselves help learners feel in control of their own learning and motivated to learn. The students become active participants in the teaching-learning process rather than passive receptacles. Thoughts and doubts are expressed as the learners shape and reshape their ideas. "Aha!" is a common occurrence as the learners share their realizations. To help the reader understand how implicit instruction worked during our course, we will describe a variety of strategies used throughout the course on a daily basis, a variety of strategies used on a one-time basis, and finally a typical day during the course.

Daily Strategies

The following strategies occurred each day of the course. They allowed us the opportunity to make personal connections to what the students expressed was of great importance in their work. We found that using these strategies strengthened the link between theory and the actual day-to-day experiences of our students. By using these strategies we could continually assess the students' prior experiences and the new insights and thoughts that were moving them toward growth and learning.

Class Meeting/Discussion. In order to build community, the day always began with a discussion based on the previous day's journaling and reading assignments. During this time the students had the opportunity to reflect and share ideas on the theme for the day. They could also bring up other topics and questions. This particular time could be likened to an elementary or secondary class meeting. During these discussions the students got to know each others' needs and fears. As time passed the group's support for one another grew. During the discussions each student spoke. If there was a student who did not speak, we made certain to ask an open-ended question in order to be sure s/he felt part of the group. These discussions gave us the opportunity to assess what the group already knew about the topic for the day and their comfort level with the topic and their co-workers. This way we could adjust our activities to the level of the group and make students feel more at ease if they expressed alienation from the group.

Webbing/Charting. In the classroom we had a large easel with chart paper. For any discussion we webbed or charted the major concepts and ideas. As the students did group work, we asked them to make webs or charts also. This strategy achieved our desire to express the diversity of students' ideas. They could observe that there were many alternatives to the topics we were presenting. All the webs and charts were hung on the walls and served as an easy reference for what had taken place earlier. This chart-making and displaying helped us prioritize, refer to, and honor the emergent goals and ever-changing understandings of the group.

Quick Self-Evaluation. The students were frequently asked to express their feelings on every topic from our own classroom management to the topic at hand. This could be as simple as a thumbs up or down or a lengthy discussion. The important part is that it allowed the students the liberty to have a voice in the class proceedings. It was another way that we continually monitored the group's understanding of a topic. We did not simply move mindlessly on through the curriculum. We checked and felt confident the students were ready to continue.

Oral Summarizing. At the conclusion of a session, the students summarized what had taken place. The students might explain a product they had made or answer questions like "What did you learn from this?" or "What questions have emerged for you from this discussion?" or "Describe how your group worked together." This strategy gave us the necessary feedback to understand how the students had comprehended the new material.

Breaks. To keep the energy flowing we had three breaks a day: one in the morning, one for lunch, and one in the afternoon. The breaks allowed the students time to socialize and regain energy. It was an opportunity for the students to have a one-to-one relationship with the instructor where they voiced their private joys and woes. During these times we spoke with the students about their projects. Breaks were also a time to check with each other about the plans or modification for the next activity.

Videotaping/Photographing. A video and a Polaroid camera were in the room at all times, giving us the opportunity to tape sessions and take still photographs of memorable moments. We hung up the still pictures as soon as we took them. Students enjoyed seeing themselves and remembering the particular activities we captured on film. This ongoing document was a way to affirm the uniqueness of the individual and at the same time celebrate the efforts of the group. Students could borrow the videotape if they wished to review a session. It also gave the students an opportunity to control their own pace by being able to review sessions.

Journaling. At the end of each day the students wrote for 10 to 15 minutes on the topic for the next day. For example, for the day on thematic units, students journaled the day before on "a favorite unit that they teach." Students then used these writings as the basis for our discussions the next day. At the end of the week we collected the journals and wrote personal comments to the students which were positive, reinforcing, and empathetic. The journals were mailed back to the students.

Pair Sharing. Pair sharing is a simple technique to get everyone engaged in dialogue at the same time. Ideally it is a way to brainstorm, begin discussion of a compelling question or issue, frame a topic of study, or assess what people know. Students pair up and bring their own knowledge and experiences to the question or topic at hand, one person speaking for two or three minutes at a time, then reversing the roles of listener and speaker.

Dialogue. Dialogues and facilitated conversations have the advantage of slowing down thinking and consequently improve listening and ensure that participants choose more carefully what they say and how they say it. Some suggestions:

1. Sit so that everyone is facing each other.

2. Limit the size of the group.

3. Prepare a set of questions that students have helped generate.

4. No interrupting. (This is the most important ground rule.)

5. Do at least one "round robin" around the circle where everyone gets to speak before raising questions or engaging in back and forth exchange.

6. Participants have the right to pass.

7. The facilitator's role is to ensure that mutually agreed-to ground rules are maintained.

8. Sometimes it is helpful to have participants paraphrase what the previous speaker has said before the conversation goes in a new direction, **OR** make a temporary rule that participants can speak only when they wish to either agree with or further explore what the previous speaker has said.

9. Keep issues and personalities separate.

10. Encourage people to use "I" statements.

11. Identify areas of agreement and disagreement.

12. Finally, assess the quality and process of the dialogue and summarize the substance and direction of the conversation. (All members of the group should participate in this summary and evaluation.)

Other Strategies

These strategies did not occur on a daily basis but were used as methods of delivering the course content. We selected these strategies because they were highly motivating, participatory, and had built-in assessment factors. It was our hope in using these strategies that they would provide a powerful model for our students to utilize in their own classrooms.

Simulations/Role Playing. Simulations, in which every student takes on the role of a person or a group who is affected by the problem (using current issues, case studies, and personal experiences) accomplish three goals: (1) They require participants to take on the perspective of "the other," (2) they provide direct practice in the arts of democracy (collective problem-solving, negotiation and compromise, acknowledging other points of view, leadership, and public speaking), (3) debriefing provides excellent opportunities for assessment. (What happened? What worked? What didn't? What would you do differently next time? How did you feel during the simulation? What did you learn that can be applied in other situations?)

Jigsaw. This cooperative learning technique was used to have the students teach each other new information. During classtime groups of students read articles and their task was to decide what was important in the article and teach this information to the rest of the class. This is a powerful tool as students realize how working as a community can increase the amount of material one can absorb. It also gave us the opportunity to observe the teaching techniques of the students in the class.

Collaborative Problem-Solving. Collaborative problem-solving engages small groups of students in a process of (1) defining a problem, (2) gathering information and assessing the steps necessary to solve the problem or resolve the conflict, (3) generating alternative solutions, and (4) selecting the means and resources to solve the problem in a way that meets some interests of everyone in the group. Some constraints (such as time limits, restricted resources, or establishing criteria which need to be considered in the solution) lead to clarity of focus, intense involvement, and deep satisfaction in the solution.

Outside Resources/Books/Videos/Guest Speakers/Field Trips. The classroom was filled with more than 100 books which we brought as resources for the students and which they were allowed to borrow overnight. Six videos and a variety of games were also available. We brought in guest speakers and had art supplies on hand. On a one-day field trip to the St. Louis area, some students went to bookstores, some to teacher stores, some to museums or other cultural organizations. We all met for lunch and shared our findings.

These resources served as motivators for the students. Students would express interests; we would point them in a direction, and they would take off. As we took note of the materials the students were using, it gave us a reading of the progression of the students' work. At the students' urging we created a bibliography from all of these resources. Each student was responsible for logging six to eight resources on index cards. One student alphabetized the cards and the department secretary typed the list. Everyone went away happy.

Final Project Sharing. Each student shared his/her final project by making copies for everyone in the class. The interesting point about asking the students to share projects with each other is that it serves as an assurance for quality work. By giving the students authentic audiences, authentic work was promoted. After distributing his/her project each student gave a five-minute presentation. The students then received constructive criticism from everyone in the class on their work.

The instructors wrote one page of feedback to each student about his/her projects. This was mailed with the student's journal. In the letter of feedback the instructors asked the student questions about parts of the project which might still remain unclear, made comments which hopefully motivated the student to push the project to a larger endeavor, and, if appropriate, suggest other audiences for his/her project.

Experience-Based Reflection. We asked the students to give us feedback in multiple ways throughout the course. At the end of a day we asked, "What worked for you today?" or "How might you use something you learned today in a concrete way?" At the halfway point we asked the students to share three pluses (things they liked about the course) and a wish (something they would like to see changed). At the end of the course we asked the students to give us a page of feedback.

Overview of One Day

The students arrived early and would socialize, look at the resources we brought, or share their own resources with us or with one another. They brought articles or books they thought would interest us. This sharing was often prompted by the discussion on the previous day. Each day a different student provided treats for the group. Students filled their plates and class began at 9:00 A.M. with a discussion of their journal topics and the readings from the previous night.

The topic for the day, "Setting Up a Democratic Classroom," had received the most votes on the pre-class survey. Our goal was to explore several tasks:

1. Making the classroom safe for everyone,

2. Allowing student choice without creating chaos,

3. Moving from a system of discipline that punishes to discipline that teaches,

4. Structuring a caring community that promotes self-discipline, and

5. Negotiating and managing social relationships in the classroom.

On this particular day we discussed the qualities that make a classroom a safe environment for learning. Certain teachers in the class who were in particularly oppressive school situations expressed their fears and doubts about democratic education. Other students in the class responded with an explanation of what they went through under similar circumstances. A number of practical suggestions for positive learning environments were shared. For example, a teacher told of an experience where the students in her high school were given the power to make decisions through their student government and then did not use the power they were given. The students in our class asked the teacher many questions about her complaint. She came to realize that the problem was the fact that the students did not know how to self-govern and needed strategies for doing it effectively.

These discussion sessions set the tone for the entire day. One of the most important things that happened was that these meetings allowed the students to share their experiences so that we were able to connect their prior experiences to what they were learning. The facilitators really heard the students' concerns and allowed them time to struggle with them as they were rethinking their roles as teachers. Often they gave examples which we could keep returning to throughout the day. The discussion lasted for one hour and was followed by a short break.

We began again with a presentation by a first-grade teacher and member of our St. Louis Institute for Democratic Education group, Terri Anderson. She explained what her classroom was like before and after she democratized it. She began by reading the class the story *Miss Nelson Is Missing*. She explained how she had changed from Viola Swamp, a tyrannical teacher, to Miss Nelson, a democratic teacher. She showed our group slides of her classroom that demonstrated the changes she made. This lasted for an hour and a half. The last 40 minutes or so before lunch, Terri answered questions about her presentation. Again, teachers voiced their concerns or wanted greater specifics on the mechanics of particular activities. Terri made connections between her own experience and their experiences. We took a one-hour lunch break. This gave us time to go over or even revise our afternoon plans based on the morning's events. It also gave the students time to socialize and return refreshed for the afternoon.

When the students came back we gave each one a long strip of paper and asked them to write a one-sentence suggestion for creating a safe classroom environment. We hung all of these suggestions on the wall, read and discussed them. Some examples of their sentences were "In the beginning of the school year find out what makes your students sad and what makes them angry," "In the beginning of the school year have the students help you make up the rules," "Find out what the students' interests are."

Students were then divided into three groups and given a different article about democratic discipline. Their task was to read the article, decide what was important to know, and convey this information to the class. Each group made a presentation and this was followed by a discussion of discipline techniques in each of their classrooms. Again the connections were made to the teachers' day-to-day experiences. The class ended as the students took 10 to 15 minutes to write in their journals on the question, "How do you resolve conflicts, both in your classroom and at home?" This would be the beginning point for our discussion on the theme for the next day, conflict resolution. The day ended in much the same way it had begun: Students stayed on to ask questions, socialize or spend time looking through resources.

Conclusions

The students' projects give ample evidence of the myriad of practices through which teachers may increasingly transform their classrooms into sites of democratic education. The cutting edge in this change may be where overt assessment is done. But the dense webbing of implicit assessment shaping virtually all that happens in any classroom means that teachers can bring the "new paradigm" to life in many ways. As practices change individually and in parallel connections, democratic ideals visibly begin to take prominence: commitment to community and to taking a responsible part; values of equality, respect for human dignity, liberty, diversity and community; habits of reflection, multiple perspective-taking. We gain increased momentum from our successes, renewed spirit to continue the quest, and an ever sharper vision of the possibilities open to us.

Epilogue

Finally, we as teacher educators must heed our own rhetoric. Too seldom do we truly practice the process of transforming our own classes into democratic communities. We need to promote new ways of teaching and learning vigorously. Teacher educators often resist change and are uncomfortable around others who are attempting to break old patterns. It is important that department chairpersons create a democratic environment where it is safe for professors to reflect and rethink their teaching practices. Some non-threatening ways to break through the silence are teacher exchanges, guest practitioners who are teachers in the pre-collegiate classroom, invitations to visit and collaborate among the professors, time out for reflective practice such as dialogue circles with professors and students, and staff development days that emerge from interests and concerns about teaching craft. The power of transformation is not just a good goal for our students, it is a liberating aspiration for ourselves.

REFERENCES

Allard, H., and Marshall, J. (1977). *Miss Nelson Is Missing*. New York: Scholastic Book Services.

Berlak, H., ed. (1992). *Toward a New Science of Educational Testing and Assessment*. Albany, NY: State University of New York Press.

Burke, A. (1971). From L. Peter, *Peter's Quotations: Ideas for Our Time*. New York: Bantam Books.

Dewey, J. (1901). The Situation as Regards the Course of Study. *Journal of Proceedings and Addresses of the Fortieth Annual Meeting of the National Education Association*, pp. 332-348.

———. (1966). *Democracy in Education: An Introduction to the Philosophy of Education*. New York: The Free Press.

Fell, C. (1992). Project for democratic classroom course: Maryville University, St. Louis. "Reflections," pp. 1-2.

Goodman, J. (1992). *Elementary Schooling for Critical Democracy*. Albany, NY: State University of New York Press.

Nadar, R. (1971). From L. Peter, *Peter's Quotations: Ideas for Our Time*. New York: Bantam Books.

Wood, G. (1992). *Schools that Work*. New York: Dutton.

SECTION III

Prospects

CONCLUSION

Prospecting for Democratic Teacher Education

John M. Novak

Where do you find democratic teacher education in North America? As this book points out, you find it in different places, manifesting itself in many ways.

You find roots for democratic teacher education in a pragmatic philosophical past that is continually making its presence known. Dewey's lifelong efforts to conceptualize and promote a down-to-earth, educationally connected notion of democracy are alive in the chapters of this book. The democratic teacher educators here have attempted to walk the Deweyan talk. In doing so they have pointed out the details, dilemmas, and deliberations found in efforts to conscientiously promote and sustain democratic teaching; in doing so they have found ways to clarify, critique, and extend Deweyan democracy. Democratic philosophy does not seem as unapproachable as some would have us think.

You also find democratic teacher education within education departments in universities. Several chapters in this book show how democratic spaces can be carved in teacher education classrooms within traditional programs and also how experimental democratic programs can be constructed. Democratic space has become available for those with imagination and initiative. Educational departments do not seem as immovable as some would have us think.

You can also find democratic teacher education in other parts of the university. For example, Women's Studies Programs have been calling into question the traditional domains of knowledge and the authority structure of the university. In doing so, they are going beyond the creation of spaces for their programs; they are challenging the taken-for-granted rules and practices of the academy itself. This democratic challenge will affect teachers in their attempts to restructure knowledge and organizations. The university does not seem as iron-clad as some would have us think.

You also find democratic teacher education in networks that are being developed between and among groups of teachers. Teachers want to learn new things and try out new ideas, but on their own terms. By giving voice to the importance of teachers' perceptions of their work and their commitment to growth, these new democratic networks are honoring the down-to-earth issues and thinking involved in the daily practices of teaching democratically. The practical focus of teachers does not seem as narrow as some would have us think.

You can also find democratic teacher education taking place as teacher educators attempt to affect societal issues and directions. Their efforts are taking them outside of education departments, universities, schools, and classrooms. Efforts to focus on a renewed sense of citizenship and the development of the arts of democracy outside of schools will affect curriculum development and teaching practices. The skills, crafts, and arts of democratic functioning in the world outside of schools can become vital means and goals for democratic schooling.[1] Social issues may not seem as unapproachable or recalcitrant as some would have us think.

So what are we to say to those teacher educators who admit to knowing nothing of democratic teacher education? Perhaps we can say that they have been looking in all the wrong places. There are committed teachers, experimental programs, and burgeoning networks of democratic teacher education. It is now necessary to take a further look, because it is happening all around us. Perhaps we can also say it is time to rethink fundamental notions of philosophy, classroom practices, university functioning, and professional and civic networking. This is where the action is in democratic teacher education. The voices are getting too loud to ignore. Perhaps we can also say that as a teacher educator you are either part of this democratic process or you are part of the undemocratic problem. You cannot merely be a spectator; that is not the way democratic teacher education works.

NOTE

1. For an important and stimulating look at the possibilities involved in democratic citizenship see Frances Moore Lappe and Paul Martin Dubois, *Doing Democracy* (San Francisco: Josey Bass, in press).

NOTES ON CONTRIBUTORS

WILLIAM AYERS is a school reform activist and an Associate Professor of education at the University of Illinois at Chicago where he teaches courses in elementary education, interpretive research, teaching in social context, and curriculum. Currently chair of the Alliance for Better Chicago Schools (a reform coalition shaping the Chicago reform), he taught young children for twelve years, and has taught teachers for the past eight years. A graduate of Bank Street College of Education and Teachers College, Columbia University, his books include *The Good Preschool Teacher* (Teachers College Press, 1989) and *To Teach: The Journey of a Teacher* (Teachers College Press, 1993).

LISA BLOOM is an Assistant Professor of special education in the Department of Human Services at Western Carolina University. She received her Doctor of Education degree from West Virginia University in 1989. Prior to receiving her degree, she taught special education in rural areas of Pennsylvania and West Virginia. Currently, she is the co-director of the Behavior Disorders Project, a federally funded project for recruiting and preparing graduate level special education teachers, and developing a portfolio model of evaluation for the graduate program.

JANET C. FORTUNE is an Assistant Professor of Education at Berea College in Kentucky. Her primary research interests concern the theological and philosophical influences on education and pedagogical practice. She received an Ed.D. in Curriculum and Educational Foundations from the University of North Carolina at Greensboro.

MARY JEAN RONAN HERZOG has been on the faculty in the Department of Administration, Curriculum, and Instruction at Western Carolina University since 1989. She received a Doctor of Education Degree from the University of Tennessee in 1988. She taught remedial reading and English in Ashville, NC and Knoxville, TN prior to teaching education and psychology at Warren Wilson College in Swannanoa, NC. She has studied teachers' experiences with school censorship and is presently conducting a qualitative study of alternative, democratic teachers who teach in traditional schools.

KEITH HILLKIRK is an Assistant Professor in the College of Education at Ohio University. He teaches courses in secondary education, staff development, and supervision. He has taught elementary school math and science as a Peace Corps volunteer in Malaysia and English literature and composition in the United States.

THOMAS E. KELLY is an Associate Professor of Education at John Carroll University. His professional interests involve identifying and enhancing democratic practices in schools. He has published in *Democracy & Education, Social Education, Interchange,* and *Theory and Research in Social Education.* He is currently working on a manuscript about his recent year-long teacher exchange during which he sought to create a democratic classroom as a high school English teacher.

CAROL MILLER LIEBER has worked in the "educational trenches" for twenty-five years, still teaching at elementary, secondary and graduate levels. She is a national trainer for Educators for Social Responsibility, conducting conflict resolution programs throughout the midwest. Her interest in developing curriculum and teaching strategies which integrate global, multicultural and democratic education is well served by her position as an Adjunct Professor for National Louis University M.Ed. program in St. Louis.

J. CYNTHIA McDERMOTT is an Assistant Professor of Education at California State University-Dominguez Hills. Her work began with inner-city student populations and continues 20 years later in Los Angeles. A lover and teacher of children's books, she collaborates with her co-learners in the methods classes she teaches and the field supervision she conducts.

BARBARA McEWAN is an Assistant Professor of Elementary Education in the School of Education at Oregon State University, Corvallis, Oregon. She is the editor/author of *Practicing Judicious Discipline: An Educator's Guide to a Democratic Classroom* as well as several articles dealing with issues of equity and classroom management.

ED MIKEL is a former junior and senior high social studies teacher, program evaluator, school district central office administrator, program developer, and evaluation researcher. He is currently employed as an Assistant Professor of Education at National-Louis University. His interests include democratic alternative assessment, integrative curriculum, and the implications for progressive theories of economics in the workplace.

JOHN M. NOVAK is a Professor of Education and former Chair of Graduate Studies at Brock University. He has been an invited Keynote Speaker to educational groups as far north as Kotzebue, Alaska, and as far south as Christchurch, New Zealand. His recent books include *Advancing Invitational*

Thinking, the second edition of *Inviting School Success* (with William Purkey), and *Education: By Invitation Only* (with William Purkey).

SUNNY DUBINSKY PERVIL has taught in the elementary classroom, secondary English in a gifted pull-out program, and at the university level over the past twenty-four years. She also worked as an educational researcher, grant writer, educational consultant, school administrator and is currently an Associate Professor of Education at Maryville University. Her interests include gifted children, integrative curriculum, alternative assessment, and action research.

CECILIA REYNOLDS is formerly the Director of the Women's Studies Program at Brock University and an Associate Professor in the Faculty of Education. She completed her Ph.D. at the Ontario Institute for Studies in Education, University of Toronto, and has 17 years of experience as an elementary and secondary teacher. Her current research interests include critical feminist pedagogy, girls and girlhood, and women in educational administration.

HILTON SMITH is a high school social studies teacher with the Foxfire Fund. He currently serves as the Director of Teacher Education and Vice-President for Programs, coordinating the sixteen teacher networks affiliated with Foxfire and participating in the pedagogical development of the Foxfire learner-centered approach to instruction. His interests include philosophy of education, aesthetics, and dilemmas teachers face in implementing new instructional strategies.

SUZANNE SOOHOO is in her second year as an Assistant Professor in the School of Education at Chapman University. As an elementary school principal and teacher, she has proven to be a long-time advocate of democratic schools. Currently, she struggles with cultivating democratic classrooms at the college level.

HEIDI WATTS is co-chair of the Education Department at the Antioch New England Graduate School and a long-time advocate for democracy in education at every level. In her teaching career, she has alternated between the elementary, the secondary and the college classroom. Her most recent work has been with adults as teachers, working in Teachers' Centers and in graduate education.

TOM WILSON is an Associate Professor of Education and Director of the Masters of Art in Education program at Chapman University, Orange, California. He has taught in public secondary schools, community college, California State University and the University of California systems. His major interests are democratic education and social change.

GEORGE WOOD is Principal of Federal Hocking High School in Stewart, Ohio, Professor of Education at Ohio University, and coordinator of the institute for Democracy in Education. His books include *Schools that Work* (Dutton, 1992) and he edits the journal *Democracy and Education*.

INDEX